4|09

Praise for *Sniper One*

"A gritty, speedball run . . . strong, cohesive, and complete . . . it plugs the reader straight into the blood and guts of the action."
—*The Times* (UK)

"A highly charged, action-filled, adrenalin-pumped, page-turning read that, frankly, knocks the socks off all previous British accounts in this genre."
—*Sunday Telegraph* (UK)

"Full-on graphic detail . . . you can practically taste the dust and the cordite. . . . Quite simply, this is one of the best firsthand accounts of combat in the Second Gulf War that I've ever read."
—*Daily Express* (UK)

"The most vivid account ever of total combat on Iraq's front-line."
—*The Sun* (UK)

SNIPER ONE

SNIPER ONE

On Scope and Under Siege
with a Sniper Team in Iraq

Sgt. Dan Mills

St. Martin's Press ᨒ New York

www.stmartins.com

Library of Congress Cataloging-in-Publication Data

Mills, Dan, 1968–
    Sniper one : on scope and under siege with a sniper team in Iraq / Dan Mills.—1st U.S. ed.
        p. cm.
    ISBN-13: 978-0-312-53126-3
    ISBN-10: 0-312-53126-5
    1. Iraq War, 2003– —Personal narratives, British. 2. Mills, Dan, 1968– 3. Snipers—Great Britain—Biography. I. Title.

    DS79.76.M475 2008
    956.7044'38—dc22

                              2008020438

First published in Great Britain as *Sniper One: The Blistering True Story of a British Battle Group Under Siege* by Michael Joseph, an imprint of Penguin Books

10   9   8   7   6   5   4   3   2

For Chris Rayment and Lee O'Callaghan,
who didn't make it home

Illustrations

Picture credits

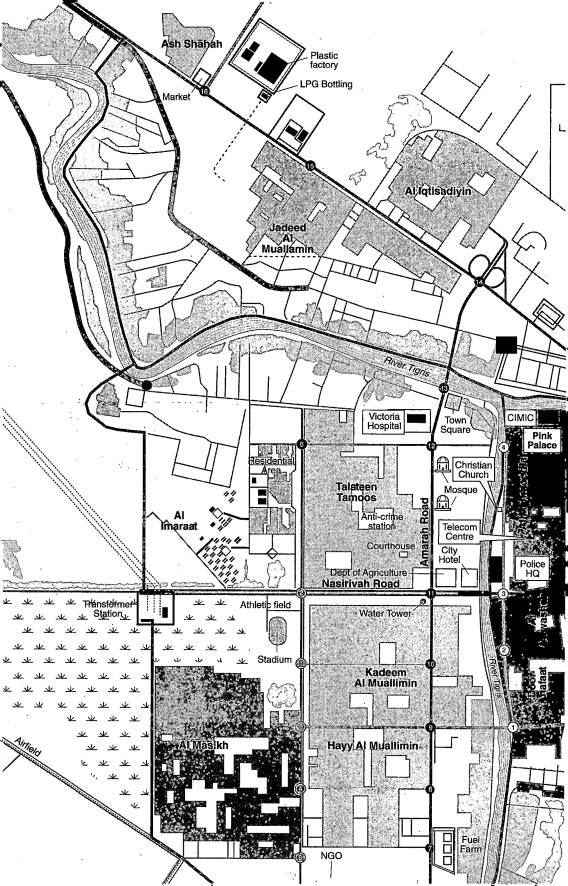

Acknowledgements

I would like to thank: Rowland White, for his faith, foresight, advice and enthusiasm from the word go; Tom Newton Dunn for the mountain of hard work, skill and dedication that made it all happen; and Carly Cook for her keen eye and excellent suggestions.

Sue for her unfailing support while I was in Iraq, and Sandra for her support and patience during the research and writing. Chris Mulrine and Adam Somers for when my memory began to fail me, Defence Public Relations (Army) for their honest advice, Rebekah Wade at the *Sun* for releasing Tom, and Mark Spicer for giving me the bug.

My daughter Elizabeth for watching over me, and my son Morgan and daughter Alexandria for giving me a reason to come home.

The men of fighting Y Company; in particular Captain Simon, Ian and Dalebert. Finally, all the chosen men of Sniper Platoon who I had the extraordinary privilege of leading and fighting alongside. Keep your heads down.

Dan Mills, January 2007

When you go home tomorrow, don't expect anyone to know what you have been through. Even if they did know, most people probably wouldn't care anyway. Some of you may get the medals you deserve, many more of you will not. But remember this. All of you are now members of the front-line club, and that is the most exclusive club in the world.

Lt Col Matthew Maer
Commanding Officer,
1st Battalion, the Princess of Wales's Royal Regiment
Camp Abu Naji, October 2004

SNIPER ONE

Prologue

'Gunman top window,' screamed H.

H was the first to spot him, from his position of height as top cover on the back of Daz's Snatch Land Rover.

As soon as I heard the call, my eyes darted to the gunman. The moment you hear a gun is trained on you, you scan for targets. And there he was, in the top window of the sinister three-storey building inside a well-fortified compound. Unusually for buildings in Al Amarah, it had a fresh coat of white paint and bars across every window.

As my eyes found him, he began to slide an AK47 through the iron grille. The metal barrel glinted in the bright sunlight as the gunman moved slowly from side to side. He couldn't seem to decide which of the nine of us he wanted to aim at first.

I was already walking backwards to my Land Rover, the other vehicle in the small patrol, which was parked up 50 metres further down the road. But Daz's vehicle was just 15 metres across a road from the compound's front gate. If the gunman was anything like a decent shot, we were all sitting ducks.

He was in animated conversation with a couple of his other stooges; one older, one younger. All of them were bearded, dressed in black dish dashes and wore green canvas chest rigs. They seemed to be jabbering away, I could almost hear them weighing up the situation: 'Shall we, or shan't we?'

Then the compound's heavy gates slammed shut with a loud metallic clunk. The four angry blokes with the same heavy Islamic beards who had been shouting at Daz and I had abruptly scrambled back inside.

They're thinking what I'm thinking. This is going to kick off. I know it.

It was only the first time we'd been this far away from base. But I'd done enough tours of Northern Ireland to realize what was going on here.

The mood was changing very rapidly from bad to terrible. My brain scrambled to keep up with the pace of events. I had already decided to get the fuck out of there and told the boys to mount up. Now it looked like we'd run out of time already.

Immediately and involuntarily, my pace quickened as I continued to walk backwards. I wanted to turn round to look where I was going, but I didn't want to take my eyes off that clown in the top window.

Fuck it. How did we get into this mess so quickly?

I couldn't turn and run to the Snatch, because that would mean we'd lose face in front of these nutters, whoever the hell they were. And the British Army doesn't do that. But I also knew it was no time to hang around.

Don't get excited, Danny Boy. Keep the heart rate slow and concentrate, you're no good to anyone panicking like a big girl.

'I've got eyes on,' shouted Smudge.

'Seen,' said Ads, along with a couple of other blokes a second later.

It had taken no more than four seconds for the three other top cover boys in the two Snatches to focus their Minimis on the top window.

Good. At least the boys are all wide awake. Then again, it wouldn't have said much for my training if they weren't during a drama like this.

The boys' reactions calmed me down a bit. Anyway, weapons aren't exactly uncommon in this desolate and forgotten corner of Iraq. Even grannies are known to walk the city's streets with AKs slung over their backs. None of this means it's going to go tits up.

I had got to within ten metres of my Snatch, and all we needed was a few more seconds to get into the Land Rovers and shove off home sharpish. No problem.

That's when the grenade came hurtling over the compound wall. We all saw it at once. Half a dozen voices screamed 'Grenade!' simultaneously.

Then everything went into slow motion. The grenade took an age to travel through its 20 metres of flight through the air. A dark, small oval-shaped package of misery the size of a peach.

On its upward trajectory, the handle sprang off, landing separately on the pavement with a light tinkle.

Then, a small cracking sound. The handle's release allowed the hammer inside the grenade to spring down hard onto its percussion cap. That ignited the gunpowder fuse, which began to burn furiously creating enough heat to ignite the high explosive charge.

My second-in-command Daz was the last to see it. He had been standing behind his Snatch with his back to the compound. As he turned round, the still ticking grenade just cleared the Land Rover's roof and hit him square in the chest with a dull thud.

Daz was left momentarily frozen to the spot, open-mouthed with shock. It bounced off his body armour's breast plate, and down onto the pavement before slowly rolling into the road and right under the Snatch itself.

In a desperate scramble, everyone else instinctively threw themselves down and covered their faces.

Another whole second of total silence.

Then *BOOM*.

A blinding flash of light, a pulsation of shock wave and deafening bang; all at once. Shrapnel flew in all directions; hundreds of red hot tiny pieces of metal whizzed through the air, pinging off the metal gate, the stone walls and my Snatch. Simultaneously, an instantaneous whirlwind of dust and detritus whipped across the filthy street, coating anyone within 10 metres with a thin layer of grime and spots of engine oil.

All I could hear was a ringing in my ears, worsened by an immediate secondary echo as the furious tirade of noise bounced off the surrounding walls and back down our battered ear canals.

At last, silence again. So I dared to look up. It had gone off right under the Snatch's bonnet, blowing the engine compartment to pieces.

Fuck, that was close.

For a few seconds, it looked like we'd got away with it. I looked up again to see the Snatch on fire. But nobody was screaming, and everyone was still on their feet.

The next thing I heard was Daz.

'Fuck. I'm hit, I'm hit. Fuck it,' he shouted again and again.

He half ran half hobbled down the pavement towards me and my Snatch. With a massive release of adrenalin squirting into his nervous system, it had taken him a few seconds to realize what had happened.

Both trouser legs were heavily ripped, and a dozen claret-coloured blood spots had started to grow on the Combat

95 desert camouflage material from his belt to his boot soles. As he hobbled, blood also began to leak out of his right boot and leave a small trail of red on the road behind him.

He made it ten metres before he stumbled off the pavement and sank to the ground right in the middle of the road. His body had obviously told him it wasn't going any further.

Remembering his first aid drills, Daz rolled onto his back and started to wave his legs around in the air to restrict the flow of blood out of his wounds.

'Fuck, fuck, fucking bastard,' he carried on, as he shook them about violently.

Unfortunately, Daz had decided to collapse in full view of every available firing position inside the compound.

I looked over to it. Most of the building's window grilles were now filling up with gunmen and at least a dozen AK barrels were pointing at us. And just as he started the upturned beetle impression, the rounds started to come in. The gunmen had taken the grenade's explosion as their cue to open fire.

Jesus fucking Christ, we've just entered another world here.

The seriousness of our predicament hit me like a smack in the face. This was for real, and it could only get worse.

Bullets smacked into the road all around Daz, kicking up small puffs of dust. They also pinged off both Snatches' armoured sides. They were spraying off whole mags on fully automatic straight at us. One whizzed just over my head with a crack as it split the air. Totally undisciplined fire, but there was enough of it to cut us to pieces.

Daz lying in the open air like that painted the perfect target for the gunmen. We had to get him out of there, but that meant running right into the bullet storm.

Shit and bollocks. No time for any more thought. I sprinted from the Snatch and, with Ads beside me, made the 30-odd-metre dash to Daz in record time.

Taking an arm each, we dragged him just as quickly face downwards back behind my vehicle and out of the direct line of fire. He screamed out in total agony as his wounds rubbed against the tarmac, but there was no other way to do it.

Somehow we reached the Snatch without taking any more hits. But still my two top covers, Louey and Smudge, weren't returning any fire. They'd trained for this moment all their military lives and they had two bloody great Minimis in their hands. But they were still in shock at what they had just seen.

Seeing anyone blown up in front of your eyes isn't pretty, let alone a good mate. The two twenty-year-old privates were scared out of their wits, and they weren't going to hang around up there in the full face of that bullet storm for any longer.

All nine of us were now sheltering in or behind the Land Rover, which had become a dirty great big bullet magnet for the gunmen. We hauled Daz into the back of it, as its armoured sides gave him just a tiny bit more cover from ricochets behind us.

Inside, I got the chance to give him a quick once-over examination.

He was in a proper mess. The shrapnel had pepper-potted both his legs with puncture holes from the top of his thighs right down to his desert boots. There were around a dozen serious wounds in his flesh. His right foot in particular had been torn up very badly, and was just a mess of ripped boot and blood, bubbling and congealing through his matted and shredded white sock.

Inside the puncture holes a host of different-sized grenade fragments that had torn through his skin were still embedded, along with any other debris from the gutter that the blast had picked up on its way into him. The pain must have been excruciating.

He gave off a strong smell of gunpowder and burnt meat. His face had also lost a lot of colour. His eyes were all over the shop, and he was going in and out of coherence.

'You stupid jack bastard, Daz,' I said, in an attempt to keep his spirits up. 'You could have collapsed in cover rather than in the middle of the fucking road, mate.'

He managed to pull a smile. For a man in that shit state, he took the criticism well. But his time was swiftly running out and we were pinned down.

Bullets were still pinging off the Snatch's sides with sharp high-pitched twangs thanks to the regular bursts of automatic fire from the compound in the background.

Welcome to Al Amarah.

I had some decisions to make — and fast. It had well and truly kicked off, and we were slap bang in the middle of it with our dicks hanging out.

We first heard we were going on a rainy November morning in Tidworth.

The battalion's brand new CO got up in front of the lot of us to announce it. His very first words to us were: 'Good morning. My name is Lieutenant Colonel Matt Maer. I'm your new Commanding Officer, and in twenty weeks' time we'll be deploying to southern Iraq.'

It was the normal overly dramatic crap new officers come out with, because they hope we're impressed by it. It worked though – we were. We were going to Iraq.

By the time we'd get out there, it would be a year since Saddam Hussein had been deposed. The Marines and Paras were long gone, and by then southern Iraq was rarely even on the TV. But we didn't give a toss. It was gleaming news. For once, we were going somewhere interesting.

In his speech, Colonel Maer also added, 'It will be a tour like no other.' And not one of the 600 soldiers in that room had any idea at the time how true those words would prove to be.

For the next few days, our camp on the Hampshire/Wilt-shire border was total madness. The phones didn't stop ringing. Soldiers serving away from the battalion were trying every trick in the book to get back off postings from all over the place. Others who had recently applied to sign off were desperately trying to steal the paperwork back again and tear it up. Nobody wanted to miss this one.

It was the firemen that had done us out of the invasion.

We missed out on being part of one of the largest deployments of British forces since World War Two because of their poxy strike. The government used troops in 1950s Green Goddesses as the emergency response while the pay dispute was going on. So while 43,000 of our colleagues were storming southern Iraqi beaches, we were saving cats from trees in Hampshire. It was pathetic.

There were some proper obscenities exchanged too when we drove past the firemen's picket lines. None of this car horn honking from us.

'Toot if you support the fire fighters,' they'd shout.

'Fuck off and get back to work, you lazy bastards,' we would reply. 'You wankers stopped us going to Iraq.'

If that wasn't bad enough, we'd narrowly missed getting Gulf War One too. Back in 1991, the battalion was so convinced we'd get the call up for it, it had started to pack up equipment in shipping containers. We'd even started painting all our vehicles sandy coloured. But then the war finished too quickly and they didn't need us.

The Paras robbed us of a chance to go to the Falklands too. We were all ready when the MoD flew them all the way back from a training exercise in Belize so they could go instead.

The truth is, the 1st Battalion, the Princess of Wales's Royal Regiment (PWRR) never went anywhere.

We're the county regiment for London and the southern Home Counties. And although only officially formed in 1992 in an amalgamation during army cuts at the end of the Cold War, we're still the senior English regiment of the line. That's thanks to our forebears, who trace back to as early as 1661 and the defence of Tangier. Our nickname is The Tigers, and that too comes from another famous forebear, the 67th Foot, because they did twenty-one years of unbroken service in India. One unit or another that we are related to has fought in virtually all the major campaigns in which the British Army has ever taken part. Then, for some reason, about fifty years ago it all stopped.

We're not flash, and we'd hardly been in the news in the last thirty years before that – except of course when we took on Princess Diana's name during the amalgamation. But that all ended soon enough too when she died five years later. None of that is to say that we weren't a bloody good fighting force of men, and one of which I was proud to be a member. A lot of the line regiments were just like us. None of us had been given the chance to prove our worth for so long, the MoD had begun to think we didn't have any worth.

I was thirty-six years old. I'd been a soldier for eighteen years and a sniper for ten. I'd done six tours of Northern Ireland, one of Kosovo, and one of Bosnia – and I still hadn't fired my rifle in anger once. Anyone who had been to Northern Ireland in the 1980s and 1990s had their hair singed by a few IRA bombs. But not actually being shot at by an enemy standing right in front of you, and not getting the chance to shoot back, used to make me question whether I could ever call myself a real soldier.

I grew up in a village near Slough in Berkshire, the second child of four. I joined the army as a boy soldier aged sixteen in 1984 after some recruiter popped a leaflet through my letterbox, and I joined the Queen's Regiment – my local county regiment – because that's what the sergeant at the recruiting office told me to do. Service is a bit of a family tradition with us. My younger brother is an engineer in the army too. And my sister was a signaller until she got out to join the police. Our dad was a fireman, and served alongside two of his brothers in the same fire station. My mum was a BT operator, and my grandfather was in the Royal Engineers.

I've been married and divorced twice and I've had three children – two daughters from the first and a son from the second. The army and marriage don't go particularly well together because you're never really there. I got out in 1998 for eighteen months because I hated being away so much. But when I realized I hated civvy street even more, I signed up again.

I've never been much of a barrack room soldier who enjoyed all the dressing up and all the formalities that go with that. In fact, my idea of hell would be to be a guardsman outside Buckingham Palace. But I've always loved being out in the field, doing the job I'm paid to do. That's why I became a sniper. It's about taking professional soldiering to another level.

As the commander of the battalion's Sniper Platoon, I'd be the first to admit that I've got pretty high standards. I certainly don't suffer fools gladly. But if they're good soldiers, I'm fairly relaxed and give them a lot of rope.

We were all well aware that Iraq was all about nation building now, not war fighting. But we were still over the moon. We were just chuffed to bits that, for once, we were going to get our turn. It wasn't the Balkans and it wasn't Northern Ireland. Who knows, we may even finally get the chance to use the blinking weapons we'd trained so hard with for all those years.

The patch the battalion had been allotted was Maysan, the northernmost extremity of the poor Shia south under British control. Its capital, which would be my company's responsibility, was the town of Al Amarah. I'd never heard of the place, but it sounded properly Iraqi and that was good enough for me.

The battalion consisted of four companies. Three of them, A, B and C, cut about in tracked Warrior armoured personnel carriers, because we are an armoured unit. And then there was us, Y Company – the battalion's 106 support weapons experts. Y Company itself was organized into four platoons: mortars, anti-tanks, reconnaissance and snipers.

I had only recently returned to the battalion from doing an instructor's job at the Infantry Training Centre in Catterick. And as soon as we got the news about Iraq, it was my responsibility to get the platoon battle ready for a serious operational deployment. I'd been a qualified sniper for twelve years and had served in the platoon on two tours previously. Now I was in charge of it – my dream job.

Sniping is one of the hardest jobs in any infantry unit. It's one of the toughest trades to qualify for, and British Army snipers are the best in the world. That's the other reason why I wanted to be a sniper. I wanted to be the best.

The platoon was fifteen-strong in total, all of them qualified snipers: one sergeant (me), three full screws (corporals), three lance jacks (lance corporals) and eight toms (privates).

When I took over the platoon, I'd decided it needed some shaking up. So I ran a reselection course which gave me a chance to bin all the blokes who weren't up to scratch. Literally dozens applied, because it's the best job in the unit. I could afford to be pretty ruthless, and really get the very best. By the time I had finished with them, they were a gleaming bunch of lads too. I'd hand-picked the fourteen best killers in the battalion.

The difference with being a sniper is you can see the man's face when you kill him. You can see everything about him, because you've probably been studying him for minutes, or even hours. So when you pull the trigger you have to be able to separate yourself from the knowledge that you're taking a life. There's no point in putting someone through eight weeks of highly physically and mentally demanding training if when the moment comes, all he's going to do is think about the wife and kids the target might have at home. He may well be a father of eight, and have four grandparents to feed too. But he's the enemy and that's that. Tough shit.

You can't teach people how they're going to feel when it comes to that moment. Which is why selecting the right character for the job is so important. If they're half decent soldiers, they should be fairly good shots anyway. So you look for mental toughness and stamina above anything else.

A sniper has to be a bit of a hunter at heart. He has to enjoy the tracking down and the kill. You can't be thick either, because there's a lot of information to learn and a fair few calculations to carry out. Just judging distance well is a bloody hard thing to do.

Pulling the trigger and hitting the target is only one small element of it. You've also got to be good at getting in and out of the right place without being seen. Otherwise, you're going to get killed too. That means putting up with a lot of discomfort and pain. You're going to be lying in a hole full of water for days on end. Or in a cramped attic, or an exposed rooftop. You've got to be used to being wet, tired, miserable and dirty. And you're going to have to have a dumper truckload of patience.

We soon became a very close-knit bunch. Snipers always stick together because we think we're better than everyone else. We also encourage resentment. Sniping is a black art that few understand and even fewer are any good at, and that bothers them. But it just made us closer as a unit. A lot of the boys were so proud of who they now were, they went out and got a tattoo of the sniper's classic logo, a pair of crossed rifles with an S above them, on their biceps.

We never used anything other than first names for each other. None of that 'sir' bollocks for us. Everyone in the platoon had a nickname. Mine was 'Monk' on account of my thinning pate. The cheeky sods. The average age of the platoon was twenty-four, so the blokes were a few years older and more mature than the average squaddie in a rifle company.

We also look different to everyone else. Our precision weapons immediately stood us apart. The main tool of our trade wasn't the regular army's 5.56mm calibre SA80 assault rifle, but the 7.62mm L96 – a single-shot, bolt-action sniper rifle. It's known as the 'long'.

We also prided ourselves on dressing scruffily. Even in barracks, we'd walk around without rank slides and looked generally unkempt, because that's how we performed our special trade. We would patter around with our shirts hanging out, sleeves not rolled up and our hair and sideburns worn long. And we didn't wear twisters in our trousers, which meant they extended down to cover most of our boots.

But we were scruffy for a good military reason. We don't like washing our field clothes because we've got to smell like the ground we're operating in. If you try and hide out in the long grass stinking of Persil, you won't last for very long. And gaping big black leather boots aren't great camouflage, unless you're trying to hide on top of a tarmac road.

That makes us loathed by the Regimental Sergeant Majors the world over. They don't like snipers because we tend not to give much of a shit about the things that really bother them. RSMs want everyone to be as smart as a pin, with shiny buttons and boots. But we're not interested in that, because it doesn't make you shoot any better.

Snipers have two textbook roles in modern warfare. The first is reconnaissance. Along with the Recce Platoon, snipers are the eyes and ears of the battle group. We obtain intelligence by either covert or long-distance observation, to build up a picture of the enemy's strength and movements. Sometimes hard information can be a lot more powerful than firing bullets. You can report back tank or troop positions, and get them destroyed by artillery without even giving your position away.

The second is to take out priority targets. Our job is to cause disruption to the enemy's battle plans and the way that they're fighting in the best way we can. Top of the list is always the enemy's command elements, their senior officers. That leaves them leaderless and sows confusion. The lowest priority is the humble soldier, because losing one or two of them won't have any effect on the enemy attack. But if they're the only targets that pop up, then you'll kill them all the same.

We're trained to operate anywhere, from behind your own lines, no man's land or even well behind enemy lines to disrupt the rear. We're always the first out, and the last in. But gone are the days of the lone sniper out in the middle of nowhere doing his own thing. Nowadays it's all down a lot more to specific tasks in patrol groups of two, four or eight men, and sometimes the whole platoon.

Our adage is one shot, one kill. Nowhere is it truer that a miss is as good as a mile than in our business. It's more than just a matter of personal pride. If you miss, it gives the target a chance to kill you another day.

Modern-day snipers work in pairs. A shooter and a spotter.

The shooter is known as the Number One. He controls the weapon, from setting up to pulling the trigger. The Number Two finds targets for him, double checks his wind and distance calculations, and covers his arse.

The elite of the platoon were the seven qualified and badged Number Ones – me, Daz, Chris, Fitz, Ads, Longy and Oost. Everyone was trained to shoot. But if there was ever the option, the Number Ones would be the trigger men. The Number Twos were Smudge, Rob, Ben, H, Sam, DV, Des and Pikey. As mine would always be the first name on the top of the platoon admin lists, I was known in military shorthand as Sniper One.

In those first few weeks after Colonel Maer dropped the bombshell of Iraq, Tidworth was a feeding frenzy of speculation on what the tour might be like. We'd latch on to the smallest nugget of gossip like it was a revelatory message from the stars.

Dale, our Company Sergeant Major, came up with one of the best in the Sergeant's Mess one night.

Conspiratorially, he glanced over his shoulder and then leaned in towards me at the bar.

''Ere, Danny, I hear the CO's done his sums. If the current tempo of events stays the same, he reckons about one in five members of the battalion is going to get into a decent contact at some stage during the tour.'

A decent contact in our books meant a reasonably sized firefight.

'Really?'

'Yeah. And Abu Naji got mortared three days in a row last week too. But be careful with those little nuggets, mate, because we don't want to scare the hens, now do we?'

He'd meant to be all grave and serious about his prized information. But when I turned to look him straight in the eye, even Dale couldn't resist a big cheesy grin. He was just as excited as the rest of us, despite his position, and we had a bit of a schoolboy giggle to ourselves.

WO2 Dale Norman was the most senior NCO in Y Company, and by far its most respected member, officer or otherwise.

A father of three from Portsmouth, he was known as Mr Unflappable – the coolest cucumber in town. Dale was a big stocky lad, and was famed for his bone crunchingly hard hand shake. He also had a big deep voice just like Frank Bruno's and always spoke naturally slowly, which gave him an immediate air of authority. Whenever he said 'fucking' though, it always came out as 'faarkin'.

He was also a good mate of mine. We'd been in the same battalion for almost twenty years. We'd gone through most of our careers together, grown up together. He never asked me to call him sir, which I should have by the book, and he was always up for a chat when I needed it.

After Christmas leave, we went straight into three hard months of operational training under the supervision of a unit called OPTAG (Operational Training and Advisory Group), the army's experts on life on operations. It was the routine package, a refresher course for all the military skills tailormade to suit southern Iraq. That meant helicopter drills, patrolling, vehicle checkpoint drills, riots, casualty evacuation, some basic Arabic. And a lot of smiling.

'Iraqis are used to soldiers with guns kicking shit out of them,' one of the instructors used to say. 'The way we prove we're different from Saddam's mob is by smiling. That way they'll know we're not going to hurt them.

'So smile, you fuckers.'

We'd smile on patrol. We'd smile at checkpoints. We'd

even smile jumping out of the helicopter. We smiled so fucking much our mouths would be in agony by the end of every day.

I pushed the platoon hard on the series of work-up exercises in Canada and Salisbury Plain. Iraq was a dangerous place, British soldiers were still being killed there regularly. So I reckoned I had a duty of care to give my guys the best chance possible of surviving.

There was initially some debate about whether we would even be taking our longs. Someone in the head shed had thought most of the kit Y Company used would appear a little aggressive for a peacekeeping tour. The locals would get upset if they saw us with too many pointy things. In the end, the CO agreed on a compromise – the mortars would stay in Tidworth, but the sniper rifles could come out. What we didn't know was that mortars were just what we needed.

2

The Hercules touched down with a heavy thump on the tarmac of Basra Air Station. The pilot threw its propellers into reverse, roaring and jolting everyone forward. We'd been swapped from the Tristar to the army's old workhorse in Qatar because the comfy passenger jet didn't have the defensive-aid suite to land safely against the surface-to-air missile threat in Basra.

It was just after half past nine in the morning on 7 April – a year to the day since the city had fallen to the British invasion force.

Everyone had been wearing full body armour and helmets since we had crossed over the Iraqi border. As soon as the loadies opened up the doors, the warm air permeated the plane drowning out its air conditioning in a few seconds. Even without the extra weight on us, stepping out into it felt like walking into a furnace. It was still only mid-spring, but the ground temperature had already reached 40°C. From the dark interior of the Herc, Basra's bright sunlight was blinding. And within five minutes, I was covered from head to toe in a proper sweat.

The first sight I saw was the happy smiles of some soldiers from the 1st Battalion, the Light Infantry, lined up to get on the plane we had just got off. They were the unit in Al Amarah we were going to replace. They were going home, and our arrival was the final confirmation of that. And the joy was plastered all over their faces.

As we filed by into the terminal building, one called out:

'Hello, lads, nice to see you.' Another asked: 'How long you boys got here then? Six months is it? Oh dear, that is a shit sandwich, isn't it. Did you know I'm flying out today?'

He got a huge laugh from his mates. It was the normal good-natured ribbing between rotating troops that happens anywhere. But the Light Infantry boys really seemed to mean it.

Before all troops arriving in theatre got to their final destinations, you had to do two weeks of acclimatization at Shaibah Logistics Base first. So we were packed on board coaches and driven to it through the desert.

I peeked out from behind the coach's blastproof curtains on the way. Iraq was pretty much exactly the shit hole I had expected it to be from what I had seen on the news. All along the route lay destroyed Iraqi tanks and armour. The desert plain looked just like a widely spaced junk yard. Endless remnants of the invasion, the first Gulf War before that, and the Iran–Iraq war even before that. Nothing had been cleared up. There was war detritus everywhere, and it's what we had all been yearning to see.

Fucking brilliant, we're here at last.

It was also still the nearest most of us had ever been to an official war.

After an open-mouthed hour with all noses pressed to the windows, our first holiday in Shaibitha began. The point of it is to get used to the heat and desert conditions of southern Iraq inside the safety of a great big base in the middle of no-where, where nobody is going to shoot at you or try to blow you up. It's also used as a place to give soldiers in Iraq a few days off from the front line – hence the Ibiza nickname.

Shaibah is the main supply hub for the 9,000 British troops in the country. It's based on an old British barracks built in the 1920s when we first ruled Iraq. But these days, it's the nearest the British Army has ever come to going to war the American way. It was a small slice of home shoved right in the middle of miles of sand. Amid row upon row of big air-conditioned accommodation tents is everything a squaddie could ever want. Apart from beer and shagging, that is. There are fast food trailers like Pizza Hut and Burger King, a massive gym, coffee shops, hairdressers, souvenirs, a cinema and even a traditional British pub – alcohol-free of course.

After we'd found our lodgings, the three other platoon commanders and I got an update on the general picture in Iraq from the company OC (Officer Commanding), Major Justin Featherstone. He'd been out for a bit as part of the advanced party. His news was dramatic.

In the last forty-eight hours while we'd been travelling, it had all well and truly kicked off out there. Across large parts of the country, the firebrand Shia Muslim cleric Moqtada al-Sadr had stirred up a shit storm. His fighters had seized police stations and government buildings, and attempted to storm a series of coalition forces' headquarters. The fighting was at its worst in the major southern cities of the Shia heartlands. In the city of Kut just 100 miles north of Al Amarah, a Ukrainian soldier was killed and Polish troops even had to temporarily abandon their base and pull out of the city altogether.

The trouble had been brewing for months. In September 2003, Moqtada declared his own shadow government for Iraq. He promised to rule it as a strict Islamic state and started rubbing out his rival Shia leaders. Eventually, the Americans' patience ran out. In March 2004, they closed down his newspaper and issued a warrant for his arrest for murder. In retaliation, he mobilized the Mehdi Army. On 5 April, fighting broke out. The al-Sadr uprising had begun.

Elsewhere across the south, 500 Italian troops in Nasiriyah

had fought a fierce battle with militia, suffering twelve casualties of their own, but killing fifteen and wounding thirty-five enemy. Spanish soldiers were fighting on the street with Medhi Army gunmen in Najaf, and the Bulgarian base in Kerbala came under heavy grenade and machine-gun fire. An American soldier was killed by a rocket propelled grenade (RPG) in the poor Shia stronghold Baghdad suburb Sadr City, recently renamed after Moqtada's father. And three Japanese civilians and seven South Koreans had been taken hostage, and the Mehdi Army were threatening to burn them alive. From what Featherstone could pick up, there had even been a bit of scrapping in Al Amarah too.

The 'good' news, Featherstone said, was that it wasn't ex-pected to last much longer. Intelligence had predicted the uprising would peter out pretty quickly after the initial outburst.

Shit. We were sitting on our hoops in Shaibitha watching everyone else have all the fun on CNN. It was the same old bloody story for the PWRR all over again. Yet again, we were going to miss the action. By the time we got up there, there would have been a settlement, or al-Sadr would be dead. The whole storm in a tea cup would be all over. Un-fucking-believable.

What was worse was there was absolutely nothing I could do about it. I had to wait for the rest of the platoon to arrive and take them through acclimatization. I was sick as a parrot.

I couldn't work out whether Major Featherstone was happy or sad about the al-Sadr uprising. Probably a bit of both. It was exciting for him like it was for all of us because he was a soldier. But it also meant an increased risk to his men, and that for him was a major worry.

Major Justin Featherstone was very much a soldier's

soldier. He was a very approachable and friendly guy, who always made a big effort to be liked by all the blokes. That really mattered to him, and so far he'd pretty much achieved it. Physically, he was balding prematurely for his thirty-five years, but well built and always carried a cheeky smile. And he was never afraid of getting his hands dirty and mucking in with any shitty task he'd given his men.

But if he had one flaw, it was that he was born a *Boy's Own* hero. He was the classic army officer amateur adventurer sort. He was always organizing adventure training trips or exciting expeditions, and the explorer's urge – which included a keen eye for the ladies – had given him a fairly lively army career.

Being given the command of Y Company, the most skilled soldiers in the unit, on an operational tour was a chance for Major Featherstone to really prove his worth to the army. He was very keen to take it. That meant keeping his nose clean doing a faultless job. Most importantly, that meant keeping all his blokes alive.

When the rest of Sniper Platoon finally did arrive over the next few days, I began the programme immediately. That meant drinking endless bottles of water, platoon runs, lots of smiling, and practising our Iraq drills. The most important one I wanted to get us good at was top cover. That's the two blokes who stand up in the back of Snatch Land Rovers to give the vehicles all round protection while it's moving. If there was any action still left to be had up in Al Amarah, I wanted the boys to be ready for it.

There were also endless lectures on hygiene. Exactly how you should wash your hands before you ate, or you'd spend the rest of the tour in the shithouse with D and V. Shaibah also has a shooting range with 100 lanes in it for blokes to zero their weapons sights. It's the biggest the British Army has anywhere, and we thought it was awesome.

But the bottom line was Shaibah was well and truly the land of the REMF – Real Echelon Mother Fucker. It was a Yank phrase from Vietnam, but it's been adopted by English-speaking military all over the world. And it was doing my head in. After four days of the place, I was chomping at the bit, so Daz and I resolved to scheme a way of getting up to Al Amarah as soon as we could. He felt exactly the same as me.

Corporal Daz Williamson was my 2i/c and, at just a year younger than me, had the seniority to be in charge of the platoon himself. But a while back he'd been demoted from sergeant for punching some gobby PT instructor in the face. We agreed on pretty much everything – just what you need from your deputy.

I had another word with Major Featherstone.

'Sir, I've got to get up there. With the current crisis, it's really important Daz and I do a good and thorough handover with the Light Infantry sniper platoon commander before he goes.'

'Right.'

Lying, I went on: 'I've heard he'll be on his way down in a couple of days. Chris can stay behind and bring the boys up in two days' time.'

'Oh, I see. Well if you think you have to, you'd better go then, Dan.'

I gave Chris the good news.

Corporal Chris Mulrine, my No.3, was very popular for his sharp wit as much as his fine soldiering. He had no time for army bullshit and, as a massive *Blackadder* fan, did his legendary General Melchett impressions when only just out of earshot of some particularly bumbling officer.

In full Melchett impression, 'Yeees, that's the spirit. They don't like it up 'em.' He shook his head.

'You bastard. I get it, I'll stay here and be a fucking REMF and you and Daz will have a right old caper. Off you go.'

That settled it. Daz had managed to find a couple of rides on a routine road convoy up to Al Amarah. They needed a couple more armed escorts. We jumped at the chance of a lift, they jumped at the chance of getting a couple of snipers to cover their arses.

We found the convoy of six eight-tonne lorries and a couple of Snatch Land Rovers by Shaibah's main gate at 8 a.m. the next day. They were loading up and almost ready to go. The driver of our lorry had done the trip once already in the last few days. He was none too pleased about having to do it again. But thanks to him, we got our first real indication of what the situation was like on the ground in Al Amarah, in a shouted conversation over the noise of the engine as the convoy pulled out.

The Light Infantry had had two weeks of misery.

The main base in the city centre had been repeatedly surrounded by more than 3,000 demonstrators. It started as just an angry protest, but the mob – which was constantly chanting the name of Moqtada al-Sadr – had got increasingly violent. Blast bombs were now regularly coming over the base's walls and armoured Warriors had to be deployed on the streets.

Over the last two nights, troops had also fought a series of clashes with Mehdi Army gunmen after coming under small arms fire.

Six British soldiers had been injured, and they had killed at least fifteen enemy in return. It was the worst violence British-controlled southern Iraq had seen since the end of the war.

And it showed no signs of abating at all.

3

Daz and I rode shotgun up country. It should have been a three-hour journey. Our convoy did it in five because the drivers got lost. That's a hard thing to do, because it's just one road.

We didn't care. This was real Iraq.

With our SA80s in our laps, and a round in the chamber just in case, our legs dangled over the eight tonner's back tailgate all the way up. It gave us a great view of the place that we were to call home for the next seven months.

For long periods of the journey we just sat in silence staring at the scenery, if you can call it that.

'Fuck me. What a khazi,' was Daz's concerted opinion.

Most of Maysan is unpopulated wilderness. A dust-blown, heat-baked, flat and featureless wasteland. The Tigris River runs right the way through it, so it's not desert. But it's too hot and dry to be any good for farming more than a mile each side of the river.

It's the poorest of all Iraq's eighteen provinces – the true arse end of a truly arsed-up country. Maysan hates the rest of Iraq, which in turn hates it back. Nobody elsewhere gives a fuck about the place, and it couldn't give a fuck about them either.

One of the reasons why it's such a dump is the 280-kilometre border it shares with Iran. The province was the scene of a lot of the hideous trench warfare fighting between Saddam's legions and Tehran's during the 1980s. That not only destroyed what little industry there was in Maysan, but it also drove away most of its population for good.

Outside of its few towns, its only real landscape features are the hundreds of decaying tank and artillery berms built by both sides during war. Those, and the network of crumbling irrigation ditches that haven't carried any water for decades.

Almost all of the houses we passed by were made out of mud walls. And what little farming we saw was totally untouched by any modern methods. At stages, it felt like we could have been driving through a land a thousand years back in time.

Not much has changed in Maysanis' behaviour patterns from the dark ages either. Much of the province is semi-lawless. Its people are and always have been furiously independent. The only authority they have ever respected was tribal or religious. Extreme violence was just part of everyday life in Maysan. Human life had no great value.

On a piss stop, our lorry driver told us a story he had picked up off the Light Infantry.

A few weeks before, a dispute had broken out between two tribes over the ownership of a cow near a little town in the south of Maysan called Qalat Salih. They had settled it in the usual way. Both sides went home and got thoroughly tooled up. They met back in a field with all their heavy weaponry and opened up on each other. By the end of the day there were ten dead and forty wounded.

'Mad fuckers or what, eh?' the driver laughed.

'Yeah, but what happened to the cow?' Daz asked.

Nine miles short of Al Amarah itself, some 240 kilometres north of Basra, was Camp Abu Naji.

In Saddam's day, it had been his 4th Corps' massive headquarters – four square kilometres of barracks, training grounds and ammunition stores. Dozens of US and British bombing raids during both wars against Iraq had turned the camp into long eerie stretches of charred foundations and rubble. For all the tens of thousands of tonnes of ordnance the fly boys had dropped on it, they might as well have used a nuclear bomb. It wouldn't have looked any different.

In the ensuing chaos, the camp had been heavily looted in the two days between the Iraqi army's flight and the Paras turning up. Every home for miles around now had its own private arsenal, from AK47s to Dshke heavy machine guns, RPGs and mortars.

Only a few flat-roofed single-storey barracks blocks remained fully standing in the middle of this desert of rubble. So the Royal Engineers had built up a compound around them 800 metres long by 300 metres wide, by pushing up four great walls of earth four metres high and digging a deep defensive ditch all around them.

The previous battle groups' command centres had occupied the hard buildings, and everyone else lived in rows and rows of giant air-conditioned tents. The PWRR did the same. Abu Naji was far enough away from Al Amarah to prevent insurgents using it as cover to put effective mortar fire down on the camp. But that didn't stop people trying.

As we were shown to our temporary digs, we passed the Light Infantry mortar teams digging themselves in for the night's activities.

Right in the middle of the camp there was a makeshift football pitch, and smack in the middle of that they were digging three mortar pits. No more football there, then. We hadn't even brought our mortar tubes. There were a few frantic phone calls back to the UK when the head shed arrived and remembered that. Last man out remember to pack the mortars.

Abu Naji had everything working soldiers needed inside it. A permanent cookhouse with three different hot meal choices per sitting, together with strawberry cheesecake and ice cream for pudding. To wash in, there were permanent, air-conditioned and tented shower blocks with hot and cold running water most of the day. And there was even a small R&R tent, rigged up with a dirty great satellite TV dish. But it was still very basic, and mind numbingly claustrophobic. You couldn't leave the compound unless you were on official military business, and even that meant taking weapons, body armour and helmets with you. Shaibitha felt a very long way away.

I tracked down my oppo, the Light Infantry's outgoing sniper platoon commander. I thought I might as well use the time before the rest of the platoon arrived to do the proper handover I promised Featherstone. It was a good job I did it then too. His name was Sid.

'Hello mate, I'm Dan. I'm here for a couple of days, so if you've got time for a decent chinwag over a brew maybe . . .'

'Yeah, pleased to meet you. Look I'm sorry, fella, we've got an hour and then I'm out of here on the next fucking bus. So what do you want to know?'

We sat down on the floor of his accommodation tent then and there. It wasn't exactly the world's longest handover. I tried to get as much out of him about the lie of the land as I could. We went over the maps of the city. In the last three or four weeks, he and his boys had been all over the place doing observation jobs on suspected ring leaders for all the crowd trouble. They had been run ragged.

As he heaved his Bergen over his back, Sid added: 'I expect you're going to have some fun in the next couple of weeks if it stays like this. I've got to dash or I'll miss the plane. See you in another life.' And off he went.

Abu Naji wasn't to be our home. So as soon as the rest of the platoon caught up with Daz and me two days later, we would get straight into Al Amarah where Y Company was to be based.

And because it wasn't our home, in true soldier's fashion the boys started taking the piss out of the place the moment they arrived. Compared to the city where we'd hoped the real action would be, they'd decided it was just another REMF hang out.

'Eh, lads, look at this place,' said Pikey, as he jumped off the lorry and dusted himself down from the journey. 'It's fucking Slipper City here.'

'No, it's not, it's Abu Napa,' quipped Ads.

So that was it. The unsuspecting tourist resort of Aya Napa in Cyprus had just given its name to British Forces HQ, Maysan Province. From that moment onwards, nobody in the platoon called it Abu Naji ever again.

Ads and Pikey were two of the platoon's strongest characters.

Private Adam Somers was a 22-year-old South Londoner, and a typical cockney. He came to the army from the City, where he had worked for two years as a trader in the Stock Exchange. He traded futures and options and even used to wear a silly bright yellow jacket. But as far as we could tell from his stories, all he learnt in the City was about whorehouses. He was eventually sacked for losing £128,000 in one day, and decided to join the army to do something exciting with his life.

Ads was a cheeky sod. He used to love calling me Granddad. But he was a right charmer too, and was always the first to crack a joke. Whenever he went out on the town, he was famed for bringing back the fattest bird he could find and shagging her as noisily as he could.

More than all of that, he was an excellent soldier. He loved fighting, in or out of uniform. A keen boxer, he would never miss a punch-up if there was one going in Tidworth. And he was the most tenacious in the platoon during combat exercises. But he was also always in and out of trouble with the army over women or alcohol – the only thing that stopped him from being made an NCO.

Private Geoff 'Pikey' Pieper was twenty years old and got his nickname from his family. They were proper gypsies, and lived in caravans. He was the best fixer I've ever known, a fantastic wheeler and dealer. If the platoon ever needed some piece of equipment, I'd put Pikey on to it.

'I'll see what I can do, boss,' he'd say – and he'd always get it. Fuck knows from where, and I didn't ask. Pikey's room used to look like Steptoe's yard, or Delboy's living room. He'd always come back off leave with something off the back of a lorry to flog to the rest of the company: shirts, watches, mobile phones, perfume, aftershave, sex toys. You name it, he flogged it. He did have a bit of a bad habit of nicking things, but never off the platoon.

I found him a thoroughly good and dependable soldier, who never avoided confrontation and was a brave little terrier in a fight. But like Ads, he also had a bit of a problem with authority, especially when his temper was up. Once when we were in the pub in Tidworth, Pikey had got too much booze inside him and he pulled a knife on one of the lads after some minor argument. He would have done him too, if I hadn't stepped in.

They might make a bit of trouble for you every now and then, but both Pikey and Ads were your archetypal British Army soldier, the backbone of the nation. They may not mix very well with peacetime, but sweep them out of the pub, pick them out of the gutter, and when they sober up give them a bayonet and tell them to charge. They'll fight out of their skin for you. From the Peninsular War to Iraq, their sort were what made the British infantry the greatest fighting force in the world. And it's exactly the same today.

The next day, another convoy of eight tonners took most of Y Company into Al Amarah. Our destination was Cimic House, the opulent former home of the governor of Maysan province slap bang in the middle of the city. It had been taken over by the coalition forces, for now. It served as both the US-run Coalition Provisional Authority's headquarters and the battle group's only foothold in the city. It was a busy place.

The journey in was our very first taste of a Middle Eastern town. It wasn't a nice one. Al Amarah was the capital city that Maysan province truly deserved. It was a squalid, stinking dump.

If you're being kind, Al Amarah is a place well past its heyday – if it ever had one. At worst, it's a filthy truckstop for petrol and a punch-up, before they take off again as quickly as they can. It wouldn't surprise me if the River Tigris runs twice as fast as it normally does when it goes through Al Amarah. Nobody wants to stay there for longer than they have to.

4

The smell of the place is the first thing that hits you. And the smell of its people's rotting shit will stay with me for ever. It was everywhere. The sewage system had long since packed up and shit and piss, along with bathwater and cooking waste, ran openly down every street's drainage gutters for everyone to see and smell. Piles of uncollected rubbish were everywhere.

We gawped out of the back of the trucks at our new home. Almost nothing differentiates the city's dull blocks of single- or two-storey houses from each other, laid out on a US-style grid system. Almost every building is sand coloured – nobody seemed to bother with paint.

Most of the cars on the streets were also in a shit state, a good indication that there was little money about the place. But money or not, I could never understand how Al Amarah's 350,000 people could care so little about their own surroundings.

If what was there wasn't bad enough, the town is pretty much constantly slapped by a strong wind that blows across the empty plains. It burns the back of your throat when it gets really hot and dumps a thin layer of dust over everything.

Children were playing in the overflowing shit-filled gutters, covered in grime and dirt. 'Mister, mister,' they shouted as we went past. It's an upsetting sight when you have kids of your own the same age.

A few groups of men hanging around on street corners

gave us the evil eye as we drove past. The uprising in Najaf led by Moqtada al-Sadr's militia had swiftly hardened the population's stance to our presence.

If there was one thing Al Amarah people do care for it was their religion. For a lot of them, Islam and Moqtada were inseparable. The biggest thugs in town were the holy nutcases, hired guns and vicious gangsters of Al Amarah's Office of the Martyr Sadr (OMS). Named after his father, this was Moqtada's official fan club and local HQ for the Mehdi Army. People did what they said – they paid no attention to the police who were by and large an irrelevance.

Depending on the political climate around Iraq, the OMS's fighting strength numbered anything from a hardcore of around 400, to several thousand. They dressed in black. The OMS was also a convenient umbrella under which people who wanted to resist the coalition's presence grouped. They welcomed all comers, from tribesmen with blood feuds against us to settle, to frustrated former Ba'ath party officials and jobless young men just wanting to earn a few dinars. With a lot of the male Iraqi population having undergone conscription at some stage under Saddam, most of the OMS's ranks had some form of military training.

It may be only nine miles from Abu Naji, but Cimic House took up to an hour to get to. Convoys in and out varied their routes as much as possible to avoid being caught by improvised explosive devices (IEDs), also known as roadside bombs. That could mean crossing the river three times.

When our convoy pulled up at Cimic House, the city was peaceful. During the daytime over the last few days, it had been quiet. The bad boys came out to play at night.

CIMIC stood for Civil and Military Cooperation, the army's term for reconstruction projects, improving the infra-structure and general tree-hugging. Getting Iraq back on its feet, and all that. It was the basic reason we were all there. The whole compound is around 200 metres long, from north to south, and 100 metres across from east to west, at the widest point.

On two sides, there is water. The vast River Tigris runs past its northern perimeter, and one of its tributaries passes by its western edge. Since the Tigris stretches from the northern mountains of Kurdistan down through Baghdad as well as a dozen other towns, it was thoroughly filthy by the time it reached Al Amarah. It escaped into the Arabian Gulf just past Basra. It wasn't uncommon to see dead dogs and cows floating by, as well as the odd badly bloated human body.

The main road that approaches Cimic House from the south also snakes past its southern and eastern boundary, a thick concrete wall six feet high and reinforced by Hesco bastion bollards and sand-filled bollards.

You get into the place by two gates, each preceded by a series of 50-metre-long chicanes. All traffic is filtered through them to stop suicide bombers. The front gate, two sheet metal doors, is at the southern end of the compound and was used most often. It opens onto a long wide paved drive-way that leads up to the main house. It was used as the vehicle park, and it was where we debussed from the eight tonners.

Cimic was a hive of activity. But we would have to hit the ground running.

Dale had gone in ahead of us, and he was in the vehicle park to greet us.

'Right lads, listen up. You've got twenty minutes to sort

your shit and then we're in the sangars on guard. The Light Infantry are getting out right now. So let's look faarkin' lively. Sentries, have your weapons cocked, but don't take your safety catch off unless you're going to fire.'

The plan was to take the Light Infantry out on the trucks we had come in on. They were pissed off, and couldn't get out fast enough. It was hard to blame them.

The rioting they had faced was up there with the worst sort of stuff the army had to contend with during the darkest days of Belfast and Londonderry, including bullets and bombs. Heavy crowd aggro was never good to come up against, but that too was all new to us and seemed pretty exciting at the time. We'd done a huge amount of public disorder training during OPTAG so we were full of confidence and determined to give a good account of ourselves.

There was just time for a quick guided tour so we knew where everything was.

As he showed us around, the Light Infantry NCO pointed out a crater where a mortar round had landed inside the camp perimeter. There was the odd bullet hole in the wooden frames of the sangars (fortified lookout posts) too. We pretended we weren't much interested in all his battle chat. But of course, we were fascinated.

In a line to the right of the driveway before the main house itself there were a series of ten prefabricated Porta-kabins, eight of which were single-storey. These were the shower and toilet blocks, or offices for the Cimic teams, which were largely made up of British TA soldiers, who in civilian life were accountants or engineers. The Light Infantry NCO said Cimic House was a cushy posting for them.

'If they've got to do a tour of Iraq, then what better way to spend it than safely behind a desk with us guarding their arses, eh?' he suggested. 'And they still get a campaign medal to go home with.'

The double-storey blocks were much larger, and were our accommodation area. Each floor was just one long dormitory, divided up into sections of four beds in each to give a little privacy. That's where we were to sleep, said the NCO.

Only Molly Phee and Major Featherstone had their own rooms, inside one of the single-storey Portakabins. With a big grin, our guide even gave us a good look inside them too, just to make sure we knew what we would be missing out on from the start.

Molly Phee was head of the Coalition Provisional Authority (CPA) for Maysan, the province's de facto emperor. A senior US State Department official in her late forties, Molly was liked by everyone – Iraqi and British. She was a small woman, but she had a reputation as a seriously tough negotiator, and spoke fluent Arabic. Molly presided over a team of twenty CPA officials, most of them Yanks too.

'Molly's all right, but you're going to love her close protection mob,' said the NCO. 'A load of septics called Triple Canopy. What a bunch of fucking nob jockeys they are.'

They were Molly's twenty bodyguards for when she went out and about. Most were ex-elite US military and of all different ages, he added. Apparently one guy claimed to be an ex-SEAL and had served as far back as Vietnam. They dressed in their own uniform of khaki slacks and black polo shirts. They all wore Oakleys or wraparound RayBans, and walked around tooled up to the eyeballs. They sounded just terrific neighbours, and we couldn't wait to meet them.

Then it was on to Cimic House itself. A large and rectangular 1960s concrete building, 30 metres long and 15 metres wide. It's not much to look at now, but it was probably the coolest thing in southern Iraq when it was built. For Maysan, it would have been an estate agent's wet dream.

On the ground floor were a series of generously sized meeting rooms, which were full of CPA officials' desks, shaped around a central courtyard of a few square metres in size, right in the middle of the building. There was even a small number of servants' rooms.

A wide staircase alongside one of the inner courtyard walls ran up to the second floor, where there were further substantial rooms that must have been originally designed as state bedrooms. They were large and airy with big windows to allow their original occupants to take advantage of the great views over the water. Several of them were en-suite, and had big air-conditioning units pumping cool air into them. A wide balcony with white railings ran the whole way around the level. All the floors in the building were made of marble.

Most of the house's rooms were out of bounds for us. We were also ordered to have very little to do with the minor CPA folk, on their own request. There was a lot of tension between us, and none of it was our making. They were keen for us to keep as low a profile as possible because they didn't want the locals thinking the military had come to make war. We were supposed to be on a smiley happy peacekeeping tour, and we had to behave like it.

The nicer toilet blocks were set aside for them too.

'You'll also have to eat meals at different times to them,' said the NCO. 'It's what they made us do. It helps them pretend we're not here.'

I supposed that made them feel like they were really helping the people of Iraq. Twats.

The tour ended with Cimic House's wide, flat roof. Up

there hung a solitary red, white and black Iraqi flag. It was there instead of a Union Jack to prove to the locals we were there for them.

As soon as we got up there, I knew immediately where my platoon would be spending most of the next seven months. Our job was to be the eyes and ears for the company; to log, report and observe anything that looked like insurgent activity. With the most potent and longest range weapons system, we were also its best deterrent. The roof was not only the highest spot in the compound, it also had a 360-degree view over much of the city. A three-foot-high wall even ran all the way around it for cover and to rest our longs on. All in all, it was our ideal location – a sniper's Shangri-La.

5

'Right boys, this is our new office,' I swiftly announced. 'No fucker comes up here without our permission. This is sniper territory from now on. Put the word around.'

It was important to claim the roof as quickly as possible, before another platoon like Recce got the same idea.

OK, Cimic House was overcrowded, our housemates were obnoxious, and outside the walls there was a jungle. But crucially, in the roof we now had an excellent place to work. On tour, everything else comes second to that.

The more we saw of our new home, the better it got. My mood was lifting by the minute. There was a proper cook-house with real tables and chairs, not a tent full of plastic furniture like in Camp Abu Naji. It was run by a couple of military chefs in a mobile kitchen trailer. They did everything from chips and curries to fry-ups and ice cream, and a fresh fruit bowl every day. On Friday nights, they even threw on a barbecue.

One last treat awaited us in the palm-tree-lined garden, a luxurious remnant of Saddam's day when his governor in Maysan lived there like a prince. Ringed by its own wall and a cooling thatched veranda was a 15-metre-long swimming pool. It was fully functioning too, thanks to the efforts of previous units. A little outdoor gym had been set up beside it, with exercise bikes and punch bags.

All in all, it really was quite a promising spot — a haven of calm in a storm of shit. Having been prepared for the worst on the grim drive in, we were chuffed to bits with the place by the end of the look around. We were also delighted to be away from the rest of the battle group stuck inside Abu Naji. It meant we could do our own thing, well away from the RSM's moaning about haircuts, saluting and all that crap.

That evening I sat on the benches outside the cookhouse beside the river with Dale. There was a patio right on the corner that overlooked the Tigris where it split from its tributary. From there, you could watch the sun set behind the palm trees while fishermen in ancient looking canoes paddled past. There was even a little table tennis table.

We treated ourselves to a fresh, cool glass of orange squash (on this dry base, orange squash was as good as it got) and put our feet up. All over the city, the mosques had started to wail to call people in for evening prayer. For a moment, sitting out there almost felt a bit like being on some Mediterranean holiday. It was certainly a pleasant change to the freezing windowless underground bunk rooms of South Armagh.

'This is all right, isn't it, mate. What does sir think of the view?'

'Well, I don't mind telling you, Danny, if it wasn't for that faarkin' toilet of a city the other side of the fence, I could spend six months here with some ease. If we have to be tree huggers, I'm all on for tree hugging in comfort. Any fool can be uncomfortable.'

Not that we thought it would ever come to it, but militarily it was also an excellent place to defend. With water on two sides, there was little chance boats would make it across without us giving them a fair pummelling first. And the front and back sangars gave good arcs of fire, not to mention our all-round view from Cimic's rooftop. Two final buildings perched on the riverbank on the northern edge of the compound completed its prospect, a tall water tower and water treatment plant.

The only downside was the Pink Palace, the governor of Maysan's office and seat of power located the other side of the road from the front gate, which we were also tasked with securing. It was an ugly two-storey block shaped in three sides of a square. It was known as the Pink Palace because it was pink. But we called it the Pink Sauna on account of how hot it got in there. If there was ever any air con in it, it didn't work now. For some reason the poor design meant almost no clean air would ever pass through it either. It stank terribly. A third-rate architect had tried to make it look like a palace, but all it resembled was a naff Arab mansion. Technically, it was the seat of the governing council of Maysan. They didn't govern anything at all, because the Americans did all that. But it didn't stop them turning up to shout at each other all the same.

I spent the rest of that first night on the rooftop with a couple of pairs who had set up their longs. Our task was to log, report and observe anything that looked like insurgent activity. Mortar firing positions were our top priority. They were easiest to locate at night because the round will give off a bright flash when it ignites at the bottom of the barrel.

There were no attacks on us. But we heard shots fired all over the rest of the city. Once we knew all our call signs out had been accounted for, we relaxed, sat back and just enjoyed the show. Little zips of red or yellow tracer would suddenly shoot up over the rooftops. Sometimes it was far away, other times closer. It was like a fireworks display.

Most of it was tribal shooting, power struggles between different gangs. Some of it was celebratory fire. To mark a birth, wedding or a funeral, it's customary for Iraqi men to unload a full AK mag into the skies. They don't give a shit where the rounds land. It's not uncommon for totally innocent bystanders to be killed.

Excrement aside, there were other fascinating smells I hadn't come across before: the perfumes of the souks, and the spices of Arabic cooking. And in the mix from somewhere, a permanent smell of burning.

Even at night, we were still sweating because we weren't used to the heat. But thanks to a good breeze up there, the rooftop was always the coolest place to be.

Then Pikey ruined the whole romantic image in one fell swoop.

'Jesus Christ, it's 1 a.m. and I've still got the Niagara Falls running down me crack.'

'Thanks for that, Pikey. Just carry on drinking as you were told.'

At the start of the tour, we were getting through 20 litres of water a day. It was the only way to rehydrate while our bodies acclimatized. Water is a good business to be in in Iraq. Vast crates of two-litre bottles would turn up on trucks, and we'd go through them like locusts. We were forever pissing – I never knew I could piss so much. But after a little while we were back down to drinking just a couple of litres a day. It's amazing how adaptable the human body actually is.

Manning the rooftop was only half of Sniper Platoon's responsibilities. We were also going to have to muck in and do our fair share of routine patrols around the city, along with the other three platoons in the company. Sadly, Major Featherstone had far too few men at his disposal to use us only in our specialist role.

Before we got too ambitious, we would all do a few short familiarization patrols around the local area. On foot first, then in the Snatch Land Rovers we inherited from the Light Infantry. It was a confidence-building exercise as much as anything else.

I was allotted a time slot of 3 p.m. the next day for my first foot patrol. That gave me the morning to make sure every last part of every bloke's battle kit had made it the 4,000 miles from Tidworth in one piece. It was an ordeal in itself.

With the situation as tense as it was, we were going out in full rig and tooled up for any eventuality. That meant a total of around 45 lbs of equipment per man.

Combat body armour went on first over your shirt. This was a sleeveless jacket with a heavy Kevlar breast plate large enough to cover your heart. The plate would stop a 7.62mm round fired from close range. The rest of the jacket was made of rubber, and only stopped blast fragments or ricochets.

On the front of our body armour we wrote our zap numbers, in large writing with an indelible marker. It's what was read out over the net so they knew who to expect in the regimental aid post – or in worst case scenarios, whose family they had to inform. Also, if the casualty's face was a mess, you could just look at his front to see who it was. Zap numbers were made up by the first two letters of your surname followed by the last four digits in your army number. So I was MI7769. As the patrol commander, I would carry a list of everyone's zap numbers with me, along with their blood groups.

Over that went my webbing. What you carry where is down to the individual. Personally, I have always hated jamming things in my leg pockets because it restricts movement, so I put everything into my webbing and shirt. Into the webbing's internal pocket went my maps. On the outside of it were two grenade pouches, which were filled with other things because the company quartermaster didn't think it was right to issue us with grenades on a peacekeeping tour. There were also four more long pouches for rifle magazines.

In a place like that, I liked the boys to carry as much ammo as they could. The standard drill was six magazines of thirty rounds in each. But we always took out ten per bloke, plus a bandolier that held a further 150 rounds, packed into a piece of green material and slung around the shoulder. That made a total of 450 rounds of ammunition per man.

Field dressings were another must. You don't use your own on others; others use it on you. The idea is that everyone can see where it is immediately and rip it off you straight away. Most people tape them on to their webbing straps, and you write your blood group on them so the medic knows immediately what blood to pump into you. I always tried to carry two or three on me. A single dressing only holds one pint of blood, and then you'll need to smack another one on.

Wherever a soldier is, he must always carry enough food and water for twenty-four hours. So into the webbing would go most of that lot too, with a floppy water container known as a 'camel back' on your back.

Crammed into any other spare space was a silver compass, a handheld GPS device that gives an eight-figure grid reference accurate to within 12 metres, a torch, water bottles, a set of plastic handcuffs, language cards with basic Arabic, camouflage cream and a notebook. Finally, a vial of morphine and dog tags went around your neck.

Then there was what we had to carry.

The patrol commander is in charge of all the comms equipment, because he's the one that needs to talk to the desk jockeys back at HQ. The main VHF set, a Clansman 350 or 351, went in my day sack on my back. In case that failed, I had a handheld walkie talkie radio and a normal Iraqi mobile phone on me as well.

Because of its remoteness, the comms were so bad at times in Maysan that we'd heard stories about units before us having to dial the Whitehall operator on a satellite phone in the middle of a firefight, and politely ask to be patched through to their battle group headquarters no more than a few klicks away.

Over the net, my patrol's call sign was always 'Alpha One Zero'. As its commander, my own personal call sign was 'Alpha One Zero Alpha'. The Ops Room at Cimic House was 'Zero', and Featherstone was 'Zero Alpha'. Being a radio operator was a bitch. Get one letter the wrong way round, and you've passed on an order to totally the wrong bloke.

So that the patrol itself could speak to each other, each soldier in it also carried their own Personal Role Radio (PRR). That was a microphone and an ear piece attached to a head strap and connected to a main transmitter box the size of a packet of cigarettes on your upper webbing. PRRs were on permanent receive, but to talk you had to press a button on the transmitter.

On your swede would be either a floppy hat or the regimental beret, to keep the sun off. You'd have to carry your hard helmets everywhere too in case things got hairy. They were only strong enough to stop shrapnel and glancing rounds. High-velocity bullets from close range will go straight through them.

A night vision monocle would also be in your day sack. It could either be head-mounted on your helmet, or worn around the neck on some string, as I did.

A decent knife, worn on the belt, was also a prerequisite

so you could cut through obstacles. These days, soldiers only kill with them in the movies. Everyone is trained to use one if they have to. But if you've got down to that you're in pretty dire straits. You have to get extremely close to someone to stab them, and it's almost impossible to cut someone's throat without them knowing – unless they're fast asleep. If you really can't shoot them, batter them with your rifle butt instead.

The two weapons we carried out on patrol were the SA80 assault rifle and Minimi machine gun. Our longs would stay back at base, unless we were going on a specific snipers' task.

Forget what you've heard, the SA80 A2 variant was a perfectly reliable and good weapon. Its predecessor, the A1, got all the bad headlines and was a bit suspect. But its German manufacturers Heckler and Koch had done a lot of work to iron out the faults. The A2 had a sturdier cocking handle and a decent ejection mechanism that no longer threw the old shells back inside the rifle to cause stoppages.

The SA80 takes a 5.56mm round and weighs about five kilograms. It has two modes of fire, single shot and fully automatic. The latter would be used only very rarely, for in-your-face tasks like trench clearing. It's very hard to aim on fully automatic because of the recoil. On single shot, a soldier is expected to hit a target at 300 metres. But you're a pretty good shot if you can hit something more than 600 metres away.

The rifle's SUSAT telescopic sight was another new addition to it, and it was also pretty handy. It had a simple needle with a sharp point at its tip to signify the point of aim. Some of the boys had added laser aimers that clip on to the barrel and throw a red dot onto the point of aim. It was also standard issue kit for Iraq. It's handy if you're in a rush, because you can just point and squirt. In darkness, we swapped the SUSAT for a CWS night sight, which works by light gathering.

One bloke in every four on a patrol would carry an Underslung Grenade Launcher (UGL), mounted under the barrel of his SA80. It was yet another piece of kit that we hadn't seen before, though widely used by the US Army for years. And we thought it was gleaming.

The UGL was fired with its own trigger, and aimed by a flick-up sight. It shoots out a 40mm fragmentation grenade to a range of up to 350 metres, which explodes after a few seconds once its fuse has burnt out, killing anything in a five-metre radius. It was a very good weapon, and easy to be accurate with.

There would also be one Minimi in every four-man fire team. The Belgian-made Minimi is an area weapon with a far heavier weight of fire than the SA80. It's designed primarily to suppress rather than for accurate target shooting, and chucks out up to 1,000 rounds per minute. Basically, the enemy is going to keep their heads down for a bit if there is a continual wall of lead coming over them. That gives you and your men time and space to manoeuvre.

The weapon also took a 5.56mm calibre round in magazines of 250, which came in either a bag or a hard box. Minimi men would also carry one or two spare 200-round magazines on them. A bipod was attached to the barrel that could be folded out to support the weapon while being fired. It has an effective range of 800 metres, but it's hard to hit anything accurately beyond 300 with automatic bursts.

It was the first time we'd been given Minimis too. They look pretty sexy, so the younger blokes in the platoon loved prancing around town with them feeling hard.

No matter what you had, in a place as dirty and dusty as Iraq you would clean your weapon every single day. That means stripping it down, wiping every surface with a cloth, cleaning out any dirt, carbon or gunpowder residue, oiling the moving parts, wiping it down again, reassembling it, and finally performing a function check by cocking it and pulling the trigger. It takes between fifteen and twenty minutes. You do it so often that the whole process doesn't require any thought at all. It becomes a ritual. And you're happy to do it, because you know that lump of steel can save your life.

Our first patrol was to be into the souks – for no reason other than I was keen to have a look at them. Ten of us went out; from the front gate, south, and then east.

'Remember boys, keep your spacing. Twenty metres apart and alternate sides of the street. Keep your eyes on each other.'

I didn't need to remind them really. They'd done it already.

Because it was our first time out, I wanted my handiest blokes there with me. I'd decided Pikey would always be my point man, the man out in front of the patrol, so I gave him one of the Minimis. Like all gypsies, he had a great pair of eyes and ears, and he had the knack of smelling out trouble a mile off.

As well as Daz, Chris and Ads, that also meant the South African connection, Des and Oost. Private Desmond 'Des' Milne and Private Cameron 'Oost' Oostuizen were two peas in a pod. They were best mates and totally inseparable. They even sniped as a pair. In their early twenties, both had left their homeland to join the British Army and see some action.

Both had bags of energy, and were exceptionally keen and professional soldiers. They were the first to volunteer for any task. They'd be packing up their kit and halfway out the door before I'd even finished speaking.

Des was quite open in admitting he specifically joined up so he could legally kill people. I've never met anyone with such a bloodlust. He loved anything to do with knives and hunting, and got extremely excitable in times of danger. He also used to love telling us how the Afrikaaners were the master race.

'Just remember, the Boers kicked your sorry little English arses once,' he liked to say. 'And we'll do it again if you're not careful.'

Des was a big chunky boy too, the fittest in the platoon. He spent a lot of time in the gym, and was careful to always eat well. He planned to go for SAS selection after the tour, and he'd be perfect for the special forces.

Meanwhile Oost prided himself on being the platoon's weirdo. That meant not shaving as often as he should and sporting the craziest hairstyle he could get away with. His favourite was shaved sides and as long and spiky on top as he could make it. He wore shades and fingerless leather gloves wherever he went, and worshipped thrash metal bands. The Foo Fighters were always playing at full volume on his CD Walkman. He was the RSM's worst nightmare. But he absolutely loved his shooting.

Both Des and Oost hated army bullshit, which is why they became snipers.

Also with us was Fitz. Lance Corporal Mark 'Fitz' Fitz-gibbon was by some distance the best shot in the platoon. Aged twenty-nine, he was slim and lanky, and was a quiet bloke most of the time. He didn't say ten words if one would do. But put a long in his hands and he'd never miss a thing. Ever. He was like a robot, it was scary. He was also a good dependable NCO who didn't take any fucking about.

And you'd certainly hear him when he threw his toys out the pram at his blokes.

Our mobile armour was Louey.

Snipers had been given three privates from Anti-Tanks Platoon for the duration of the tour, to be our drivers and even up the numbers a bit. Two were Caribbean, Gilly and Louey. And the third, Private Mark Potter, was known as Harry for obvious reasons.

But with Louey, we'd really won the lottery.

Private O'Neal Lewis was an absolute ox of a man. Aged twenty-four and from the island of St Vincent, he was six foot four inches tall and built like a brick privy. If we ever needed a bit of muscle on a job, I'd send Louey in first. We nicknamed him 'The Swede' after the giant prize fighter in the Clint Eastwood movie *Heartbreak Ridge*. He was so powerful that he was always pinged to play the 'red man' during riot training. The red man was the chief rioter that had to be snatched out of the crowd, and he'd wear a big red rubber suit. It took literally dozens of blokes to subdue him because he'd fight them all off, one after the other. And his party trick was to lift up the corner of a Land Rover single handedly while someone else changed its tyre.

But despite all of that, he was one of the most reserved and polite people I'd ever met. Louey had a huge respect for authority, and was very well mannered. He loved his soppy R 'n' B ballads, Whitney Houston being his favourite. And he was the only man in the platoon who'd insist on calling me Sergeant throughout the whole tour.

None of that stopped him from having eyes like a hawk. And make him angry, he'd tear your fucking head off.

Bringing up the rear was Private Adam Smith. Only a young lad aged just twenty, Smudge was already a good all-rounder. He had a fantastic street awareness, just like Pikey.

That probably had something to do with his obsession with image.

In a platoon not short on posers, Smudge took the crown. Baby faced and with bright blond hair, he was the platoon's pretty boy. His shades were always perfectly placed on top of his head, and the last thing he'd do before we went out on patrol was check to see if his hair was OK. He also insisted on having his photo taken with every different sort of weapon he could get his hands on. But he was a very cool customer when we were in the shit, and thoroughly slick at his skills and drills. He'd make a great NCO one day.

The weight load was hard going in the heat to begin with. But the boys were a fit bunch and soon got used to it.

The souks were a fascinating sight. Market stall after market stall, all run by busy chattering shopkeepers, and grouped together by their specialities. First there were the metal stands, then the fruit sellers, vegetables, meats, spices, electricals, coffin makers; it went on and on.

As we walked about, we could also see that if only someone cleaned up all the muck and filth, central Al Amarah could be a half decent place to live in. Cafes were doing a roaring business all along Tigris Street. Men were sitting out puffing away on hookah pipes and families were having picnics in the park by the river's edge. If you held your nose and squinted, it could be Istanbul.

We were only out for a couple of hours, because I didn't want to push our luck.

But to our great surprise, most of the people we had come across seemed generally happy to see us. We got a lot of 'hello misters' and a whole load of smiles, which we of course were quick to return. Only one child got a firm cuff round the head from his father for talking to us. Even some

45

of the women mumbled positive noises from behind their veils (which OPTAG had told us would never happen).

As we made our weapons safe inside Cimic's front gate, Daz said: 'I dunno, mate. Perhaps the good people of Al Amarah have got bored of scrapping with us, no matter what's going on in Najaf. They've had a couple of weeks of it now after all.'

'Yeah,' I agreed. 'Judging by last night on the roof, killing each other seems a load more fun.'

It wouldn't be very long at all before we were both proved badly wrong.

6

The PWRR Battle Group assumed command of Maysan Province at 7.30 a.m. on 18 April 2004. It was a Sunday.

For the platoon, the day meant our first vehicle patrol around Al Amarah. We were in charge now, and everyone was looking forward to getting out and about on the streets.

It was going to be just simple stuff again. Just a bit of a drive around the main routes to get the boys used to the place, the feel of the vehicles on the streets. Our official task was also to drop in on a few police stations and make ourselves known. We set off from Cimic House at 3 p.m.

As the patrol commander, I rode in the passenger seat of the front Snatch Land Rover. Sam was my driver. Private Sam Fleming was a shy and quiet redhead. Aged just twenty, he was new to the platoon and was really just learning his way. Iraq was his first full operational tour. But he was a skilled and confident driver, and a nice lad with it.

Louey and Smudge were doing top cover for me, so Louey had a Minimi. Daz commanded the second vehicle, with Chris as his driver and Ads and H on top cover.

Daz also had a passenger in the back of his Snatch, Major Ken Tait, a Territorial Army officer from the Black Watch in his late forties. A school teacher from Glasgow, Ken was posted to Cimic House on a six-month call-up to be a tree-hugger on one of the reconstruction teams. But Ken was a true soldier. A heavy smoker, he was already bored with his desk job after only four days of being there, and asked

47

me if he could come along for the ride and have a look about too.

We weren't gung-ho, but we were confident and professional, and exactly where we wanted to be.

'Remember to smile, all you happy people,' Daz said over the PRRs as we pulled out of the front gate.

We headed north, and swept out around Al Amarah's eastern outskirts first, before cutting back into the city centre through the southern suburbs. I got the boys to dismount to carry out a quick spot vehicle checkpoint at the road junction Blue 5.

Al Amarah's main roads are codenamed by colours and numbers so the enemy wouldn't know what we're talking about if he intercepted our radio transmissions. We only ever knew a few streets by their real Arabic names. Its five main north to south thoroughfares roughly follow Al Amarah's grid system, with the Purple route the furthest west, red next, yellow in the middle, blue after that and finally the green route on the north-eastern flank. Main junctions on each coloured route are numbered upwards from south to north. Yellow isn't very long, so there are only four junctions on it. But red is the main arterial route through Al Amarah from Basra to Baghdad (Route 6 on the Iraqi road maps), so it has fourteen junctions. Sounds a nightmare, but imagine a bloke from Bermondsey trying to pronounce Al Muqatil Aj Asaneyya Street in a hurry.

After ten minutes, we drove off again up the Yellows, and made a right turn east at Yellow 3 onto a main road that hadn't been given a codename for some reason. There we stopped, and dismounted for a poke about at Al Balda police station, which was one on our list. The vehicles parked up 50 metres apart, on the south side of the road. All but one of the top covers in each Snatch dismounted to watch over

48

the patrol, as the rest of the boys inspected the ground around the vehicles for IEDs, the routine drill.

I walked over the road to the police station's front gate-house with a silly big grin on my face and attempted to strike up a conversation with the three officers lazing around there. I was keen to improve my crappy Arabic with the language cards we had been issued with.

The first thing that wasn't quite right was when the cops started to look very uncomfortable as soon as I approached. They had been doing what we had been told was the usual for Iraqi policemen – sitting around lazily in the shade and not really being arsed to do anything at all. But they proved even less interested in having a chat with me. They all squirmed, and looked away.

'Yeah, whatever then,' I said. Probably just don't like us. I shrugged my shoulders and walked away.

Daz approached two other coppers who were leaning on a motorbike, 50 metres down the road. They were standing in front of a well fortified compound that housed a large three-storey concrete building, painted white and divided into offices and a mosque area. Unusually for buildings in the city, it had a fresh coat of white paint and bars across every window. The front gate was made out of sturdy wrought iron, and an imposing six-foot wall ran around the whole of the rest of the exterior. Fifteen hundred metres from Cimic House, the place clearly had a pretty high status. It was just off the city's main promenade and overlooked the Tigris River.

As I walked over to Daz, four men with big Islamic beards came out of the compound very agitated. They were shouting at us full pitch in fast, aggressive Arabic and jabbing their fingers at us. We asked one of the policemen what their problem was.

'Their neighbourhood. Don't want foreign jundi in it.'

'OK, fine,' I said. 'Tell them they have nothing to worry about. We've only come to have a word with you and we'll be leaving now.'

But instead of passing on my message, the cops jumped on their motorbike and sped off.

It didn't take a brain surgeon to realize that things were obviously in danger of going Pete Tong. It was time to back off. We could argue the toss over our right to walk the public streets another day.

'Back to your vehicles lads, and mount up. Top cover first,' I ordered.

That's when H spotted the gunman in the top window.

As he shouted the warning, the four angries were already slamming the compound gate shut with them inside it. More likely than not, it was one of them who then chucked a grenade over the wall.

It exploded largely into Daz. That seemed to be the cue for the now five gunmen in the sinister-looking building to open fire in unison. Hot lead was everywhere. Daz struggled a few yards towards me, and then collapsed into the middle of the street.

Jesus, how the fuck had we got ourselves into this?

Rounds were pinging off the tarmac. But Ads and I somehow escaped them and hauled Daz into the back of the Snatch. The patrol's two trained medics jumped on top of him immediately and began slapping field dressings on his multiple leg wounds. The first batch instantly turned bright red, and had to be doubled up with a second lot immediately. Daz was in a shit state and there was no mistaking it. But I managed to get a half-smile out of him with a bad joke. That was a good sign. So I threw him the VHF radio handset and told him to send the contact report back to the Ops Room. Staying occupied was the only thing that would keep him awake and take his mind off the pain.

Daz and the two blokes working on him were in the back of the Snatch, and the other six of us were sheltering behind it. We were getting our arses kicked, and it was my responsibility to do something about it. Sharpish.

I did a rapid 360 scan of our position. As chance would have it, my Snatch had parked up perpendicular to a long alleyway of two chest-high walls at right angles. It was about six feet wide, and there were courtyards and dwellings off it all the way down it. And it was just ten feet away.

'Everyone not helping Daz behind that alleyway wall. Now.'

Nobody needed to be told twice. And for a few seconds, it seemed to work. Once we were out of sight, the rate of fire from the building eased up. We were now about 80 metres away from it, with a large empty garden between us and them.

As the blokes got their breath back, I peeked up over the wall's edge with my SA80 at my shoulder to have a look at the building. It was a good job I did.

A gunman was busy climbing over the building's exterior compound wall. In his thirties, he was dressed in beige-coloured dish dash. He had a scruffy dark beard, beady eyes, and an AK47 in his left hand. Moving as stealthily as he could, he dropped down into the street and began creeping up towards my Snatch. It was obvious he thought he was about to steal a number on us. Sneak up on Daz and the medics and finish them off. I will always remember the exact expression on his face. It was one of complete and total intent.

Oh really? You think you're a right crafty little sod, do you? Well I'm not having any of that.

And that's when I knew that I was going to kill someone for the very first time.

I tracked him through my Susat sight to within 20 metres of the Snatch. Most of his body now filled the lens. It was far enough. On single shot mode, I squeezed the rifle's trigger three separate times: bang, bang, bang, soaking up the recoil comfortably into my shoulder. The three 5.56mm rounds tore straight into him, penetrating with dull thuds. His body soaked them up like a sponge. The first two went in just below the neck and the third right into the middle of his head. On the spot, he tumbled to the ground in an unnatural, lifeless heap.

Straight away, I raised my rifle and put a quick burst over the building's wall in case anyone else had the same idea.

To my right, Ken Tait had watched it all. Half in wonder, half in shock, he said: 'Jesus, his whole head has come apart.'

I felt an overwhelming need to shout. Only one thing came into my mind.

'Yes!' I screamed. 'Have some of that, you fucker.'

There was no chance to think about it. Even if I'd wanted to. After I opened fire all hell broke loose again. Gunmen in every available window in the building opened up on us for a second time. But this time, the boys had seen my lead.

Seeing one of the enemy go down liberated them. Everyone thought yes, get some of that. With their adrenalin soaring, they too all opened up in the direction of the building. Gunmen were crawling all over it now, at the windows, on the rooftops, on the top of the walls, and at the main gate. There were too many to count.

But the lads were on to them. The best training in the world had kicked in, and the battle was on. Coolly, seven guns spotted for targets and engaged them with cold-blooded accuracy. With every SA80 banging and Minimis chattering along one long firing line down the alleyway wall, it made a deafening noise. The smell of cordite filled the air and burnt the nostrils. Every few seconds, a whizz of burning red phosphorus would zip through the air as a tracer round piled into the enemy's stronghold. Puffs of chalk and brick dust erupted off its walls around the windows as the lads honed their accuracy.

It was a good firing position. And after a small while, the targets started dropping. You knew when one of the lads had hit someone because they would let out a whoop in delight. It was too hard not to. Adrenalin, stress and fear were all working overtime at once.

Ads even managed to knock an enemy fighter straight off the roof with a direct hit in the chest from one of his UGL rounds. The grenade still exploded at the point where the bloke had been standing, but he was already long gone.

'Fucking 'ell, d'ya see that? Fucking awesome,' Ads shouted. He was sweating like an Eskimo in a sauna. We all were.

My mind was on a million things at once. As well as spotting for targets without showing too much of myself to the enemy, I was also trying to keep an eye out for the rest of the platoon and direct their fire when I could. Then there was keeping the Ops Room fully informed, and making sure Daz was still alive. And all the while, I had to scheme how the hell we were going to get out of there. I didn't have the time to be scared.

Ken scampered over to report what had just come over the VHF from the Ops Room. It explained a few things.

'Hey Danny, you know what that fucking building is? It's the OMS's headquarters. Some bonehead at Cimic has just

53

checked out our location with Abu Napa. Nice of 'em to tell us, eh?' he panted.

Jesus Christ. The OMS. Moqtada al-Sadr's pet loony tunes. We had unwittingly managed to put our heads right inside the lion's mouth at the very first available opportunity. No wonder they had taken exception to us snooping around on their doorstep. We must have looked like prize buffoons.

At that moment, two RPGs fizzed through the air in the direction of Daz's Snatch. It was still sitting outside the OMS's building about 60 metres away from us. The first missed and ploughed straight into some poor fucker's house instead and exploded. But the second was a direct hit. The explosion rocked it a foot into the air, before landing down on its wheels again. It set the Snatch on fire, and thick black smoke started billowing out from its engine casing.

Shit, another problem for us. We had some highly classified radio equipment in the back of it. We couldn't let it fall into the hands of the enemy. Somehow we had to get it back.

I made the short leap from the alleyway to my Snatch to check on Daz. His condition was worsening and he was drifting in and out of consciousness. Blood and discarded wrappers covered the floor and walls of the Snatch. The medics had done a good job. Field dressings had been tightly strapped all over his legs to keep pressure on the wounds, a jacket had been put over him to keep him warm, and a roll mat was under his neck for support. His eyeballs were all over the shop from the morphine. He would last a little bit longer like that, but not for ever. In terms of commanding the men, he was now clearly incapable.

I got on the PRR so everybody could hear it.

'Chris, you're now 2i/c.'

'Right. No problem mate, I'm right behind you.'

Chris knew what he had to do as second in command. He was a professional. Immediately, he starting scampering up and down the line to keep the boys' firing tempo up and help them spot for new targets.

But it wasn't just Daz I had to worry about in the Snatch. There was Sam too now. As its driver, it was Sam's job to stay with the vehicle and man the comms. But Sam was going down with shock.

The vehicle was totally exposed and presented a big target for the enemy. Bullets kept pinging off its armour. Sam had also seen what had happened to the other Snatch, and he didn't like it one little bit. His face had gone white as a sheet.

'Dan, I've got to get out of the fucking vehicle. I don't want to stay here.'

It's given the tag of armoured, but a Snatch is just a regular metal Land Rover base with a composite fibreglass shell bolted onto its back. The two rectangular driver and passengers' seats in the front give way on to a space like that of a small van in the back. In it are a couple of mini plastic seats, with double wooden doors that open outwards and two tiny windows at the rear, and a big square cut into its roof for the top covers.

The name comes from Northern Ireland which is where they were developed and used — to snatch the ringleaders of riots off the streets. They're liked because they are speedy, tough and reliable. But their downside is they're Spartan and pretty uncomfortable, and, worst of all, they won't protect you from anything more than a 7.62mm round. RPGs and shaped charges shred them.

Sam knew that too.

'No. I need you here, mate,' I replied, trying to keep my voice calm. 'Listen to me, I need you here for the following reasons. You need to keep your eyes on Daz, you need to guard the vehicle so someone doesn't throw a grenade in the back, and I need you on that net.'

'Fucking hell, I've got to get out of this thing. Please Dan, let me go over to the wall with the others.'

'Sam, stay calm. Think about Daz.'

But he was too worked up to listen to reason. I tried to suggest a compromise.

'OK, mate, we'll do this. You get yourself out of the door on the right side in cover from the incoming, and sit down there behind the front wheel. I'll pass the handset out to you.'

He did it, and it seemed to calm him down.

'Good lad. Now shoot any fucker who comes near you.'

'Right, Dan.'

I ran back to the wall. We were still putting down good suppressing fire and they weren't getting anywhere near us. But we were also stuck. There were too many of us to get into the one remaining vehicle and we couldn't just leg it back to base through the streets *Black Hawk Down*-style. We had no idea what could have been waiting round every corner. And sooner or later, our bullets would run out.

Sergeant Ian Caldwell came on the VHF, so I leapt back over to the Snatch again to talk to him. He was the commander of the Quick Reaction Force (QRF) tasked at Cimic to come and rescue us. A tall thin bloke like me but with a big nose, Ian was a good mate of mine. Also like me, he had a reputation for speaking his mind. He told me he was on his way in two Snatch Land Rovers. Good. We could certainly do with a bit of rapid help. I had already given the Ops Room the best roundabout route to get to us away from where I suspected there would be ambushes.

'You know the best way to come, Ian?'

'Yeah, yeah, the Ops Room told us. We'll be with you in five minutes.'

'Fucking brilliant. Do us a favour mate, put your foot down.'

Two minutes later, Chris was at the end of the firing line by my Snatch.

'Three Snatches, Danny. Just driven past our position.'

Blimey that was quick. And I thought Ian said he was only in two Snatches?

As they came up level with the OMS building, the vehicles drove into a fresh shower of bullets. The drivers immediately threw the vehicles around with a screech of tyres and they pulled up at the top of the alleyway.

'Cover them, lads.'

We had to put a lot of fire down onto the OMS to cover the Snatches' arrival. I slapped the rifle onto fully automatic and raked it with a full mag of rounds. That should get the fuckers' heads down.

As I turned round and ducked down to change the mag, a posh-looking bloke was crouching beside me. He was wearing just a T-shirt under his body armour, but no sign of any rank. I had been expecting Ian.

'Who the fuck are you?'

'Hello there. I'm Lieutenant Colonel Jonny Gray. I'm the Commanding Officer of the Argyll and Sutherland Highlanders.'

'Oh, hello, sir. Erm, very nice to see you.'

'It looks like you're in a spot of bother. Can we help?' It was the sort of calm and convivial tone you'd use with someone who'd just got a flat tyre.

The colonel and his men were on their way back from training an Iraqi army battalion nearby. By total chance, they'd just happened to drive straight into our fight. Now they were all clustered around the lip of the alleyway, watching us put the rounds down.

I gave him a quick sit rep, and asked him how many men and weapons he had.

'We're twelve chaps in three vehicles. You're in charge here, Sergeant, we're in your hands. Oh, we've also got a GPMG with us.'

This was gleaming news. I could do with a Gimpy. The General Purpose Machine Gun is a big old dragon that gives you some excellent fire power. Its 7.62mm rounds were going to punch much bigger holes into the screwballs we were up against than our SA80s.

'Right, bring that Gimpy over here and I'll place it, if you don't mind, sir.'

No sooner had the colonel scampered back to his men, than right round the corner came a dirty great big jock, well over six feet tall, with the machine gun in one hand and a big ammunition box of 800 rounds in the other.

Just the sight of him put an enormous smile on my face. Oh yes, a big scary bloke like that is just what we need. He was with a team of four, who were all carrying belts of Gimpy ammo too. Excellent, we could fight for hours with that. I told the jock to take his team down to the other end of the alleyway to protect our right flank.

The Argylls' arrival had proved to be pretty timely. The sound of another big blast echoed out, but from a little further away. It must have come from the other side of the OMS building, and it was followed by repeated AK fire. Then we heard the slightly higher pitched firing noise of SA80s.

It was Ian's QRF being ambushed. He'd come the most direct way he could, which was straight past the OMS building. That's exactly where they hit him, just as I had predicted. All my instructions to the Ops Room had been ignored. Ian wasn't going to get to us in a hurry now.

Then more bad news came over the radio. The Warrior armoured vehicles of the battle group QRF from Camp Abu Naji had finally been tasked to come and extract us. But they were still forty-five minutes away. What had they been fucking waiting for?

This was a problem. Even if the twenty of us could hold out against probably the ever larger number of enemy before the cavalry finally arrived, Daz wasn't going to last that long. We had a drip in him, but it was just saline solution. He had a lot more than one hole in him and he was slowly bleeding to death. He would need a surgical team to stabilize him.

It was time for Plan B. I told Sam over the PRR to leave us the VHF and drive like the clappers back to Cimic House with Daz. I don't think he's been happier to hear anything in all his life. As the Snatch wheel spun off down the street, you could hear rounds still pinging off it. As for the rest of us, we would just have to slug it out until either Ian's mob fought their way through or the Warriors turned up.

The Gimpy was up and running now, and spitting out fire when targets popped up in the street at the other end of the alleyway. The Gimpy team and Daz's departure had created a lull in fire from the OMS. I decided to take advantage of it, and rescue the sensitive radio equipment from Daz's burning Snatch. I spotted a doorway into the garden next door from the main road, and another out of it again next door to the OMS building. I reckoned we could get most of the way there out of the view of the OMS if we got into the garden next door and kept low against its lefthand wall. Then, we could leg it out to the Snatch, do a double quick smash and grab and be away with what we needed.

I told Colonel Gray my plan. To my surprise, he immediately insisted he would come with me. Someone as senior
as him is normally stuck behind a desk and would hardly
ever get the chance to get his hands dirty any more. It's not
at all what COs should do, but he just couldn't resist it.

'Fuck it; this is going to be my VC moment. I'm going
to be bloody H Jones and get shot trying to be a hero. I
can't believe it. I'm supposed to be going home in seven
days' time.'

It wasn't exactly the behaviour of a Glasgow school
teacher either, but Ken said he was up for it too. Just like
the colonel, Ken was also past his best years but he didn't
want to miss the excitement either.

'Ads and I are in too,' Chris said. 'Some peacekeeping
tour, eh?'

The five of us put fresh magazines in our rifles, pulled
back the cocking handles, and flicked the safety catches off.
We were ready for action. But Ken still had something left
to do.

'Hang on a wee sec there, Danny.'

Just as I was about to give the word to go, Ken pulled a
cigarette from a packet in his pocket, put it in his mouth,
and lit it. He stood up straight with a smouldering Benson
and Hedges stuck between his teeth, and stuck his chest
out. Now he really looked the part. He inhaled deeply, then
he let the smoke go.

'Right,' he announced, 'let's kick us some fuckin' arse.'

When you need a fag, you just need a fag I suppose.

7

We sprinted out of the alleyway into the main road and ducked straight back into the courtyard between us and the OMS building. They didn't see us. We spread out low and crept up in a line along the brick wall that bordered the main road up to the second gate. Daz's Snatch was just five yards away. My plan was for Ads, Chris and me to leg it to the Snatch while Ken and the colonel covered us.

I poked my head out of the gate. Unfortunately, a sharp-eyed little fucker on the OMS building's roof top spotted me immediately. He started shouting his head off. Thinking we were now trying to sneak up on them, the bastards directed all their fire on to the metal gate. The sheer weight of rounds began to shred it. Shit.

We all scrambled back behind the brick wall. How the hell were we going to get through that wall of lead?

I looked at Chris for inspiration. But he thought that was his nod to go for the radio. Chris turned round to look at Ads. They stared at each other in horror.

'Fuck off, Danny, I ain't doing that,' said Chris firmly.

'OK, OK.' My heart was in my own mouth now. 'I didn't tell anyone to do anything. Everyone just calm down.'

'We are calm, mate. You calm down.'

Ads turned to Chris. 'I ain't going to get that fucking radio, Chris.'

'Don't worry Ads, neither am I. No fucking way.'

Screw the radio, it's not worth three dead bodies.

'OK, OK. We'll bin the fucker. Everyone back the way we came.'

'I think that's a rather sensible decision, sergeant,' agreed the colonel. And we sprinted back to our alleyway.

There was a reason why the enemy had gone quiet. They had been pulling a flanking manoeuvre, and a load of fighters had now sneaked up behind us. Just after we got back, a grenade came over the alleyway's back wall and landed just a few metres behind our firing line.

Oh bollocks. We're going to get some of this.

Everybody stared at it. There wasn't any time to do anything else but throw ourselves to the floor. It exploded with an enormous bang, spraying shrapnel out in a wide circle. Because of its design to plant metal into people at waist height, amazingly nobody was hit. We'd all got down in time. But we all went deaf for a minute. Ads thought it was hysterical.

'Fuck me, how the hell did we get away with that?'

Even I couldn't resist a smile in relief. But as I was standing up, I heard the very loud whoosh of an RPG. It sounded like it was coming fast from behind me, so I instinctively ducked down again. It turned out to be a wise move. The rocket swept right over my head and out over the alleyway wall beside the garden.

We now had enemy rear. I got Colonel Gray to put his men and mine in an all-round defence. We now had a line of guns against the back wall of the alleyway as well as the front. The GPMG was still on the right flank. But we were suddenly very vulnerable because we were in a crap position to engage the threat from the rear. We couldn't even fucking see it. We had to move.

Ten yards up the alleyway on the rear side was a much smaller alleyway. Halfmoon-shaped, it lead from ours back onto the main road further away from the OMS building. With its hard concrete walls 10 feet tall on either side and partially covered by scaffolding, it would give us far better protection. So we withdrew into it. I put a couple of sentries at each end to engage opportunity targets. Meanwhile, the rest of us reloaded our magazines from the bandoliers we were carrying.

Almost as soon as we had vacated our old positions, the enemy started to move into them. Gunmen took up positions on the lip of the first alleyway where my Snatch had been. And rounds smacked into the other end of our new alleyway where it joined the main road. One RPG after another screamed over our heads. At the moment, the angle was still too tight for them to plonk one in on top of us. But it was only a matter of time.

'Danny, come in.' It was Ian Caldwell of the QRF on the VHF. He asked me how we were.

'Been a lot better, mate. I take it that was you getting into a little bother on the other side of the OMS building then?'

'Yeah, that was us all right.'

'Why the fuck did you come down that way?'

'It's what the Ops Room told us to do. Why, did you tell them differently?'

Great. Why had I even bothered getting on the radio to them?

'Look, I'm sorry, Dan, but there's no chance I'm going to get to you right now. We're getting hammered here. I hate to ask this, mate, but, anything you can do for us?'

The first of Ian's two Snatches had got smacked straight on by an RPG as they approached Yellow 3 on Tigris Street. They debussed, but were immediately pinned down by a wall of small arms fire. They fled to the only cover available, a bit of metal fencing under a bridge. They were still taking heavy fire from three different sides with just the river behind them. They were in a very bad state, and Ian knew it.

'Fraid not, mate. We're still in the shit pretty spectacularly down here.'

There was a silence.

'OK, well I guess we're both on our own then.'

We both knew what was going on, and it was a bit of an emotional moment. I tried to keep positive.

'OK, mate, well I'll see you when you get back in. Keep your head down.'

'Yup, same to you, mate.'

It's the sort of lofty optimism soldiers exchange when things are looking pretty bleak. Actually, I wasn't sure that I would ever see him again. But he certainly didn't want to hear that.

Then the worst news yet from the Ops Room. The Warriors weren't coming to us any more. They'd been retasked to help Ian's QRF as well as another battle group call sign who had also got themselves in deep shit while trying to get through to us. Both were now in a worse state than us so got the priority billing. That's how it goes.

The other call sign was my Commanding Officer's rover group.

It's not often that a lowly sergeant gets the chance to have not one but two colonels fighting for him. But it was that sort of day.

Lieutenant Colonel Matt Maer was in Cimic House on a visit when news of our contact came over the net. Then Ian's lot got hit too. As the nearest available troops left with working vehicles, Colonel Maer had nobly decided it was his responsibility to see what he could do for us too. Also,

64

his boys were as keen as any of us to taste a bit of action.

The RSM, 'Chalky' White, acts as the CO's bodyguard when he's out and about. Chalky was in the barber's chair having a haircut when the CO rushed out. Unfortunately for Chalky, he had to leg it after him with only one half of his head shaved. He looked like Robert De Niro out of *Taxi Driver.*

The CO's two Snatches also piled straight down Tigris Street. They got within a few hundred metres of Ian's bridge when they also got smacked by an RPG attack. The OMS had worked out which way reinforcements were coming now. It wasn't exactly hard. They had been lying in wait.

A young lance corporal, Kev Phillips, jumped straight out of one of the Snatches and took a bullet right through the neck and out of his left shoulder. He was bleeding heavily. From that moment onwards, their priority was to get him back to the regimental aid post as soon as possible. In other words, they were going to be fuck all use to us as well.

Louey was one of the sentries on the alleyway's lip with the main road. He had the best view of what was going on outside. Having the balls of steel that he had, he'd dodged sniping fire repeatedly to stick his head up and out to identify enemy positions.

'I'm sorry to bother you, Sergeant. It's just that I've done a quick count-up, and there are about forty points of fire on us now from 360 degrees.'

'OK, thanks, Louey.'

We'd only been stationary there for a few minutes, but the enemy had been on the move again. They were like a vast pack of wild hyenas moving in on their prey. They had the taste of blood in their mouths. And they were slowly surrounding us.

Shit, this is getting serious now.

Literally hundreds of the lunatics had now joined the battle against us, and their numbers were growing every minute. Word had obviously got around. They'd all gone home to get their weapons and have a go at the foreign jundi. We were massively outnumbered, and it was getting a little scary.

We had only a few minutes left to get the fuck out of there before an RPG finally came in on target and turned us all into a big vat of claret. There was only one option left open to us. The lot of us would somehow have to extract in the Argylls' three Snatches.

Colonel Gray and I thrashed out the new plan.

'OK, Sergeant, I think this might work. Our Snatches aren't that far away on the main road, maybe about 40 metres at the most. If we're quick, with your help we can reach them. Cover us going out to them, and then we'll cover you coming to us.'

In groups of two and hard targeting, the Argylls started to leg it. Rounds pounded into the tarmac around them, and I just waited for the first bloke to drop in an agonizing body twist. But they all reached their vehicles unharmed.

Safe under the vehicles, the Argylls started to return fire on the enemy's positions. That was my patrol's cue to start legging it. Smudge was next out, but just as he peeked into the main street, a gunman opened up with his AK out of a window almost directly above his head, from the nextdoor building to the lip. He hurled himself back in just in time.

'Fucking bastard. That cunt's completely cut us off.'

I stuck my head out to look for the guy and another burst of rounds smacked straight into the wall behind me less than a foot above my head. He was right. The gunman was right between us and the Argylls.

We had to clear another route round to the Argylls. That meant going back out into the original alleyway and into the direct fire of the enemy again for a few metres until we found a way into the next compound down. We had to outflank the bloke who was cutting us off.

'You're fucking crazy aren't you, Dan?' said Chris. 'That's whistling death out there in that alleyway.'

'Don't worry lads. I'm leading the way. If anyone's going to get shot it's going to be me. Just follow me and you'll be all right.' It was a lie. I had no idea if we were going to be all right. 'Come on boys, let's fucking do this.'

We ran at the alleyway at full sprint, sparking a crescendo of noise. I could feel the air parting as the rounds whizzed past my head, with a zipping and a slapping sound. Puffs of brick and dust kicked up when bullets hit the walls and the ground around us.

Luckily, Iraqis aren't very disciplined with their fire. They think nothing of emptying a whole magazine at you in one go. You can't aim properly on automatic. They also think it's very uncool to shoot from the shoulder, so they all blast away from the hip like Rambo, which reduces their accuracy even more. In that moment, their overexcitement was the only thing that saved our lives.

Thank Christ that three metres down the alley on the side we needed was a door. I kicked at it manically and broke the lock. All seven of us all pretty much piled through it at the same time. Inside it was a small single-storey house.

Nobody was inside. A good job too, because being confronted by seven sweating blokes, eyes bulging out on sticks with adrenalin would have given them a heart attack.

It was pitch dark and we couldn't see a bloody thing. Every window was covered by drapes or boards. And the whole squalid place stank of piss. Chris and I cleared the house's three rooms. I fell arse over face on a coffee table in the first room, so we did the rest of the place on our hands and knees.

'Clear,' I shouted, after the second room. Chris crawled into the third, ripping at everything on the walls in the search for light.

'Fucking hell,' he shouted. 'There's no fucking way out of here. Fuck it.'

It was a dead end.

We had no choice but to go back out into the alley of death and try again elsewhere. But the thought swiftly came to me that it could take us hours to find a successful way through that maze of shit holes.

Meanwhile, the enemy was getting closer. We could hear them shouting commands from the nextdoor compounds. If we didn't keep moving, they'd be on to us in a few seconds. Don't think any more. Just do.

'Fuck it, lads, we're just going to have to leg it the 100 metres to the end of the alleyway. We'll do a right, then a right again and that will take us back to the Argylls.'

If they were still there, that is.

'OK, Danny, whatever. Let's just fucking get on with it then,' said Chris.

I switched my SA80 to automatic. It was trench-clearing time. I led off out into the alleyway again with my index finger already semi-depressed on the trigger. The first person that appeared at the other end of the alleyway was going to get the full mag and no mistake.

As I sprinted down it as low as I could, I could hear gunmen chattering on the other side of the alleyway wall. They could hear us too. Halfway down, two hands and an AK poked over the lefthand wall just in front of me and squirted a burst down into my path. I threw myself tight against the wall and the rounds narrowly shaved past me.

I heard the bolt go in the bloke's rifle. Dead man's click – his mag was empty. I returned the compliment, and gave a similar burst back over to his side of the wall also without looking at what I was firing either. There was a groan. Then nothing more.

I carried on running. The closer we got to the end, the more I felt we were going to make it. It was foolish optimism.

'Come on lads, we're almost on the road.'

And with just 20 metres left to go, we saw it. It was obvious it would be there. Only the most deluded of all wishful thinking had persuaded me otherwise.

Straight in front of us, on the other side of the road from where the alleyway ended, was an RPK medium machine gun. It was set up on a bipod underneath a red Toyota car, and it was pointing straight at us. Two gunmen with AKs raised were standing either side of the vehicle.

They had waited until we were close enough to be sure they could hit us. Then all three opened up at once.

'Contact front! Contact front!'

Immediately we were down on our knees and aggressively returning fire. Then, we slipped into pairs. The years of training took over. While one bloke got up and sprinted ten feet back up the alleyway, the other emptied all the rounds he could in the direction of the gunmen. Then, the pair swapped roles. Fire and manoeuvre, fire and manoeuvre.

It was just like the bank robbery scene in *Heat*. It's amazing how well you remember it when you need to. But still the RPK poured lead at us. A whole burst went straight between my partner Smudge's legs just as he was stopping to turn and cover me. We looked at each other in amazement.

69

'Average,' I said, and we carried on. 'Go.'

It was working. They weren't hitting us, because our fire was causing so much havoc they were screwing up their aim. And it felt awesome. So we did it all the way back up to the top of the alleyway.

'Go,' screamed Smudge for the umpteenth time, adopting the cover position again. And I spun round to see 33 beautiful tonnes of Warrior sitting right there a few metres in front of me.

The methodical thumping sound of the Warrior's chain gun was slapping a target good and hard on the other side of the road, and its heavy diesel engines were still ticking over with a permanent growl. *Yes please, I'll have some of that if you don't mind.* The battle group QRF had turned up at last, and were waiting to extract us.

Colonel Gray was crouching down beside the Warrior, waving frantically and shouting at us to jump in.

'I need to get my other blokes in there first, sir.'

'Don't worry, Sergeant, they're all in already. Jump in quick.'

I did as I was told.

'All in,' someone shouted to the driver, and the door closed automatically with a heavy metallic clunk.

An overwhelming and incredible relief rushed through me like a drug. There were ten of us fully tooled up in a space built for seven with bodies everywhere, but I couldn't have cared less. I then realized how thirsty I was, so reached for a two-litre bottle of water and drank most of it straight down.

After what felt like a lifetime with RPGs still whooshing by overhead, as well as a lot of foul abuse to the driver from me, we finally chugged off. The Warrior tore up the hot tarmac streets with its giant tracks as it moved over them.

Ten deafening minutes later, we ground to a sudden stop. What was the problem? Who was attacking us now?

The back door began to open up again. As soon as I saw daylight through it, I piled out with my three fire-and-manoeuvre lads following me close behind. We all jumped straight into a square-shaped ditch, the first cover we could see.

'All round defence, lads!' I ordered, scanning desperately for the next target. The only people near us were calm clusters of men wearing British Army combat fatigues. They were just standing around chatting. Among them was Ian Caldwell and his QRF team. What the fuck was going on? Why weren't they taking cover, the idiots?

With a broad smile on his face, Colonel Gray calmly strolled over to us.

'Stand down, Sergeant Mills. This is the new Iraqi Army's training camp on the town outskirts. You're safe enough in here, I assure you.' As he walked off, he added, 'Good drills all the same.'

It was over.

We were surrounded only by what looked like the entire battle group. A huge fleet of Warriors was in the last stages of preparation before going into Al Amarah again to establish law and order. But we'd done our bit. And another fleet of Warriors arrived shortly to run us back to Cimic.

There was one final 'fuck you' lying in wait for us from the OMS. Just as the lead Warrior in our convoy got to within 100 metres of Cimic's front gate, an IED hidden by the roadside exploded right beside it. It was an old Iraqi army 155mm artillery shell. It made an almighty bang, but none of its shrapnel got through the vehicle's armour. Instead, it just covered it in shit.

Daz had already been flown in a medivac helicopter down

to a field hospital in Basra by the time we got back. He went down in the same chopper as Kev Phillips. They'd both live, we were told.

That night, we were treated differently by the rest of the company. Word had got round like wildfire what we'd been through. We had done our jobs, and we had done them well. That won us a fair amount of respect, and even a little awe. Of course it didn't last for long; they'd all get their turn soon enough.

Personally, I was just pleased as punch for my lads. The patrol had ten enemy kills that we could confirm. But, for all we knew, the real tally could have been triple that. We'd hardly had much of a chance to check many bodies for pulses. The guys had been fantastic and followed me everywhere I had asked them to go. Apart from retrieving the sensitive radio kit maybe, but that was certainly no bad thing. They'd fought like lions together, and I couldn't have asked for more. And as scary as it was at times, for all of us the adrenalin rush had been unbelievable.

After getting some scoff, I sat down alone to think it all over. I ran through the afternoon's events in my mind again and again. I wanted to work out what I'd done wrong to get us into that mess. I came to the conclusion that there was really nothing I should have done differently. We were just in the wrong place at the wrong time.

Nobody had told us that the very building we'd dismounted in front of was the OMS's Al Amarah headquarters. Also, the OMS weren't stupid. They'd seen all the movement around Cimic over the last few days, and they would have spotted our different berets. They knew there was a new regiment in town, and they would have wanted to test our mettle. Today's events gave them an opportunity to give us our first workout.

Then my thoughts turned to the sneaky OMS fighter I'd slotted climbing over the wall.

In the movies, you're supposed to feel sorrow and remorse about having taken life. You're supposed to contemplate the tragedy of man, and all that. But the truth is the only feeling it gave me was satisfaction. That, and a bit of curiosity answered. This man along with a lot of his pals were trying to kill us. They meant my men and me serious harm and they had already badly hurt my good mate Daz. We had got them back and that felt good. I felt not a single second's guilt, neither then nor since. It was quite simply him or us, and I'm far gladder it was him.

The honest truth is I didn't give a shit about him. He was the enemy, and all I gave a shit about was that he was dead. He's wasted. Move on.

There was one more thing to do before I went to bed. I went to see the company quartermaster.

All quartermasters are tight as a gnat's chuff when it comes to giving out kit because they get good marks for saving money. Ours would give the very tightest a run for their money. While we had been stuck down that alleyway today, grenades would have come in very handy indeed on more than one occasion. I felt the day's events had earned me the right to dispense with pleasantries.

'I need grenades, and I need them fucking right now,' I told him.

It was deeply disappointing. He didn't even put up a word of argument. He just meekly pushed over a big box of the things, and I stuffed as many as I could into every pocket I had.

8

The next morning, Major Featherstone called an O Group. They were normally held in the evenings, but that day it was first thing. There was urgent business to be discussed.

Every company and battalion has a regular O Group. O stands for orders. You can do it anywhere, on the battlefield or with your feet up in barracks. It doesn't matter. It's when the head sheds all get together during an operation to discuss – or be told – how the unit is going to progress. For Y Company, it meant all four platoon commanders and their deputies, the sergeant major, and the company 2i/c.

Featherstone's O Groups were more relaxed than most. Wanting to be a man of the people, he liked to hear our opinions.

That day he began with an apology.

'First off, guys, I'm sorry we didn't have any idea the big white building at Yellow 3 where Sergeant Mills was contacted is the OMS's headquarters. Unfortunately, battle group HQ in Abu Naji hadn't seen fit to tell us that. We know now. We've got no idea how long they will want to fight us, but we do know that there's no sign to any end of the standoff in Najaf.'

Moqtada al-Sadr was still hiding out in a large Shia shrine in Najaf. He was being protected by thousands of fanatical supporters who had barricaded themselves into the shrine with him. The US military were encamped on the outskirts of the city. If they wanted al-Sadr, they would have to go in and get him. That would mean a massacre on both sides, and both sides knew it.

Featherstone continued his speech. As he spoke, he chucked a karabiner from one hand to the other in a purposeful gesture.

'What we do know though, thanks to yesterday, is that the Al Amarah OMS have made their intentions towards us very clear. The CO is adamant that we must be able to do all we can to protect ourselves while this whole business lasts. That means we're going to stop pretending we're having a picnic here and everything's nice and dandy. Cimic House is the centre of law and order for this province, and that's the way it's going to stay – even if it has to become a fortress to do that.

'We're also going to start giving some of it back to these bastards if they want it.'

It was what we all wanted to hear. The gloves were coming off. We could stop smiling like clowns everywhere we went and start doing a soldier's job.

The mood of frustration in Cimic hadn't been helped by the RPG attack on the front sangar in the middle of the night. There is an alley directly opposite it only 60 metres away on the other side of the main road, from where the compound is most vulnerable. Without the sangar's sentries spotting him, an OMS fighter had crawled into it just after 2 a.m. and opened fire. He scored a direct hit. The grenade's explosion blew the sangar's three occupants clean out of it and onto the ground 20 feet below. All three blokes had to be medivaced out with blast injuries and broken limbs. From that night onwards, it became known as RPG Alley.

The previous day's events had also put an end to the bold prediction that only one in five of the battle group would see some proper action at some stage of the tour. It was only Day Two, and the majority of us had already been caught up in an ocean-going-sized contact. There were still officially 173 days of it to go. But if they did want a war, we were going to be ready for them.

As part of the CO's new regime, Cimic House was to be thoroughly militarized. Not only did we badly need better protection, but it sent a message to the OMS that we were here to stay.

Forced against their will to labour under the fallacy that they were on a peacekeeping tour, the Light Infantry had been prevented from doing almost anything to fortify Cimic House. That included not being able to deploy snipers on Cimic's roof, until the very end. It was all because the CPA were adamant that the place musn't look like a combat zone for the sake of the trust they were trying to build with the locals. As a result, the lads were getting homemade blast bombs regularly chucked over the compound's walls. The poor sods just had to sit there and take it.

The CPA bods weren't going to like our militarization at all – especially because the very first thing that went was their treasured views over the Tigris. We erected ten-foot-tall anti-sniper screens made out of locally made reed fencing all along the compound's perimeter. That would stop people taking pot shots at us as we moved around inside. On top of the sheeting went a thick coil of razor wire, to dissuade any suicidal nut from getting over the walls in a hurry.

The front and rear sangars were rebuilt more sturdily and filled with proper sandbags. We had to dig up most of the garden to fill them. We also threw out all the old local weaponry that the CPA had asked the Light Infantry to put in the sangars. They were lined with RPKs, AK47s, old Iraqi army boxes of ammo, and even RPGs – again, all to make the place look more Iraqi-friendly rather than foreign occupied.

Screw that. We replaced them with our own weapons. That meant a GMPG in each and NATO standard ammunition. Our weapons were tried and tested, and had been properly zeroed. The local jumble sale collection were unzeroed, we didn't have the proper cleaning kits to maintain them, and we had no idea how accurate they were.

And from now on, the front gate would be manned at all times by Y Company troops, not just Iraqi policemen. We'd seen how reliable they could be.

As the roof was our domain, my platoon was responsible for fortifying that part of Cimic. The key to sniping is being able to see as much as possible in comfort. So we rearranged it just how we wanted it. First off, we taped down all the wires up there for the radio antennas and the Sky TV satellite dish. They were trip hazards.

Then there was the crappy half sangar the Light Infantry had built. A sangar is the army term for a fortified lookout post, normally at height. We moved it from the south-west corner to the south-east, which gave us a far clearer view straight down Tigris Street. And we rebuilt it up to chest height with a base three sandbags thick. We gave it a flat roof with some timber and another couple of sandbag layers, and laid a camo net over its sides. It wouldn't have stopped a dirty great mortar round bang on target from killing everyone inside. But it did give us something to dive into if we saw or heard a mortar launch. And it gave us a little bit of protection from the heat. From then on, it was known as Top Sangar.

We also built a second half sangar on the small roof of the enclosed stairwell block that led up to the flat roof. It was just three metres square. But it was the highest point of the house and that meant we wanted to be there. We made a ladder to get up there, and gave it a three-foot wall of sandbags and a lining of mattresses. Only six blokes maximum

77

could comfortably work in it at any one time, but it gave us another eight feet of elevation and a great 360-degree view of the town from one single position. Its position was known as Rooftop.

All this work was done in the middle of the night, so we could use the cover of darkness to climb about the place.

In the morning, the CPA bods woke up just as we were finishing off. Molly Phee had cleared the lot, so we had nothing to worry about. But that didn't stop a few of them sharing their feelings with us.

The prettiest woman in the compound by a country mile was an American CPA official called Jodie. She was young, had long brown hair, big boobs, and always wore tight denim jeans. A very nice bit of eye candy and no mistake. And just the sort of thing you don't want to see when you're trying to concentrate on a difficult job. But we all still used to gawp at her.

That morning was the first time any of us had really seen her open her mouth. And the dream was ruined in an instant.

Dale had been supervising a couple of young lads put the finishing touches to the sniper screens by the water on the western wall. Jodie flicked her hair over her shoulder and marched straight up to him.

'What the hell do you bozos think you're doing? This is not an army boot camp, you know. This is a peaceful office of the government of Iraq. You've made us feel like we're living in Fort Knox.'

'Sorry about that, ma'am. We're only doing our job.'

'You may think it's your job, but the only reason we're being attacked is because you guys are here.'

'I'm not sure that's really the case, is it, love?'

'And anyway, what sort of image does all this give the local

Iraqis? They'll be scared to death about coming in here to see us now, which means we'll be back to square one.'

Then, as an afterthought: 'You people might as well be Saddam Hussein.'

Dale's a heftily patient man. But that really did it.

'Now you listen to me,' he said, his voice a low, slow rumble. 'The only reason we're here is to protect you and what you do in this place. And if we hadn't been here over the last few days, there's a middling to strong chance the OMS would have crept over the walls in the dead of night and chopped you and all your CPA buddies into little bits with kitchen knives. So go and have your breakfast, let us do our faarkin' job.'

We heard no more from Jodie about our renovations.

To prove Dale's point, we were mortared for the first time since we'd been in Cimic that day. It was a burst of four rounds, and only one landed in the camp perimeter. It exploded on the driveway with a loud bang leaving scorch marks on the tiles. Luckily nobody was around. The reality is there is little you can do if one of these things lands on you. Unless the mortar launch is close enough for you to hear its dull clump, the first you know you're getting incoming is the telltale whistle of the round coming in about three seconds before it lands. It's an intimidating weapon to deal with mentally because it takes your fate almost entirely out of your own hands. If you're in the wrong place, you're fucked. Simple.

One of the very few strategic negatives of Cimic House was the giant water tower within the compound right next to the main house. As the tallest building in Al Amarah, it gave the OMS's endless supply of mortar teams the perfect aiming point. Getting mortared is a nasty experience to begin with. But after a while, we learnt to stop being bothered about whether we were going to get it from the next shell and trust in fate. It was hardly as if we had a choice. With only a couple of attacks a day, the odds were still massively in our favour.

On the roof, we had to learn about our new city's skyline fast. At any moment we could be called upon by the battle group to try to bale someone out of the shit with our longs. That meant familiarizing ourselves with the view until we could see it in fine detail with our eyes closed.

From Rooftop we could see clearly for two kilometres in every direction. It was a great panorama.

Going clockwise and immediately to our west, a dam was slowly being constructed on reclaimed waste ground to control the Tigris tributary's flow. On the other side of that waterway was Al Amarah's main hospital. Further west still was the vast Olympic Stadium, a great big arena built in an art deco design that was now substantially unused. At some stage, some buffoon had decided Al Amarah actually stood a cat's chance in hell at competing with places like London, Paris, Tokyo and Sydney to host an Olympic Games, so they built it to the cost of millions. Severe delusion. That deserved sectioning.

Sweeping towards the north, a big dual carriageway road bridge crossed over the main Tigris River that ran west to east. It was known as Yugoslav Bridge because it was built by Tito. On the north-west bank was 'Vietnam Wood', a thick grove of date palm trees that had a jungle feel about it when we patrolled through the place.

On the eastern outskirts of the wood was the remnants of the Iraqi Army Corps' massive ammo dump. Tank and artillery shells were piled up in dozens of mounds as tall as a man, just rusting away. Most of the serviceable stuff had already been pinched by the locals and the OMS but there were still regular scavengers around it. Unlike at Abu Naji, they didn't need to steal the stuff in the city centre. Here they just picked it up off the street.

Directly north over the Tigris was one of the most pathetic sites of all, the shattered ruins of the Corps' city centre camp. It was completely flattened by the USAF twice, in the Gulf War and then in the invasion. Since Saddam's downfall, it had been inhabited by hundreds of refugee families. I don't know how they managed to survive in that slum, but they did. It was overrun by packs of wild dogs and covered in unexploded ordnance, along with the rusting hulks of abandoned T55 tanks. Most of the refugees had nowhere else to go. Behind them, there was a busy bus depot and a big school.

To the east after another major road bridge were the crowded rooftops of Al Amarah old town, a district known as Al Mahmoodia where there was the endless maze of market souks from our first foot patrol. The old town's houses were a lot older, and it was the only place in the city that wasn't built on a grid system. Again with a squint, some of it looked quite charming.

Behind the old town and over a third Tigris bridge as the river swung right was the OMS stronghold suburb of Aj Dayya. It was a stinking slum of a place. Al-Sadr's most fanatical followers ran it with a rod of iron so it became very fundamentalist, as well as home to a large body of the enemy. We went there as little as we could.

Swinging to the south, over 200 metres of rooftops, was the old town's major east–west thoroughfare, Baghdad Street. South of that was the main business district of the city. In it was the telecom centre, the police HQ and a series of oily factories. Then, the Pink Palace, and finally Tigris Street which led down to the OMS building at the bottom of it, with a pontoon footbridge that crossed the Tigris tributary halfway down it.

We struggled to see further than that, even with our high-tech viewing aids. But that was no bad thing really. About three kilometres south of Cimic, the shops and work yards began to give way to slum housing estates. Apart from Aj Dayya, the city's southern half was its main residential area. We passed through it on our way in from Abu Naji. And it was a true dump in the very highest of Maysan traditions.

The southern half was split into four estates of varying degrees of upkeep. From west to east, they were Al Masikh, Kadeem Al Muallimin, Al Awwashah in the middle and Al Muqatil on the east. Independent from the OMS, each of the estates also had its own militia, normally formed on tribal backgrounds. At any one time, they could be at full-scale war with just us, the OMS, each other – or all of us at once. There appeared to be little rhyme or reason to any of it. They couldn't tell you either. It was just what they did. For them, the British Army was just another rival tribe. Someone else to shoot at.

On the city's far southern outskirts just beside Route 6 was the city prison. We had codenamed it Broadmoor. Of course, it was empty when the Paras arrived here after the war. So the NGOs moved in as it was one of the few secure locations they could find from which to defend themselves if need be. These were the people who were really going to rebuild Iraq, from the UN right the way down to various US government-sponsored organizations and Christian charities.

We had at least five different standing tasks on the roof at any given time. The most important was to keep an over-view for as long as we could on any patrol that went out. If they came under fire, we would help out by trying to spot for the gunmen. And if any of them got into the shit at night, we'd be ready to pop up an illume round from a 51mm mortar tube.

The 51 is small and light enough to fit in a backpack. It has an accurate range of anything between 200 and 800 metres. We mostly used it for illume. Like all mortars, you simply put them down the tube and then pull a lever which smacks a hammer onto the round's firing pin, igniting it. And an illume is just a bloody great lump of burning magnesium that falls slowly down to earth on a little parachute. It burns with the brightness of 10,000 candles. It's like turning on a giant floodlight over the town for sixty seconds. If need be, it could also fire high explosive rounds.

During daylight I made sure there were always at least two sniping pairs on the roof, one in Rooftop and one in Top Sangar. Often, there were many more than that. Many of the lads used to come up in their free time as well because they enjoyed the work so much.

As with any soldier there, we had an automatic clearance to shoot people, and kill them, if we really thought it was necessary. We didn't need to ask for permission. But I was careful to remind the boys of the British forces' strict rules of engagement at that time. .

'Remember boys, do not open fire unless you perceive a direct threat to life. We need to catch these sods in the act of trying to kill us or someone else. That means grenade in hand about to be thrown, or AK47 brought up to aim. You know the drill.'

They didn't really need telling. Each and every one of them was a professional and knew you don't kill unless there is a clear military purpose. It's a waste of a perfectly good round.

We had all our kit laid out next to us. Everything was at arm's reach when we needed it. The place soon began to resemble a craftsman's workshop.

'I'm like a pig in shit up here,' Pikey announced to Ads.

'Yeah, you smell like one too, mate.'

The L96 took a box magazine that holds eleven rounds. So as well as the one in your rifle, we'd also lay out three to grab if they were needed. The rifle takes ball ammunition, exactly the same sort as a normal 7.62mm bullet. The only difference is it's green spot ammunition. Green spot is the first batch hot off the presses from a new mould. If you've just made 50,000 rounds, the first 5,000 will be the very best, so they mark them with a little green spot. After a while with metal clunking against metal, small nicks and dents will develop in the bullets. They could minutely affect the round's trajectory in flight. That's why the best stuff is always held over as sniper ammunition. We never use tracer, which lights up a few metres out of the barrel to show you where you are shooting. First of all, we know where we are shooting. Second, it will betray our position.

The L96 is accurate enough to kill at 900 metres, and harass at up to 1,100 metres. The restrictions are not human nor the fault of the rifle. After that sort of distance, the 7.62mm round just hasn't the explosive charge powerful enough to allow it to fly any further. It then starts to drop out of the sky.

The standard sight that goes on the rifle is a Schmidt and Bender. It gives from ×3 up to ×12 magnification, which is thrice that of the SA80 rifle sight. Its crosshairs are just two simple black lines that turn into dotted lines at its epicentre. In darkness, we clip a SIMRAD night filter on top of it. It's half the length of the normal sight, but three times the thickness. It works by sucking up any spare ambient light into itself and turns everything you can see into different shades of light green.

One of the first things we did on the roof was make up range cards. Everybody had one. It's the drill when you take up a static position that you're going to stay in for a bit. They are a series of pre-calculated points of distance in the panorama around you. When a target pops up and you need to shoot quick, you can immediately refer to the range card to get a rough distance and feed those coordinates into the sight's distance drum. It saves you having to make the distance calculation afresh every time you have a shoot on. We used a couple of laser range-finders to plot out all the major landmarks around us – the hospital and Yugoslav Bridge to the east, Vietnam Wood and the bus station to our north, RPG alley and Aj Dayya to the west, and Pontoon Bridge and Baghdad Street's rooftops to the south.

You also need some sort of stable platform from which to fire your rifle. At the same time, the sniper should be as comfortable as possible because any physical awkwardness might make the body shake. That butt must be as tight into your shoulder as possible and the barrel must be steady. There are a series of designated sniping positions to achieve all of that. The Prone position is lying down flat on your stomach. The Hawkins position means resting the L96's barrel on your thumb while you're lying down. Alternatively, you could use its bipod legs, or even a tripod.

While kneeling and standing, it's unlikely you can get the stability of aim you will need unless you then rig up a sling or a hook. The Tree hook position involves screwing a hook into a wooden surface and resting the rifle in that. Again, a lot of it is personal preference. You do whatever works best for you. On the rooftop, for most of us it normally meant wedging the longs into a decent ledge on top of the sandbag walls, with our knees or arses resting on the mattresses.

While the Number One worries about his position, the Number Two has his own viewing aids to set up. His responsibility is to get the Number One onto the target, and help him execute the shot. He has at least three sets of binoculars to hand. One is a basic set that gives him strong magnification. Another will be a SOFIE, which are thermal and pick up body heat signature. And finally a laser range-finder. Not all the kit has to be hi-tech though. Most Number Twos also like to carry small periscopes that allow them to see over parapets without exposing their heads. The best snipers' periscopes were made in World War Two, so we still use them.

Throughout their work, One and Two talk to each other incessantly. Sharing information is crucial. You'll discuss everything you see while spotting for a target. And once you have picked one up, Number Two will give a permanent running commentary on everything the target does from that moment onwards.

'Target still stationary in the driver's seat. Though he's fidgeting now, looks like he might be about to get out the car,' Number Two would say.

'Yup.'

'Target getting out of the car now. Closes the car door. Going to the boot, and opens it up. Has a rummage about.'

'Aha.'

'Target is taking a long wrapped package out of the boot. Could be a weapon. Target closes the boot.'

'OK.'

'He's taking the package back to the front seat again, this time passenger's side. Puts package down beside him into the foot well. Target stationary again. Target now picking his nose.'

'OK, mate. Roger all of that.'

Number Two will still commentate even if Number One can see everything perfectly well for himself. A running commentary confirms what his own brain is already telling him. That allows him to focus his mind 100 per cent on carrying out the kill.

Our personal weapons would also go up to the roof with us along with our battle webbing, just in case we needed them in a hurry. And we also made sure there were at least two GPMGs set up in or close by to each of the roof's sangars. Nothing we had was going to stop a determined bomber quicker than a Gimpy.

Technically known as an L7 General Purpose Machine Gun, the Gimpy has been the much loved mainstay of the British infantry for decades now since it first came into service in the 1960s. It was designed to put down 750 rounds a minute of heavy suppressive fire. And that was just how we used it outside the OMS building during our first contact.

The Gimpy weighs 14 kilos and is fed by belts of 200 rounds, which come in tin boxes that hold 800 in each. With its flip-up sight and mounted on a tripod, a GPMG can be effective at ranges up to 1,800 metres, thanks to its 63 cm-long barrel. But you can also use them in what is known as map-predicted mode, like mini-artillery pieces. If you point the barrel up into the air, the rounds will fall down onto the target in an arc, giving you ranges of up to 3,000 metres. It's a very skilled art form, but very impressive when done properly. Because of the 7.62's higher calibre, you have to change its barrel after every 2,000 or so rounds fired, because the barrel will have become so hot and in danger of melting. It can literally glow orange. So each machine gun is set up with a bag of two fresh barrels next to it.

As the fighting in Najaf and Baghdad continued, we also got regular taskings from the Americans to look out for Mehdi Army battle casualty replacements passing through our AO. Route 6 was one of the two main roads to both cities from Basra and Iran. Thousands of Shia Muslims flocked from both to join their brothers pitted against the Great Satan. They often travelled together in coaches with flags and posters hanging out the windows. I'd put up an extra pair to scan for them along the Red Route – which was Route 6 when it hit Al Amarah – and where it crossed the Tigris at Yugoslav Bridge. Once we'd identified them, the Americans would often lie in wait for them further up the road.

The task was known as Operation Tiger. Sometimes, it was just speculative spotting. On other occasions, there was specific intelligence that the Americans wanted us to confirm. They often gave us not only the colour and make of the buses, but a four-hour time window when we could expect to see them. It was amazing how accurate some of the intelligence was.

Des and Oost loved volunteering for Op Tiger. It allowed them to salivate at the enemy.

'Hey Oost, look what we've got coming,' the Number Two Des would say, staring through his binos. 'Two white buses 50 metres apart. What was the int again?'

'Two white buses.'

'What time is it?'

'It's 5.46 a.m. That's almost bang in the middle of the time frame. The Yanks said between 4 a.m. and 8 a.m. Fuck, their green slime are good.'

'Yeah. Shit, man, I wish we could just slot a few right here and now.'

'Yeah I know, man. Would save the Yanks the effort. Maybe we could just say that my finger got a spasm.'

Despite their bloodlust and the immense temptation, Oost and Des never did open fire on the Mehdi Army convoys. They were too professional for that.

There were also the permanent watches over the regular trouble spots that we had identified. After a few days, the enemy's octopus-like pattern of movement slowly began to come clear.

Four of their favourite sites for shenanigans became so infamous that we gave them their very own codename. It saved a wordy explanation each time we wanted to report activity over the radio to the Ops Room.

They were christened after precious metals. Gold was a stretch of waste ground on the north bank concealed from our eyes by ruins. It was a popular mortar-firing position. Silver was a road junction over to the north-east where the OMS used to set up their own illegal vehicle checkpoints. It was also a regular ambush spot. Bronze and Zinc were two more favoured mortar points, the first 300 metres to our east amid the old houses, and the second a park 1,500 metres to our south down Tigris Street, conveniently on the other side of the road to the OMS building. The lazy sods could pop a few rounds down the tube while they were waiting for the kettle to boil.

The CO had been right to take the gloves off the battle group as early as he did. What Daz and I thought might have been the end of the OMS's resistance in Al Amarah proved only to be the end of its beginning. From the day Daz was blown up, they kept up a regular barrage of violence against us. During the day that meant opportunistic attacks on patrols. And every night without fail, at least one RPG or mortar strike on Cimic. By the end of our first ten days, the whole company had seen their first contact. Some had already had to fight their way out of two or three.

We had no choice but to keep up with the pace the enemy had set. We had to learn how to do that fast.

9

As snipers, we were busy as buggery. Our dual role of manning the roof and keeping up with the patrol programme ran us ragged. With all our skills, Major Featherstone had decided we were his most potent force and wanted us to be doing as much as possible. It was ironic. Only a month ago back in Tidworth, we had wondered whether there would be a role at all for the platoon in Iraq.

The daily routine was particularly hard on me and Chris. One of us would be up commanding activities on the roof half the night. When he staggered in, the other would go up to take over. Then in the morning it was time to crack on with the patrols again. But we wouldn't have had it any other way. The excitement kept us going.

'It's weird, Danny,' Chris told me. 'I should be bleeding unconscious with the lack of kip I'm getting, but I feel right as rain. D'ya think they're putting cocaine in the scoff?'

We learnt most out and about on foot patrols in town.

We got to know the warning signs when trouble was about to kick off. Empty streets in the middle of the day always spelt bad news. Before the shooting started, the OMS would often tip the locals off first to allow them to get under cover. Men running about on rooftops was another combat indicator. The enemy used high spots to signal to each other, flapping bits of cardboard around. We also learnt we should never stay in one place for longer than five minutes. That's all the time the OMS would need to organize an ambush. Going too close to houses with black flags hanging off them was also a bad idea. It was the colour of the OMS and its owners would see our presence as a challenge. For the same reason, the city's mosques were also put out of bounds. There was no point in picking a gun fight just for the sake of it.

Not all of Al Amarah's people hated us. We still got friendly smiles from the law-abiding majority as we patrolled. Some even willingly engaged us in conversation to practise their English. But from one street to another the mood could turn dramatically and without any warning. On one early patrol, we popped our heads into a metalworks to say hello. We had been told it was a friendly area. Nobody would talk to us. Instead, all the workers started banging away as loudly as they could at their desks. It was calculated to intimidate, and it did. We quickly left.

We also learnt about Al Amarah's history. One place more than any other brought that home to us. We first came across it on a foot patrol. We had known it was there, and it was marked on our maps. But we had been foolishly expecting to come across neat rows of gravestones because of what you see in northern France. Behind a big park on the southern banks of the Tigris, at the western edge of the old town was the Commonwealth War Graves cemetery.

'Keep your eyes open for the cemetery, Pikey,' I told my point man. 'It's supposed to be around here somewhere.'

'I am, boss. I can't see a bloody thing. It's all just waste-land. The only thing around for miles is this brick tower thing. Hang on, there's some English writing on it. It says "Amara War Cemetery".'

We had walked right into the middle of the place without having any idea. The cemetery was the size of a couple of football pitches, but there was very little left of any head-stones. Most had been smashed up into fragments, which had themselves been overgrown by weed. The tall red brick obelisk with a domed black roof that Pikey had spotted had once been its front gate. But it was now badly chipped by bullet holes and desecrated by Arabic graffiti. The cemetery's ramparts by the river had also fallen down, leaving the plot susceptible to regular flooding and water damage.

There was a total of 3,704 British and Commonwealth troops under its ground. Most were killed in the bloody Mesopotamian campaign against the Turks and Arabs in the First World War. It wasn't our finest hour. We lost an entire division of 10,000 troops during the grim 147-day Siege of Al Kut in the winter of 1915–16, and a further 23,000 casualties from the relief force that failed to break it. It was seen at the time as the greatest British military disaster since the Charge of the Light Brigade, and far more costly in numbers. And it was fought in horrific conditions where soldiers had to resort to eating rats. Al Amarah itself was the scene of a major battle in June 1915 as the invasion force struggled north to Baghdad.

In one corner, a long stone memorial wall was just still standing. It had the names, rank and regiment of all the dead buried there on it in alphabetical order. Many of the names on the memorial wall were still legible. Two Victoria Cross holders are buried there, the Royal Navy's Lt Commander Edgar Cookson and Lt Colonel Edward Henderson, of the North Staffordshire Regiment. Both were killed winning them. I could also make out the names of several of our regiment's illustrious forebears. Among them were The Queen's Own Royal West Kent Regiment, The Queen's Royal Regiment and The Buffs. Many of their soldiers had died young, the same age as a lot of my blokes in the platoon.

It was a sobering thought. For us, Al Amarah was a brand new experience. But for the British Army, it was very old territory. Along with every other cemetery for British war dead in Iraq, it had been entirely abandoned after the first Gulf War in 1991. Saddam refused the Commonwealth War Graves Commission access to pay their caretakers and gardeners. They still hadn't found it safe enough to come back.

As soldiers, it was a desperately sad site. You deserved more than that if you had made the ultimate sacrifice for your country. We had a wander around the place and reflected on it. Nobody said much.

'The poor sods,' said Chris. Even he knew a *Blackadder* line wouldn't have been appropriate there. 'Here we are, back here all over again. Why are we always fighting the Arabs?'

We didn't stay for long. I could see some of the younger lads getting a bit too thoughtful, so we all took a few pictures for the albums back home, and moved off again. It was not a place to hang around.

In case we were in any doubt, during those days we also got final confirmation of whose side the Iraqi police were on.

The patrols involved regular visits to town police stations to check their armouries. We supplied them with new weapons and equipment to give them some pride and confidence, and so they could take on the OMS themselves. That meant AKs, brand new German-made Glock pistols, body armour and helmets, all painted nice and blue for them. Then we'd go back a few days later, and half the stuff would already be missing. 'So and so has got it', or more often 'it got stolen' were the regular excuses. But through the sights of our longs on the roof, we'd see OMS men cutting about with the Glocks stuffed into their trousers on the very same day.

On the surface, we'd still turn up to train the cops and offer advice. But it was all a façade, and we'd talk to them through gritted teeth. It was one big game. Both sides knew we had to carry on playing it to please our masters in Baghdad.

Some idiot young Iraqi coppers pushed it too far one day when we were on our way back to Cimic at the end of a patrol. There were three of them, in their mid-twenties, and they were lazing around on the roof of a small single-storey police station on the corner of Baghdad Street. They looked a shambles, all skinny and unshaven with their shirts hanging out.

As we patrolled past on the other side of the road, Pikey gave them the usual friendly wave. In response, one of the coppers put an imaginary rifle up to his shoulder, aimed it at us, and pretended to pull the trigger. His other two friends thought it was hysterical. We didn't.

Pikey was straight over to them in a flash. The coppers stopped laughing instantly, and shat themselves. He ordered them down from the roof with hand signals and made all three stand to attention against a wall.

'Not funny. Now listen to me, you fucking idiots. If you ever do that again, I'll kick the shit out of you. Do you understand me? Do you?' he screamed.

Smudge was right in behind him. To reinforce the point, he made his SA80 ready by loudly cocking a round into the chamber.

'You wankers are supposed to be on our side,' he added for good measure. 'That's why we're fucking paying you. Think about that next time you want to crack a funny.'

Despite the language barrier, you could tell the cops got what Pikey and Smudge were saying. They were wide eyed and shaking. They didn't do it again.

Frustration had been building in the platoon over how

we'd been shackled from carrying out a kill, particularly over a hefty desire to attack the mortar crews who'd been chucking stuff at us pretty much every night. Several times the boys had asked permission to engage targets that were borderline under the rules of engagement. But Major Featherstone, who was very cautious, had repeatedly refused.

The OMS weren't stupid. They had worked out our rules of engagement. So they gladly took the piss in the full knowledge there was fuck all we could do.

For three nights in a row, Ads had spotted a mortar team in a truck moving north over Yugoslav Bridge into the wasteland that they used to engage us. They would set up and fire behind buildings where they knew we had no direct line of sight on them. Brazenly, the team would then come back right in front of us. If the team were trying to wind up Ads, it worked.

One night, Ads – known for his sharp eye – even spotted the top of a mortar barrel in the back of an open-topped truck crossing back over the bridge just after we'd been hit. There were two men in the back with the equipment as well as the driver in the front. Ads radioed down to the Ops Room on his PRR.

'Ops Room, Rooftop. I have three UKMs [Unknown Males] driving a flatbed pickup with a mortar barrel in the back. Am I cleared to engage?'

'Can you see them setting up the mortar?' was the response from Major Featherstone.

'No, they've just finished. But I know it's them. Can I engage?'

'No, only if you can see them setting up a mortar.'

'Well, can I fire a warning shot then, over the top of the vehicle?'

'No.'

Silence, while Ads thought about the diplomacy of his next response. But not for very long.

'Well, what's the fucking point in us being up here then, sir?'

'Wind your neck in, Somers,' said Featherstone.

The next day, I was pinged to do a shift manning the radios in the Ops Room. I hated being stuck in there, but it was another of my responsibilities as a platoon commander. We all had to take it in turns. During a routine afternoon patrol, a multiple from the Mortars Platoon were ambushed at Blue 11, a major road junction east of Cimic on the river bank. They were pinned down by a huge weight of fire and taking incoming from a full 180-degree angle in front of them.

The twelve guys dived for shelter behind a garden wall in front of them. They couldn't retreat because it would take them straight into one of the arcs of fire. They were in deep shit because one of them had taken a bullet in the chest and was bleeding badly. Dale had rushed up to the rooftop to lead the company's response. As he leapt three stairs at once, he summoned every available sniper up there with him to help out. I heard all the action play out on my PRR.

With Maysan's radio gremlins at work again, the only way Cimic had of speaking to the patrol was from Dale to one of its NCOs, Cpl Daz Wright, who was carrying a back-up set. And Daz Wright had to shout loudly over the sound of rounds going down all around him to make his contact reports heard.

'Do you copy? We're pinned down, Sarn't Major. We've got no fucking comms with anyone apart from you. We need a Warrior down here to extract us. Now.'

Dale was always a calm and reassuring presence. 'Keep going mate, you're doing a good job.'

Daz Wright explained where the enemy's main four firing positions were. The most lethal was on the north bank across the river, almost at right angles to them. With their longs at the ready, Ads and Fitz were in Rooftop Sangar facing directly east. There was no time for a Number Two to set up. On hearing Daz Wright's report, they immediately started scanning the area he had identified on the north bank. From Cimic, they had a good and uninterrupted view over most of it.

'If you see anything at all let me know immediately, lads,' boomed Dale as he crouched beside them and peered through a set of binoculars.

It was time for Ads and Fitz to use all the empathy they could muster. You have to ask, Where would I want to be if I was the enemy? Normally that means the high ground, buildings or rooftops – anything that offers good cover. Then, you tell yourself to look out for any shape or aspect that seems unusual in the landscape. Nine times out of ten, that's exactly where they are.

Ninety seconds later, Ads spoke up. 'Sarn't Major, I've got him. I've got a shoot on here.'

Ads was lying flat on his stomach with the L96's bipod legs up. The rifle's long, camouflage-sprayed barrel was pointing over the small lip of the wall. At a distance of more than 800 metres away, all he had seen was a long thin piece of metal poking out from a large bush. A hard looking shape sticking out of a round mass of greenery was unusual enough to attract his attention. He had concentrated on it for 20 seconds. When he finally saw a long spurt of yellow flame blast out of it, he knew what he was looking at was eight inches of an AK47 gun barrel.

'Are you sure, Ads?'

'Yes, Sarn't Major – hundred per cent.'

'If you're happy, mate, take the shot.'

It was a hell of a long way away, so Ads got to work quick. First, he ranged the gunman's position. He was 828 metres away. So Ads did his calculations, and adjusted the sight's range drum by eighteen clicks, setting it to precisely 830 metres. He looked back through the sight, and ever so slightly raised the L96's barrel to put the bush back into his crosshairs. In the movies, snipers aim off and above targets to take account of distance and wind. That's a load of bollocks. The crosshairs are always dead on the target.

There are a total of thirty-two different clicks on the windage drum. You choose which one to set it on depending on whether there is a light breeze or a Force Nine gale blowing. Ads looked harder at the bush through his scope to see if any leaves were moving on it. It fitted comfortably into the middle third of the sight. It was perfectly still, so he left the drum on zero.

Next, the gunman himself. From just the end bit of the barrel that Ads could see, he estimated exactly where the gunman's head might be. You aim for the largest part of the body visible. Normally that means the torso. You don't need to demolish someone's brain to take them out of action, a 7.62 in the kidneys is more than sufficient. But this time it had to be a head shot, because the gunman was lying flat on the ground and his head offered the greatest surface area. Ads looked down into the bush directly following an imaginary line from where the barrel was pointing. The head was roughly 12 inches further back from where the barrel ended, he calculated, and set his eyes on one specific leaf behind which he believed his prey lay. He was ready.

It had taken him no more than three minutes from start to finish. A novice might have taken half an hour, and still only be in with a fifty–fifty chance.

The sweat was running down his brow hard, but he ignored it. He controlled his breathing, gripped the weapon firmly and took up the pressure on the trigger. Then, he took in a deep breath and held it. After staying perfectly still for five more seconds, he took the shot. One slow and steady movement of his index finger, not a snatch. Total control.

A 7.62mm ball round fired from an L96 travels at 875 metres a second. So Ads's round took just a fraction less than a full second to hit the target. Immediately, the barrel sticking out from the bush fell onto its side. Its iron sight was no longer visible, and it didn't move again.

Five seconds later, Ads exhaled slowly. With perfect calm, he sat up and quietly announced, 'I got him.'

He pulled back the bolt of the L96, pulled out the bullet's empty casing, and popped it in his pocket.

'I'm keeping that.'

He lay the L96 back down on a sandbag next to him, and lit up a Lambert and Butler cigarette. A cheeky little grin then spread right across his face. He had killed the gunman stone dead without ever even setting eyes on him. One shot, one kill. It was perfection.

For Daz Wright's patrol, the kill had the effect of taking a considerable amount of fire off them so they could begin to look up over their garden wall and return fire. That gained them a foothold in the battle. Ten minutes later, Warriors arrived to extract them with the patrol suffering no further casualties. Daz Wright later had a chance to inspect Ads's work behind the bush. The gunman was still lying there. The shot had taken the whole of the back of his head off.

For the rest of the day, Ads was the platoon hero. He taunted Pikey repeatedly about it.

'Who's the fucking daddy, eh, Pikey?'

The kill had a great effect on all the platoon's morale. Everyone was proud of Ads, but it was a platoon triumph as well, as it could have been any of us. We had proved our trade by saving comrades in dire peril. The satisfaction wasn't warped bloodlust. It was entirely professional. Just like a bricklayer who's just built his first house, and knowing he can do it – and damn well at that.

Company morale was also high at that time, despite the steep learning curve we were all going through. But that doesn't mean there wasn't the odd bit of tension. With 106 fully grown men living in such close proximity, it would be a miracle if there wasn't the odd tense situation.

It came in the shape of Louey, and his arch nemesis Private John Wedlock. An enormous Fijian in Recce platoon in his mid-twenties, John Wedlock was the only bloke in the

View of Al Amarah city centre from above its southern edge, over a Lynx helicopter gunner's shoulder

The Cimic House compound beside the River Tigris, from the north, with the Pink Palace behind it

Sniper Platoon,
1PWRR.
Back row, left to right:
H, Smudge, Des, DV,
Dan, Daz, Rob, Chris,
Fitz, Ben and Ads.
Front row:
Pikey, Longy, Oost,
Sam, Harry, Gilly
and Louey

Yours truly on the
look-out for enemy
activity on Cimic
House's roof

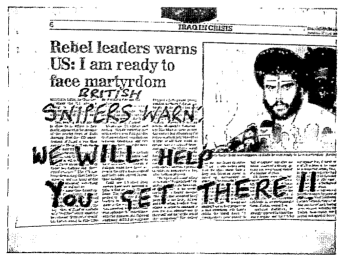

Article picturing rogue
cleric Moqtada al-Sadr,
pinned on the wall
of Sniper Platoon's
living quarters

A typical roof-top scene post-battle

Cimic House's swimming-pool, before its redecoration by mortar shrapnel during the siege

Louey and Des in the rear sangar

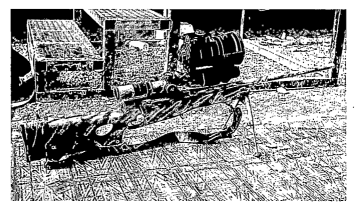

An L96 sniper rifle with a SIMRAD night sight

The view of the OMS building from behind the wall
where Dan's men first returned fire at the enemy, on
18 April

RPG Alley

View of the OMS building from the neighbouring park, a favoured launch location for enemy mortar teams

Major Ken Tait on his return from a fighting patrol before he was banned from going out

The remains of Daz's burned-out Snatch after the 18 April contact

Like having the gods on our side. The awesome AC-130 Spectre Gunship

Chris, me and Sgt Ian Caldwell in the driveway of Cimic House, preparing to leave on an arrest raid

Chris snipes and Des spots while concealed on a roof-top in downtown Al Amarah

Ads snipes and Oost spots early in the morning from the roof-top of Cimic House – after a hard night's work

Fast Air. An F-16 drops a laser-guided bomb

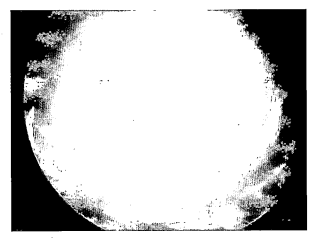

Dale fires illume mortar rounds from Cimic
House's roof – his birthday treat!

whole company even bigger than Louey. He was a very keen rugby player, and he was seriously hard. When he initially applied to join the British Army in Fiji, he was told he couldn't because he had too many tattoos on his arm. So he cut them out with a pen knife.

Louey and Wedlock had a massive rivalry over who was the biggest bloke in the company. They hated each other with a rare passion, and it went back as far as anyone could remember. They had already had a few scraps back at Tidworth. His rivalry with Wedlock was the single and only time Louey ever got into trouble. But in Iraq it got even worse. As far as they saw it, they were now representing their platoon's honour in a war zone. Louey was Sniper's big boy, Wedlock Recce's.

One day early on in the tour it flared up again. Wedlock mumbled something under his breath as he passed Louey while coming in from a patrol on Cimic's front driveway. That was Louey's cue to launch his favourite Wedlock piss-take. In his cool Caribbean lilt, he mercilessly took the piss out of the Fijian's broken South Pacific accent.

'Orr, hellor Wedlock. You do nice patrol or you bit hot boy now?'

Wedlock retorted with his usual insult at Louey.

'I may be black, but you're a lot darker black than me, man. Look at you, you're ugly black.'

Louey stood up straight and tall and eyeballed Wedlock with a stare that would have turned most of us to stone.

'Say that again, Wedlock.'

Luckily, Major Featherstone walked out of Cimic just at that moment. With reluctance, the two giants parted looking daggers at each other.

The only racism I ever heard in the battalion was between those two. And they were both black. How they were going to peacefully coexist within the same 100 square metres for the next six and a half months we had no idea. It was Clash of the Titans, and secretly, everyone longed for the next instalment.

That evening's O Group finally brought news about Daz. It had been twelve days since we had last seen him or known anything about him. Once a bloke disappears out of the battalion's area of responsibility, it's very hard to keep track of him. But the news was good. Having lost a lot of blood he had been in a critical condition when he arrived at the Basra field hospital on a Chinook. But the surgeons had done a great job of putting him back together, and he was expected to make a full recovery.

He was now in Selly Oak hospital in Birmingham, where all military battle casualties go. He'd also heard what we'd been going through since he left. He was furious he was missing all the fun. Apparently, he had already pissed the doctors and nurses off considerably by continually demanding to know the date when they would release him so he could get back out. A proper soldier.

Inside the platoon, the only teething problem we were having was Gilly. He was another new arrival for the tour and was a lazy bastard. Like Louey, Gilly had been attached to us as a driver. But if we'd won the lottery with Louey, with Gilly we'd lost the ticket. He was a 27-year-old recruit to the British Army from the Caribbean. He had made a mistake in joining the infantry, and he knew it. Sitting in trenches wet and tired all day long wasn't his bag at all. But the real problem for me was that he couldn't hack Iraq. Its extraordinary pace exposed him as the crap soldier he was. He could hide that easily enough in Tidworth. He was a quiet character who was just happy doing as little as possible for his money. But in Iraq there was nowhere to hide. If you didn't give your all while everyone around you was, they'd notice pretty quickly. It meant you would become an extra burden, and we didn't need that. Gilly would do everything he could to avoid going out on patrol, and he absolutely hated leaving camp. The thought of it terrified him. And he hadn't even been shot at yet.

He couldn't drive either. I learnt that the very first time he drove me around Al Amarah. He had no confidence behind the wheel of a Snatch. He kept tailgating cars in front, which is dangerous because it means you won't be able to manoeuvre around them if something happens. Then, as we approached the police station we'd planned to visit, I told him to hang a left into its driveway. Gilly turned right instead, straight into a garage. He was as nervous as a virgin on prom night. He'd got himself in such a state he was no longer listening to me.

'Gilly! What the hell are you doing? I said turn left, not right.'

'Sorry boss.'

I'd seen enough. 'Right. Stop there. Gilly, get out and get in the back. Sam, get out the back and get behind the wheel. Now, Sam, take us into the police station please.'

Gilly didn't drive for anyone again.

A few days later, he asked me for a transfer. Someone had obviously told him you got an easy life in the Royal Logistics Corps. It was bollocks, because loggies get shot at as much as the rest of us. But none of that stopped Gilly from going on and on at me about wanting to join 'the RLCs'.

'Gilly, do you even know what RLC stands for?'

'Er, well, er . . .'

'You haven't a fucking clue, have you? When you know a bit about the new unit you want to join, come back and see me, you silly sod.'

We were in a combat zone now. The company needed all the blokes it could get, even if they were as useless as Gilly. If he couldn't do anything else, he could hump water or ammo about the place. There was certainly no shortage of shitty jobs to do in Cimic. Passing him on to the RLC would also just be passing on the problem to some other poor sergeant in a loggies regiment. Perhaps Gilly just needed some more time to adjust. It was a brand new experience for all of us after all.

Gilly aside, in just a short time the battle group had made considerable progress in learning how to defend itself against the OMS and their tactics. In fact, we were getting pretty good at it. But there was also no ignoring that instead of it abating, the level of OMS-orchestrated violence against us was only increasing. Rapidly. The frequency of their attacks on patrols was going up day by day. At night, more and more mortars would thump in. The more we hurt each other, the greater the animosity on both sides. Notwithstanding events in Najaf, our own little war in Al Amarah began to develop a healthy life of its own. Every time the OMS escalated it, the battle group was forced to react.

On a vehicle patrol around the OMS stronghold suburb of Aj Dayya, a blast bomb was thrown at my Snatch. A long burst of machine-gun fire also rattled just over the heads of the two top cover. The bomb exploded a fraction early, a second before we would have driven into its full blast. But it still scorched and fragged the Land Rover's right side and windscreen. It was a close call. But it also proved to be the death knell for Snatches.

After the carnage that resulted from our first vehicle patrol along with the ever-increasing roadside bomb threat, it was decided that troops inside Snatches were too vulnerable. All Snatch Land Rovers were banned from leaving Cimic. Our patrols were to be on foot from now on. That way we would have more visibility around us and we could get into cover quicker. Warriors would be dispatched to extract us in an emergency, if we couldn't fight our way out.

For that purpose, two Warriors turned up at Cimic on permanent attachment. The forty-minute trundle from Abu Naji was too long for patrols in the shit to wait. They also provided the base with another excellent layer of protection. One was stationed just inside the front gate, and one ditto for the back.

Warriors are built to carry ten men: the driver, gunner, and commander and seven dismounts in the back. They were seriously ageing by then, but they still provided some handy firepower. The chain machine gun was gravity fed, loading long belts of 7.62 into itself upside down. It's fired by the gunner stamping on a pedal under his foot.

Hence the popular phrase among us in a contact, 'Give 'em some fucking pedal.' In the turret next to the chain gun was the Warrior's main armament, a 30mm Rarden cannon. With a range of 1,500 metres, its high explosive rounds would silence most enemy positions that fancied engaging us. But it was never easy to fire something as powerful as that in the middle of a built-up city. We didn't want to kill everyone.

Of course, the CPA bods made more irritated noises about us putting a couple of tanks on their lawn. But they didn't complain with any real conviction any more. With the fighting on the increase, even they were secretly quite pleased to see them there now.

At the very end of April, our official mission in Al Amarah was hit by another serious setback. For the last two days in a row, some of the civilian NGOs' 4×4 Land Cruisers had got badly shot up. On both occasions, gunmen lay in wait for them at Red 11. It was a major road junction on Route 6 just over the river from the OMS's HQ building. It was inconceivable that anyone else but the OMS could have been responsible.

The two organizations they had got were the American Heart Foundation and the Mines Awareness Teams. Both had been totally unarmed. One of their workers was shot in the leg. He lived, but it made the NGOs finally decide they couldn't stay any longer amid the town's rapidly deteriorating security. It was simply too dangerous for them to do any meaningful work. As a group – and with little regret – they packed up and left. This was bad news for us because it meant the only people left to rebuild Al Amarah now was us. Because of the fighting, most of our reconstruction effort had ground to a halt too. And that was really the only reason we were there in the first place.

That night, Cimic took its heaviest pounding yet from the OMS mortars. They opened up from three different positions just before midnight. They also used an 82mm tube on us for the first time. Previously, they had only chucked 60mm rounds. But an 82mm is getting on for the same sort of calibre shells used by light artillery guns. It was set up among the slums of the north bank and made a hell of a racket too. One of its giant shells scored a near direct hit on a Snatch in the vehicle park. It tore the arse out of the thing.

While we hunkered down under hard cover during the ferocious mortar strike, the operations officers at Abu Naji were already hard at work. For the CO, the NGOs' disappearance was the last straw. We had let the OMS take the initiative this far. But enough was enough. It was time for the battle group to attack.

Operation Pimlico was planned to begin at 2 a.m. the next

morning, May Day. It turned out to be a very bad joke. But the Abu Naji planners could never have foreseen what was to happen that day. None of us did.

On paper, the plan was a good one. We represented law and order, and the OMS were the criminals. So that's how it was decided to treat them.

Intelligence had revealed that six of their main players lived on the same shitty estate, the Kadeem Al Muallimin, in the south-west of the city. So we were going to go in and arrest them. But it was to be done in the dead of night for the maximum element of surprise. The arrest teams – a company of Royal Welch Fusiliers in Saxon armoured cars from Abu Naji who were attached to us for the tour – would be in and out before the city even woke up. If they did, Y Company would hold the fort in Cimic. The operation was named after a London tube station because all of ours on that tour were. No significance, just the easiest names for everyone to remember.

A backlash of some sort was expected. So from the early hours, most of the platoon was up on the roof. The rest of the company either doubled up in the sangars or waited in full battle kit as an emergency QRF.

The plan worked. The OMS men had no idea what was coming and were nabbed in their beds. The teams also picked up a fair stash of arms and explosives. But best of all, they got out with just a few volleys of fire at their rear. At Cimic, it remained quiet too.

We had to wait until sunrise to discover what a hornet's nest we had kicked over.

The OMS were absolutely livid that the battle group had the audacity to kick down the doors of some of their top men's homes. It was the first time we'd gone after them and they were in outraged shock. As far as they were concerned, it was a declaration of outright war. By the time it got light, they began to mobilize everybody they could, and their fighters started to come out in serious force. The town went crazy. We watched from the roof in amazement as the whole spectacle unfolded.

The city was a wall of noise. Trucks with loudspeakers were driving around and around blasting out angry messages in fast Arabic. The imam of every mosque was up in his minaret on their Tannoy systems. Cars packed full of blokes dressed in black cut about the place at full speed with guns poking out of every window, and car horns were honked incessantly. All over the city, thick plumes of black started to snake up. Many were the result of rubber tyres being set alight. It was an easy way to block a road.

'Jesus Christ, this is going to be interesting,' I said to Chris as we looked out over the mass hysteria. 'Do you think they've just been told they've won the Olympic bid after all?'

Chris thought the whole thing was hilarious. His General Melchett impression was in full swing.

'I don't care if they've just rogered the Duke of York with a prizewinning leek. They've all gone completely fucking kookoo.'

We asked Khalid, one of the Iraqi interpreters who worked for us at Cimic, up on to the roof to translate what all the loudspeakers were saying.

'They say, "Tell everybody to go home and get a gun. Come and fight infidel oppressor." They say this is jihad.'

11

The OMS were putting it about that our raid was a personal attack on the authority of Moqtada al-Sadr. And in Al Amarah, that was as good as an attack on Allah himself.

Khalid had started to get nervous. He could see his well-paid job coming to a swift end.

'Sergeant Mills, this is very bad. They are going to come in here and kill you.'

Des interjected. With the pride of a seasoned Boer hill scout, he stroked his long's barrel. 'Don't worry, Khalid. They're going to have to get past ten of these little puppies first. I'd just love to see them try.' And he meant it.

Cimic became a frenzy of activity. Everyone was now either standing to, or preparing to. The place was feverish with anticipation. There was another major hurdle we were going to have to overcome that day. We were overdue a big resupply from Abu Naji. We were low on food and ammunition, and it wouldn't wait. A column of Warriors was going to have to come into the city again to do it. The smart arses at Slipper City hadn't thought of that one.

What we didn't know was that there was a little bit of method to all the OMS's madness. By noon, they had mounted their own fortified checkpoints on all the roads leading into Al Amarah, and many of the major road junctions inside it too. The city had been effectively sealed off. With us inside it. And the enemy was ready and waiting to unleash seven shades of shit on anyone who tried enter.

They had also taken a load of senior policemen hostage. We had no dialogue with the OMS. So they broke the news in a phone call to Molly Phee. They would execute all of their hostages unless their prisoners were returned immediately.

I sent some of the boys down to get us a bigger supply of ammunition. If it was going to kick off, we might as well be prepared. They brought a shed load of it back up, and we made a massive central pile in the middle of the roof; boxes of green spot for the longs, belts of 7.62 for the Gimpys, tin after tin of 5.56 for the Minimis and SA80s, and crates of illume rounds for when it got dark. All the weapons we could lay our hands on we brought up and lay next to each of us. I personally had four beside me: a Minimi, GPMG, SA80 and my long.

Not everybody in the platoon had got a kill yet. So there was still a bit of idle banter going about, as soldiers do.

Pikey and Oost were particularly chomping at the bit as they had stayed back on a roof watch the day of our first vehicle patrol. Still crowing from his wonder shot, Ads didn't miss the opportunity to take the piss.

'You never know, boys. You might just get the chance to fire your weapons today. Start catching up with us.'

They did.

The plan for the resupply was to send the Warriors all the way up the Red route past us on the other side of the river, and over Yugoslav Bridge. They would then swing right around the north bank, down the Greens, and over into Al Amarah old town from the east, crossing the bridge at Blue 11. That way they'd avoid having to pass straight by the OMS building and the centre of the enemy's strength, at Yellow 3.

At 1 p.m., two foot patrols from the Mortar and Anti-

Tank platoons were pushed out from Cimic to meet them. Their mission was to secure the convoy's two major choke points. They were roundabouts either side of the bridge it would cross, at junctions Blue 11 and Green 9. Our job again was to provide overview.

Unfortunately, the OMS had the same idea. They also wanted to control the choke points, as one of just two ways into Cimic. And they'd beaten the foot patrols to it. As soon as the boys turned up, they got taken on by a huge amount of gunmen in doorways, windows or on rooftops directly overlooking them. They were getting cut up pretty badly by small arms fire from all angles. We heard the ambush, but couldn't see it. Blue 11 is just out of the roof's view. There were too many enemy weapons firing to even be able to count them. It sounded pretty bad.

I legged it down to the Ops Room to see what they knew. A few seconds later, the inevitable confirmation came over the radio, called in by one of the platoon commanders, Captain Paul Hooker.

'Zero, this is Alpha Three Zero Alpha. Contact. Wait out.' The first words said over the net in any contact. It clears the airwaves because when anyone hears that they know to shut the fuck up.

'We're getting engaged by around fifty enemy. Multiple positions.'

Then it went from bad to even worse.

'Contact casualty. Wait out.'

A good young private called Baz Bliss had taken a bullet in the side. It tore through his body armour, bounced around a bit inside, and came out his front, taking a bit of his right lung out with it. He had been shot by a sniper armed with a Draganov, the Soviet-made equivalent of our L96s. A seriously nasty weapon. If there was a bloke with a Draganov out there and who knew how to use it, they were in serious trouble.

Realizing this, the patrols had sprinted for cover randomly, wherever they could. They were totally split up with some having made it over the bridge, and others not. The lucky ones found market stands and a concrete wall to cover them; the unlucky had only the two-foot wall of the roundabout itself.

RPGs had now also started to tear over the roundabout lot's heads too. I could even hear the loud bangs of their explosions from the Ops Room. It sounded totally desperate.

There was no let-up. The longer it went on, the more panic crept into their radio transmissions. You could even hear them losing their tempers with each other over the net.

'Listen, you need to get us the fuck out of here,' said another voice over the net. 'There's fuck all we can do. We can't move an inch. We need some fucking help down here.'

Hearing your mates desperate and panicking is not a nice thing.

'OK. The Warriors are on their way,' insisted Featherstone. 'Try and keep calm.'

I charged back up to the roof to help the boys spot for targets. I hoped we still might be able to see some of the enemy's positions from our vantage point, if not the round-about itself. By the time I got up there, they were already busy engaging a series of muzzle flashes. *Good work, lads.*

'Keep your eyes peeled for a sniper, boys. We've got a fucker with a Draganov out there.'

They needed no more motivation. The targets were all at distance, so we concentrated on shooting with our longs.

From the roof, we could also see more OMS gunmen as they moved through the streets trying to get to the battle area as well as our Warriors.

Soon after, more heavy gunfire and explosions erupted to our south.

Jesus, must be the resupply convoy.

Sticking to the original plan, the long line of Warriors from Abu Naji was now approaching Yugoslav Bridge on the Red route, and had also begun to take a heavy kicking. OMS fighters were coming out to have a go at the Warriors from dozens of pre-planned ambush positions. There were RPG nests in ditches at the side of the road, others fired from the top of compound walls and some didn't even bother to conceal themselves as they stepped out directly in front of vehicles to loose off whatever they had.

I moved a couple of pairs on the roof's southern wall to see what they could do for the Warriors. At least they had a bit of armour.

Just when we thought it couldn't get any worse, the Cimic compound itself began to get attacked. Most of it was hopeful small arms fire from a fair few hundred metres away, but it was coming in from all around us, 360 degrees.

'Right, we don't want these twats thinking they can come too close to Cimic. A pair on each of the four walls. One in Top Sangar, and two in Rooftop.'

It diverted more of our resources away from the foot patrols, and that was a pain in the arse.

A couple of OMS in a crappy old red and white Toyota even attempted a drive by. They screeched round a corner from behind the Pink Palace and gave Front Sangar two full AK mags. The lads in the sangar took cover in time and nobody was hurt. For some reason that escaped us, the Toyota's boot was wide open throughout. We put some rounds into it anyway as it sped off in case another gunman was going to pop up.

Despite the chaos, the mortaring still remained the biggest personal threat to us on the roof – the OMS teams worked overtime that day. We were hit by a total of nine different barrages, so we were also spotting for the mortar teams every time they fired.

No matter what else was going on, the company's priority still had to be Captain Hooker's men. They were in the deepest shit. On top of the Warriors, Featherstone also dispatched a thirty-strong foot patrol to try to reach them by cutting through the old town instead. They had to fight the whole of the way down Baghdad Street to get anywhere close. Once they'd passed by, the locals put burning road blocks in behind them. The OMS had seen what was happening and the more troops they sucked in towards Blue 11, the more they tried to trap in there. They wanted to kill as many of us as possible.

In response, Abu Naji dispatched the entirety of the armoured QRF which was C Company. Now practically the whole battle group had been sucked into the city. But the more reinforcements we poured in to get to Captain Hooker's guys, the more they got smacked on their way in too.

Hooker's guys finally made some progress at Blue 11. The soldiers stuck on the other side of the bridge had managed to get back across it. It was thanks to the enormous bollocks shown by a big Fijian private called Joe Natameru. In frustration, Joe had jumped up, run into the open, and taken up a highly exposed fire position. He dropped a pair of enemy that had been cutting them off on the other side but he took a bullet through his calf for his efforts.

Being reunited with the rest of the patrol had given the men a much stronger firebase. Then, the Cimic Warriors, the Abu Naji resupply convoy and Featherstone's fighting patrol all arrived at about the same time. Together, they held the enemy at bay long enough to all extract. The Warriors weren't large enough to carry everybody, so some had to jog back alongside them. *Black Hawk Down*-style, they put rounds down all the way as they ran.

I went down to the front gate to help them in. They were gasping, and there was a lot of 'fucking hell' and 'thank fuck for that'. Blokes had collapsed, and kit and weapons were strewn everywhere. It was a complete palaver and a very sorry sight.

But there was still one sorrier sight to come. Back up on the roof fifteen minutes later, we heard an appalling grating noise approaching from a long way off. The grating noise appeared to attract gunfire wherever it moved. It sounded like a Warrior that had a full bag of spanners thrown into its engine. Swap spanners for a truckload of shrapnel, and that's exactly what it was. Around the corner from the direction of Blue 11 came four truly miserable looking Warriors. Christ knows where they had been. The lead vehicle was in a horrific state. It was the one making most of the racket. There were at least five RPG blast holes in it, smoke was pouring out of the back, and all its hatches were wide open. That included the driver's hatch. Most astonishing of all, the driver had his bonce stuck right out of it – and rounds were still coming in at him. His name was Private Johnson Beharry. Chris saw it first.

'Look at the state of that! What the fuck have that lot just been through?'

'Never mind that. What the hell is Beharry doing with his bonce right outside like that?' asked someone else.

'What a waste of time slapping on all that armour,' I replied.

The battalion's whole fleet of Warriors had been up-armoured for the tour. That meant attaching dirty great big chunks of it to the side to make the things RPG-proof. It had taken hours to do. Judging by Pte Beharry's recent experiences, it hadn't exactly worked.

Because of its state, we didn't think Beharry's Warrior was going to make it all the way to us. It was unlikely he would either unless he pulled his head in. But it carried on creaking its way along Tigris's south bank at just a little faster than jogging pace. When it passed the back gate, it drew the inevitable volley of rounds from the OMS gunmen we had been playing hide and seek with up RPG Alley. But Beharry carried on in spite of it all and the machine eventually creaked to a final halt right outside the front gate.

Beharry's Warrior was, unsurprisingly, full of casualties. There was a mad scramble at the front gate to get them all out and into safety. The snipers did their bit by getting the enemy's heads down. We rammed as many rounds into their positions as we could.

Only when everyone was inside did it emerge what had happened. They were part of the C Company QRF, and had been sent into the city to rescue any one of a series of different call signs they could get to. Like everyone before them, all they had managed was a proper smacking of their own.

Beharry was a shy young lad with a disarming smile from Grenada. He'd been in the battalion for a couple of years, and was driving for his platoon commander. They were hit as soon as they turned on to the Blue route that ran north through the eastern side of the city. The platoon commander and the Warrior's gunner in the turret were both knocked unconscious by a barrage of RPG direct hits. The explosions also knocked out all of Beharry's radios, and destroyed his periscope. If he wanted to see anything at all from then on, he would have to drive with his hatch open.

Leaderless, the whole platoon of four Warriors were now badly in the shit. They were taking furious incoming, they were boxed in by burning barricades, the radios were fucked and their commander might be dead. In a call that took balls the size of watermelons, Beharry decided he had only one option. He charged the barricades in front of him and smashed a path through for the rest of the platoon to follow. With rounds pinging off all around him and RPGs whooshing over his head, he continued to press on all the way with his swede sticking out until he eventually reached Cimic. When he got there, he then helped evacuate his casualties under the sniper fire until he himself passed out with heatstroke. After they dragged him in, a 7.62mm AK round was found embedded in his helmet.

His platoon reorganized, rearmed and got some much needed water down them. They then evacuated the most seriously injured in Cimic back to Abu Naji. Once the resupply was finished, its Warrior convoy also made a beeline for Abu Naji. Even though the incoming they took on the way back was less it was still plentiful, and every vehicle still got a piece of it.

Beharry's Warrior was going nowhere though. We kept a watch on it by the front gate until it could be moved safely the next day. Fitz put warning shots into the tree beside it every time scavenging teenagers got too close. Like Daz's Snatch a few weeks before, the Warrior still had the same highly classified radio equipment in the back and we couldn't lose that.

Then one of the cheeky little sods crept up behind the Warrior out of Fitzy's sight and tried to scramble up on top of it.

'Want me to put one on the turret to get that fella off, Danny?'

'No, it might ricochet and kill him. Can you do the driver's optics? That's about the only thing that isn't metal.'

'No problem.'

The driver's viewing optics is a strip of thick glass, three inches high by twelve wide. At a distance of just over 250 metres, it was bread and butter to Fitzy. He put a 7.62 straight into the middle of it. It scared the hell out of the teenager, who jumped off the Warrior and sprinted for his life.

When it started to get dark, we also had to shoot out the Warrior's headlights because the power in it had been left on in the rush to debug from it. They were facing right into the camp and screwed up the view through our night vision goggles. They were harder shots. Fitzy took both of them out, and then calmly moved on to its indicators and three identification lights. A total of seven targets, all at over 250 metres, each just measuring a couple of square inches. Like the legend he was, he hit all seven first time.

As the sun dropped down over the horizon leaving a crimson-red sky, Chris slumped down against the sandbags in Rooftop Sangar next to me. He'd been down to the Ops Room.

After a full day's excitement for the OMS, their pot shots on Cimic had started to die down too. But we were still on a sharp lookout for mortar teams. They'd caused us misery all day, and so far they had got away with it. They were a particular concern to us. On the roof all the time, we were the most exposed to their fire.

'That's all of our call signs accounted for now, Danny. Everyone's safe inside here or Abu Naji.'

'Christ, we got away with that one, didn't we, mate? May Day. That'll be right. More like Mayhem if you ask me.'

'Too right. I tell you what. That Beharry boy deserves a medal for what he just done. Fucking astonishing effort. He's only twenty-four years old and all.'

'Yeah. How are the casualties?'

'Not great. We've got a lot of unwell people still, but they've all been passed down the medivac chain to Basra. It looks like they're all going to live.'

Unbelievably nobody had been killed. Again, we had the typical Iraqi undisciplined fire to thank for that. The OMS with their macho promenading were particularly bad at it. If we had been in their place and they had been in ours, we would have massacred dozens of them. Thank God for Rambo films.

As usual, we had spoken too soon.

Thirty minutes later, a series of explosions rang out to our south again. They were followed by a huge weight of AK fire. It was too far away to see much through our sights. Bright yellow flashes intermingled with hundreds of red darts of tracer, and then a lot of smoke. It looked like it was coming from Red 11, the main Route 6 road junction on the other side of the Tigris opposite the OMS building – the OMS's favourite ambush spot.

'Whoa, someone's getting fucking whacked over there. I thought you said all our call signs are back in base, Chris?'

'They are. At least that's what the Ops Room told me. I don't know what the fuck is going on over there.'

Chris radioed it down to the Ops Room. They checked with Abu Naji, and confirmed what they had already told him. The shooting continued for a further ten minutes. Another huge ball of flame shot up over the ambush site.

'Shit. That looks like an oil tanker going up. Who are those fuckers?'

Chris had been right. The ambush was not on any of the

battle group. It was only when a fleet of Warriors reached the scene that anyone managed to work out what on earth had happened.

It was a giant convoy of US Army engineers. Specifically, the 84th Engineer Battalion of the 25th Infantry Division. They were passing through on their way out via Kuwait. It was the end of their year-long tour and they were going home to their base – in Honolulu, Hawaii. You can just imagine how happy they must have been.

At least 60 OMS gunmen were lying in wait in drainage ditches on both sides of the main road to smack anything painted in desert khaki that passed by. They couldn't give a stuff if it was the Yanks or us. They probably didn't even realize.

When the rounds started coming in, the American soldiers had bomb burst all over the town in a desperate bid to get away from the gunmen. Two were killed, a 32-year-old staff sergeant from Chicago and a 22-year-old private from California. Eight others were wounded. Most made it to nearby police stations. But two were missing in action.

The battle group launched a massive search operation for them. That meant coming back into Al Amarah yet again and drawing yet more OMS fire. Helicopters were also sent up. But the soldiers had ducked into the southern estates, and it was like looking for a needle in a haystack. They were on the run for hours.

At first the engineers hid, but were soon spotted. In a desperate flight for their lives, crowds chased them through the back streets and shit-filled trenches of the estates. They wanted to lynch them. Eventually, around midnight, they ran out on to a main road and straight in front of a passing Iraqi police patrol car. Normally in Al Amarah that would have meant curtains for them. But they'd got a lucky break.

The two coppers inside happened to be some of the very few honest policemen in the city. They ran them down to Abu Naji's front gate and dropped them off.

Half of the engineer convoy's thirty-four vehicles had been totally burnt out. They were abandoned where they were hit and left a charred and mangled line of metal almost a kilometre long up the Red route.

We also heard that there were so many OMS gunmen firing on the convoy that the idiots even managed to waste four of each other in their own crossfire. We thought that was exceptional.

The battle group had known absolutely nothing about the convoy. That meant nobody had been given any chance to warn them about what a nest of hatred they were about to stroll into. It was dark when they came over Yugoslav Bridge. So with us busy spotting for mortar teams, we hadn't seen them either. Nobody should have been operating in Al Amarah without all of us knowing about it. You pass through another unit's AO, you fucking well tell them. Otherwise, this happens.

But it looked like the engineers weren't to blame either. Before they had set off from Baghdad, they told the CO in Abu Naji that they had been briefed that there'd been no trouble in Al Amarah for ten days, and no coalition forces were based here. Now two of their men were dead. A lot more had holes in them, and millions of dollars in equipment had gone up in smoke. Somebody in Baghdad had fucked up, big style.

With the Americans' drama over, most of Cimic's now burgeoning occupancy crashed out wherever they could. It had been a seriously long day. But it wasn't finished yet for the snipers.

12

Nightfall only saw the mortaring against us intensify. On top of the nine during the day, we were on the receiving end of eleven more mortar strikes that night too, some of them frighteningly accurate. It had become pretty obvious to us that there was a new team in town. They were good. And they were the ones with the whopping great 82mm mortar tube.

A mortar needs to be fired on a flat hard surface to be sure of any accuracy. To relocate repeatedly and still get the rounds reasonably accurate is not an easy business. We'd always plot the coordinates of their firing position. But by the time we'd done and got all our sights lined up, they'd be off again to another location. The new team also used smoke rounds first to spot whether they were on target or not. When they were, it would be five or six high explosive rounds straight down the tube at us. It was good drills and we were impressed. It also meant they'd had some good military training. A rumour went around that they were Iranian.

After a while, I sent most of the lads to bed. There was little we could do about these fuckers in the darkness and without the ability to send an ambush patrol out. Unless we got very lucky. Three of us stayed up in Rooftop Sangar to mount the usual watch. Fitz and I were on the longs and Des was spotting. Dale had also come up on the roof to keep us company. It had been a busy day. He knew everyone was fucked, so he had volunteered to do the night commander's shift. He'd even brought us out a brew.

'Mighty fine of you that is, Dale,' I said, as I took a long hard slurp of hot sweet tea. 'Cor, I needed that.'

'My pleasure, Danny boy. Mind you, it should be you giving me the presents really.'

'Why?'

'It's my birthday today. I'm thirty-five.'

'Really? I didn't know that. Happy fucking birthday, mate!'

'Thanks. I'd forgotten all about it too. Don't worry; you can save the faarkin' cake till later.'

The adrenalin of regular mortar incoming was enough to keep us awake through the long hours. Then, just after 3 a.m. Des spotted some heat signature through the SOFIE binos. It wasn't too far away from us on the north bank amid the Iraqi Army camp ruins. He looked again through a SIMRAD night sight. It was a flat-bottomed truck moving slowly with its lights off.

'Hold on, Dan. I think I've got something here.'

We lined up our sights in the direction where Des was looking and found the truck too.

Eventually it stopped. Five blokes got out and started unloading equipment from the back of it. Des started getting excited.

'Hey, did you see that? It looks like they're setting up a fucking mortar here. They're all armed too by the looks of it. AKs slung on their backs.'

Then Des got very excited indeed.

'Dan, Dan, Dan! I can see the fucking mortar tube. There it goes out of the truck now! Long fat fucker. It must be the 82 mil. Hey, we've really got the fuckers now. We're going to fucking waste them!'

'OK Des, keep your voice down. Range them.'

'I've done that already — 550 metres.'

The mortar team had made a mistake. They'd got cocky with all their success. In their desire to get closer to us, they'd set up in a direct line of sight. Just because it was three in the morning didn't mean we weren't still watching them like a hawk.

'Dan, this is really fucking it, you know?' Des had started to pump his fist under the sandbag wall.

'Yes I know. Right, we need to get some illume up. Dale, can you get on the 51mm mortar and do that?'

'Sure thing. Leave it to me.'

'Think of it as your birthday present, mate.'

'Gladly received.'

We took a few more seconds to get our weapons ready. Because there were so many of them in the team, a couple of longs wouldn't be enough for the job. They were also close enough for us not to need them. They were going to get the Gimpy from me.

'Fitz, you grab that Minimi. As soon as the illume goes up, open fire.'

'Roger that.'

Crump, crump. The team had got their first two rounds off at us. Nothing to worry about. Probably just smoke anyway.

Calmly, we rested the machine guns' barrels on the lip of the sandbag wall, and pressed our feet into its base for support. Then we looked through the weapons' iron sights. The mortar rounds thumped into the river just to our left. Then Dale let rip.

They were caught like rabbits in our headlights. Right out in the open with nowhere to hide. Two of the crew were crouching down tinkering with the mortar and its base plate.

The other three were humping mortar rounds from the flatbed to them.

Fitz and I opened up at the same moment. After a couple of rounds, the GMPG had a stoppage. So I threw it out the way without even safety-catching it, and grabbed a second Minimi lying beside me. With Fitzy already blazing away with long fully automatic bursts, I opened up again for all I was worth.

We aimed for the two men around the mortar tube first. I went for the one on its right, Fitzy the left. For a few seconds, they were all frozen to the spot staring up at the illume with disbelief. The tracer rounds, one in every four, did a great job in bringing us on to the targets. The bloke on the right went down first. He collapsed in a series of spasms as my rounds ploughed into him. In panic, all the bloke on the left could think of was to ram a round down the tube as quick as he could. He went down with the round still in his hand thanks to a long burst from Fitzy right into his guts. We made sure they both stayed down too, just in case. Both were riddled with another long burst.

The other three mortar men weren't so noble. They dropped the rounds they were carrying on the spot and just legged it. After 50 metres or so, one thought he was out of the shit enough to show a little bravado and put a few rounds back at us. Pulling the AK off his back, he turned and raised it in our direction. Bad mistake. It was just the justification we needed to engage him too, so he was the next to get the good news.

Each Minimi had a bag of 250 rounds on it. We went through them at a fair pace, firing in bursts of twenty. We'd pause for a few seconds to let the working parts settle. Keeps the barrel cool. Then we'd open up again. As we fired, bullet casings spat out of the machine guns and littered the floor with a tinkling sound like confetti.

Des began shouting. 'Danny you should see these fuckers run.' He was jumping up and down on the spot, clearly mesmerized by the whole thing. 'Run Forrest, run,' he shouted at them at the top of his voice. His eyes were glued on to his binos as he watched.

Just before one illume went out, Dale threw another one up so they would overlap and we'd have permanent vision. He was swiftly working his way through a whole crate of twelve.

The remaining two mortar men managed to make it 150 metres or so to a small mud hut. Des sized the place up through the binos. The door faced us. There was a window on its righthand side, and an old car was parked outside.

'Don't worry guys, I don't think there is any back way out of the hut. We can get those scumbags too.'

We trained the Minimis on its doorway. All we needed now was for them to engage us again to reclassify themselves as legitimate targets.

With less than a minute gone by, the two men bolted to the car and grabbed its front doors open, blatting away madly with their AKs in our general direction. Another silly mistake. In their panic, they forgot all the rules of their own game.

Fitzy didn't need to be told.

We opened up again simultaneously, hosing fuck out of the car as well. Bits flew off all over it. The men quickly scampered back inside, but we carried on firing. We smashed every window, lacerated the tyres and turned the bodywork into a pin cushion. They weren't going anywhere in that now.

Another few minutes' silence.

'They're coming out again,' Des shouted feverishly. 'Still

armed.' So they got another long burst through the door.

Downstairs, Chris was getting in and out of his bunk like a yoyo. It was the first time we'd fired Minimis off the roof, so it was obvious to him and everybody else something pretty interesting was going on. After a burst, he'd leap up and start pulling on his boots. But then we'd stop firing just as quickly and it would be all quiet again.

Oh bollocks, it's all over. I'll go back to bed, Chris thought. He did it at least six different times. Finally he just decided to settle for our running commentary to the Ops Room over his PRR.

Fitzy and I kept up the sporadic fire on the hut for a good couple of hours every time the blokes inside tried something on us. They were rats stuck in a trap. They knew it, we knew it. It became a trial of who was prepared to wait the longest. But we were snipers. We were used to hanging around for days on end to wait for a shot. Every time they poked their barrels out, we'd suppress them with rounds through the door. Sometimes we'd put a 7.62 round from a long through the window for good measure.

While we waited for the men, we also shredded the abandoned mortar tube in case anyone fancied picking it up.

As the periods of silence between our bursts grew longer, the extraordinary day began to take its toll on Dale. Determined to see it all out, he fought heroically against sleep but all he ended up doing was nodding dog impressions with the mortar still between his legs.

'Go to bed, mate.'

'Eh?' He woke with a start.

'You've done your bit. It's beginning to get light anyway,' I told him.

'Er, yeah, OK then. It's been a faarkin' awesome birthday present. Thanks for that Dan.'

Eventually the door stopped opening. It's possible the men used their fingernails to dig through the back wall. We never found out, because we never saw them again. Hopefully they went the same way as their mates. It didn't really matter. We'd destroyed the mortar team that had posed the biggest threat to Cimic. A total of 550 Minimi rounds and thirty green spot very well spent. It felt great.

As the sun began to come up, Chris, Ads and Oost appeared on the roof. They were the early morning breakfast shift and our relief.

'Well, you boys have had a good night, haven't you?'

'Sorry mate, did we keep you up?'

Battle debris lined the whole roof: spent cartridge shells, empty ammo tins and mortar crates, our abandoned rifles and machine guns, half drunk bottles of water, empty cups of tea. I finally got my head down at 5.30 a.m., on the morning of 2 May. I was shattered. We'd been up since 2 a.m. the night before and we'd gone through sixteen and a half hours of solid fighting. It wasn't bad for a day's work.

Sleep was a luxury none of us had time for though during that period. There was just too much to do. I was up, breakfasted and back on the roof by 7.20 a.m.

The US engineers had not been so lucky. But, somehow, the battle group had escaped the repercussions of Operation Pimlico without losing a single man. That didn't mean the day had been a victory. Yes, we did have a few of the big OMS men locked up, and we'd killed a lot more. And they hadn't ended up topping any coppers. It was just a bluff. But the only lasting effect of the day's events was to up the OMS's tempo of attacks on us yet further. The battle of wills was now in full flow.

Since the threat level of going out and about on Al Amarah's streets had gone through the roof, all vehicle movement was heavily restricted. From then on Warriors would only go between Cimic and Abu Naji when they absolutely had to. Foot patrols were also reduced. But it was vital that they didn't stop altogether. We had to keep on going out – if only to show the OMS that we still could. To lock ourselves inside Cimic would be to hand the whole town over to them.

Sniper Platoon had gained a bizarre addition to our foot patrols. She wasn't originally invited to join us, but often she left us with little choice. She came in the shape of a six-month-old mangy mongrel puppy called Tigris.

The thing had been taken off the streets and semi-adopted by Molly Phee, who named her after the river. Cruel little street kids had tortured her and cut her tail off. But Molly had thoroughly domesticated her, and she would be eaten alive by the packs of wild dogs if she went out of Cimic alone now. That didn't stop her following us about playing the tough girl when we were on the streets to protect her furry arse.

She was both a help and a hindrance. Her yapping did little for our stealth profile if we wanted to move around the place quietly. But whether it was her sense of smell or not, she also had a strong sixth sense of what was around the corner. We'd often know if there was someone in wait because she would get excited and start barking. It was a handy early warning system.

I've never been much of an animal person. Dogs' fleas and shit around military camps are bad for hygiene. But I allowed her to hang around the blokes because it helped to ease the tension. Half of the company fell in love with her. Dale and Major Featherstone were her greatest fans. She became known as Tigris, Dog of War. Some of the lads got truly pathetic. One NCO even used to shower with her and used his own shampoo to scrub the muck of the streets off her coat. It was understandable in a way. To them, she represented a domestic comfort to take their minds off Al Amarah for a few minutes. A lifeline to home.

When we were inside Cimic, the OMS knew mortar fire was still their best way to try to hurt us. So they jacked up the ferocity of their aerial bombardment. We might've killed their best mortar team, but, like snakes, many others swiftly took their place.

The traditional use of mortars on the battlefield is to suppress or kill dismounted enemy infantry. Unless they score lucky direct hits, their high explosive charges (of between eight and twelve pounds) aren't big enough to destroy vehicles or armour. Instead, they throw out hundreds of hot, sharp shards of shrapnel at high velocity – just like a giant grenade. With metal casings that are designed to fragment as much as possible, a mortar bomb can be lethal up to 50 metres away.

It's known as an area weapon; the more you can launch, the better chance you'll have of killing. That's why they totally pummelled us.

From 1 to 10 May alone, a total of 525 individual mortar rounds were fired at us. A lot went wide, short or long. Others landed inside the Cimic compound but were blinds; they didn't go off. But with that amount of incoming the OMS were always going to notch up some good direct hits.

Things started to get smashed up. The compound's generator took a real battering. That plunged us into darkness for a good few hours until a couple of talented mechanics patched it up again. The swimming pool in particular took a fair bashing, demolishing its nice thatched veranda and blowing the little outdoor gym to smithereens.

There were also two direct hits on the two-storey prefab accommodation blocks. The rounds tore through the thin plastic roofs and exploded in the middle of their long dormitories. Luckily, they hit in the middle of the day and nobody was in them at the time. Instead, shrapnel shredded kit, mattresses and the thin walls and the blast covered everything else in a layer of dust and ceiling. If they had hit in the middle of the night, they could have killed a dozen men.

It was decided from then onwards that nobody would sleep in the dormitories any longer. Too many men could have been lost at once. Instead, we all had to crash out under hard cover in Cimic House itself or the cookhouse. Mortar rounds can't dig through concrete. That meant the place quickly became a vast overflowing jungle of sweaty bodies. Sleeping mats lined every available piece of floor at night, and every soldier had to live out of his Bergen.

Because not all of us could fit into the house, platoons also had to start taking it in turn to live in the Pink Palace for a few days. That was a truly miserable experience. There was no furniture at all in the rooms we were given to doss down in. It had also begun to stink. By the second week of May, mortar damage meant the plumbing had totally packed up in the building's Arab-style squat-hole toilets. But that didn't stop the Iraqi police from still crapping and pissing in them all the same. Soon, shit and piss lined the whole of the toilet floors. Its rancid pong permeated the whole building and clung to your clothes. Sniper Platoon managed to swerve its fair share of Pink Sauna shifts because of our need to be on the roof. But sometimes we just couldn't escape it.

More incoming mortar rounds also meant our odds were shortened on personally avoiding them. Everybody was well aware of that, especially us on the roof. But we were professional soldiers and we had a job to do. We had little choice but to get used to it. You learn to put what you can't control to the back of your mind.

For some reason, the most intense barrage of the day would always rain down on us between 11 p.m. and midnight. It became known as the 'Golden Hour'. When we heard the crump of a launch or the three-second whistle warning, the drill was to dive into the nearest sangar and get behind a sandbag. Since we worked without our helmets on because you can't see through scopes as well, we'd make a desperate grab for them next to us or hanging off our belts. If you were caught out in the open, you'd just lie flat on the ground and get your head down as best as you could. It wasn't unheard of for the occasional round to land right on the roof. There was more than one close shave.

But the more we sat out under them, the sharper our ears got at picking up the launches, and the better we got at predicting how accurate they were going to be. Listening to them for sixteen hours a day, we got very good at it. Chris, who came to Snipers from the Mortar Platoon, was a genius at it.

'Hmm, that one's coming our way,' he'd say almost academically, on hearing a crump two miles off. Then in a scream, 'Every fucker take cover!'

Clambering down the ladder from Rooftop for more water or ammo was known as running the gauntlet. You didn't hang about.

Throughout, never once did I have a shortage of volunteers to go on the roof. I never once had to order a sniper up there. On the contrary, I had to order them off it to go to bed. Just like Dale, the lads would be falling asleep where they sat with their longs still in their hands. The truth is being up there was also one hell of a rush. We thrived on it.

Considering herself a fully signed-up member of the platoon now, Tigris the pup wasn't one to shirk what she saw as her duties up there either. She had got into the habit of coming up to the roof with us at night as well. She enjoyed its cool breeze and liked to keep us company. The feeling was mutual. So much so, that whenever we heard incoming, someone was always sure to grab her up first before diving into the sangars with the grateful mutt in their arms.

Major Featherstone was once brave enough to question our judgement on incoming mortar rounds.

The Golden Hour had just passed, and six rounds had just been thrown at us. Five had gone off causing just light structural damage to the compound. But the sixth had been a blind. You only see them if they go off. So tracking down blinds in the camp was a pain in the arse. They could go off at any stage, a minute or a month later, so they always had to be found, day or night.

Ads was on the roof. He had developed perhaps the best set of ears in the platoon. From what he heard of it, he was convinced the blind landed within the compound. Featherstone came up to the roof.

'Right guys, everyone happy the blind landed outside of Cimic?'

'Sir, I don't think so. It got in.'

'I don't think it did, Ads. If it had, we would have heard it hit something as it came down.'

'Not necessarily, sir.'

'Did you see it then, Ads?'

'No.'

'Well then. It's late and we're not going to launch a hunt

133

now because you've got a feeling about it.'

'OK, fair enough, sir. But I'm telling you there's a blind in this camp.'

Ads was a cocky little private, and Featherstone was the boss. The debate was over. The major got on his PRR.

'Ops Room, it's the OC. Can confirm the blind landed outside of the compound. We're all clear. I'm bolloxed so I'm off to bed.'

Five minutes later, poor old Featherstone stormed back into the Ops Room.

'Right, bin my last report. I've found the blind. It's in my fucking bedroom.'

The 60mm mortar round had come straight through the roof of his Portakabin and landed neatly a metre inside the door. It was half-buried in the floor, with its tail fin still protruding out. Someone who saw it described it as a neatly coiled dog turd. It could have gone off at any moment. If Featherstone had gone to bed half an hour earlier, he could have been dead.

Generously, he added: 'The next person who questions Private Somers' ears, I'll have court-martialled.'

From then onwards, he slept under his desk in the Ops Room under Cimic House's hard cover too.

The intensity of the fighting wasn't without the odd bit of its own comic relief.

On one occasion we were watching an OMS tractor trundle over the north bank the morning after Fitzy and I had blatted the mortar crew. It had come to pick up their bodies, and the driver didn't mind doing it in full view of us either. As he reached the spot, he slowed down. Then BANG. The tractor had gone over one of the crew's own mortar rounds, exploding it. The bloody great machine launched up in the air in a big puff of dust, and landed on one of its giant wheels on an angle that put its axle permanently out of business. The driver was fine. Thinking it must have been us, he scrambled out of the cab and legged it. It was hilarious. Everyone on the roof fell about in stitches. To us, it was poetic justice and put the icing on the cake.

Another light moment came in the shape of Private Daniel Crucefix. When I first heard the 22-year-old Kiwi's surname, I thought it was a nickname. It proved very apt. The movement ban meant that if you weren't seriously injured, you wouldn't get an immediate medivac back to Slipper City. So there were a lot of walking wounded hanging around the place. But Crucefix really took the prize. He sat it out at Cimic for three days with a piece of shrapnel the size of a credit card stuck in his nose.

He was one of a handful who had been in the back of Pte Beharry's Warrior but hadn't managed to fit on the convoy back to Abu Naji that night. Two RPG direct hits on the back of the Warrior had blasted him in the face and helmet with shrapnel and knocked him unconscious. Corky the Cimic House medic had decided it needed to be removed by a proper surgeon. So for the time being it would have to stay there. Having a lump of metal in his face didn't make him immune from wisecracks either.

'Love the nose job, mate, it's a big improvement,' was the most popular line.

The wound must have really hurt. But Pte Crucefix didn't complain once. He even insisted on doing his bit on the end of pot shots in the sangars. That was the spirit of Cimic House. Though we were taking a heavy pounding, we weren't going to let it get us down. The OMS could go and fuck themselves. And we were all in it together.

The fighting also threw up its fair share of the totally

surreal. At times, Al Amarah resembled a scene out of a Monty Python film gone badly wrong.

One afternoon, we were in the middle of a particularly heavy mortar bombardment and gun fight with some OMS on old town rooftops. I was with a few sniper pairs in Rooftop Sangar facing the threat towards our south. Out of the corner of my eye, I spotted movement to my left. I turned to see a bloke on a bicycle calmly pedalling down the northern riverbank in the direction of Cimic. He was around forty, with dark hair, and was wearing a grey dish dash. It was obvious to everyone within five kilometres that we were on a serious two-way range. But he didn't seem to give a monkey's. He wasn't even in a particular hurry.

I stared at him for a few moments. Then, just as he passed by Back Sangar, a mortar round landed three metres away from him right in the middle of the road. It blew him off his bike, and ripped most of his left leg clean off. Quick as a flash, he jumped up again balancing on the leg he still had. He picked up the mangled bicycle, then picked up the severed leg, popped it under an arm, and hopped off down an alley wheeling the bike alongside him. The shrapnel must have severed a main artery, because he left a long trail of claret behind him. With that rate of blood loss, he was probably dead within minutes.

A few of the other lads had also seen it. We just stared at him in shock and utter disbelief as he hobbled away. No way was he leaving that bike for some tea leaf to pinch, no matter what state he was in. It made me feel a bit sick.

I radioed it in, like I had to. Another stupid, pointless death.

'Ops Room, Rooftop. You're not going to believe this.'

The more I thought about it, the angrier it made me. *Why*

136

the fuck did you have to go for a bike ride in the middle of a battle?
Perhaps it was our fault, we should have done more to warn
him. But it wasn't our fault. We didn't fire the mortar.

He wasn't the only one either. It was the way a lot of the
city's population behaved during heavy combat. On another
occasion, a fat woman carrying a big bag of shopping
waddled right down the middle of a road that divided us
and the OMS fighters. We all stopped shooting while she
passed. It was like they'd all had a lobotomy on the parts
of their brains that flagged up danger. We kept on having
to tell ourselves that combat on their streets wasn't new to
them. They'd lived through three major wars in the last
twenty years. And on top of that there was the normal daily
tribal scrapping. The air might be full of hot lead and
shrapnel. But as far as they were concerned life still had to
go on. In a way, they were right.

Worst of all, there were the utterly innocent civilian
victims of the fighting, who had no choice but to sit it out
and take it all. They were the law abiding peaceful sorts who
just wanted to get on with feeding their children and staying
alive. Most were appallingly poor. The longer it went on,
the more we began to feel for them.

I felt sorriest for the family who lived in the house right
on the corner at the end of the block that faced Cimic's
back gate. Because they were the closest building to the
water tower outside of our compound, they were hit time
and time again by stray mortar rounds meant for us. Rounds
ploughed down onto their roof, off their walls and into their
small back yard. The house was made out of concrete and
could withstand direct hits. But soon a crack appeared on
its front wall. Every time it got hit again, the crack got bigger
and bigger. With sadness, we used to chart its progress down
the wall.

God knows what it did to the family's nerves. The whole lot of them had to live inside this shitty little house. At least three kids, grandparents and all. They didn't have a pot to piss in. It was just their plain bad luck that someone had gone and put up a fucking British base right on their front lawn.

One day we popped over the road to see if they were all right. We asked if there was anything we could do.

They told us they had hated Saddam and they were pro-coalition forces. But no matter how many times we asked, they refused to leave their godforsaken mortared-up house.

Heartbreakingly, the man explained: 'This is our home. There is nothing else. We have nowhere else to go.'

It was no way to live. For them or us. The truth was, despite the odd foot patrol, we too had become little more than prisoners in Cimic. The longer it went on, the more we realized that 1 May had been an outright victory for the OMS. The day's events had pushed their fighters out on the streets. They had stayed on them, while the reality was we had largely been forced to abandon them. It meant the OMS were the ones in real control of the city now.

We couldn't allow that to happen. So the planners at Abu Naji went to work again. This time, they came up with a proper solution. In the early hours of the morning of 8 May, the battle group launched its second major offensive on the Office of the Martyr Sadr in little more than a week. And it was truly awesome.

13

There was one major reason behind our second offensive's stunning success. This time, we held nothing back. We went to war, and with every single weapon we fucking well had at our disposal. None of this peacekeeping one-arm-behind-our-backs shit any more. As the Yanks say, it was whoop-ass time.

It had even been given the name of a decent tube station this time. It was called Operation Waterloo.

Full credit to the Slipper City planners, they did some serious telephoning around before this one began. Everybody we knew was invited to the party. The battalion's A Company, who had been sitting down in Basra as a reserve force for the division, were called up for it.

Beautifully, brigade had managed to lay their hands on six Challenger II main battle tanks for our squadron of Queen's Royal Lancers attached to our battle group for the tour. The tankies were delighted. It meant they could bin the poxy Snatch Land Rovers that they hated and get back to doing what they did best. But when the news went round Cimic that we were going to have six times 62 tonnes worth of hurt on our side, I promise you we were happier.

But best of all, a US general in Baghdad agreed to loan us two AC130 Spectre gunships as close air support for the night. Spectres have been around since the end of Vietnam. They have the normal frame of a basic propeller-driven Hercules transport aircraft. But mounted on it is a devastating array of machine guns, cannons and various hi-tech sensors. Their poor vulnerability from ground rocket and missile fire means they can only come out to play at night. But it's well worth the wait. They are quite simply flying dragons of doom.

The Spectre smacks anything that moves for you, no matter how big or small, with three different weapons systems. Its two twin 20mm Vulcan Gatling guns spit out 7,200 rounds a minute each. They dump so much brass on the aircraft's floor that their gunners have to use shovels to clear up the spent cartridge casings at the end of the night. Then there's the larger 40mm Bofors cannon, firing 100 rounds a minute. But its pièce de résistance is a 105mm howitzer. It fires any 44lb shell, from concrete-penetrating rounds to airbursts, at a rate of ten rounds a minute. To feed that lot, the plane carries up to 10 tonnes of ammunition per sortie.

Flown and operated by a crew of thirteen, the Spectre can either be called in by forward air controllers on to specific targets or plod around happily self-generating its own. It can even engage three different targets at the same time, if you'd like it to.

We'd never seen one in action before. To say we were looking forward to that would be the understatement of the century.

Waterloo was also given an H hour of 2 a.m. But this time we weren't trying to avoid a confrontation. Instead, we went out looking for one. It was a ballsy trap for the OMS leadership, with their own bloated egos as the bait. The battle group was going to go right into the town centre as tooled up as possible, and just sit there on the OMS's doorstep. It was hoped that would cause them such affront, they wouldn't be able to resist a full-out assault. Once they were out in the open, we'd destroy them with overwhelmingly superior firepower. Essentially, it was come and have a go if you're hard enough. And there was even a classic snipers' job for us to do written into the plan too.

I briefed the platoon on the plan in Cimic's QRF room before we left.

'OK lads, this is what's going to happen. The two Warrior companies from Slipper City are going to form the main attack column. At the tip of it will be four Challenger IIs.'

'Awesome,' chimed in Des. Ever a fan of firepower.

'They're coming in via the front door, right up the Red route. The main road junction at Red 11 is where they're going to stand and fight. If it's aggro you're after, we all know they're going to get it there.'

Not only was Red 11 the OMS's favourite ambush point, but it was also only 500 metres from their HQ over a big bridge on the other side of the Tigris. As a meeting of two major dual carriageways, the expansive shape of the junction also gave any defender very clear 360-degree arcs of fire.

'Now our job. We're to mount a blocking screen between the town centre and the main source of the OMS's manpower, the Aj Dayya estate. Our orders are to take up covert positions at Blue 11 overlooking the roundabout there, report enemy reinforcements, and destroy them if need be.'

Pikey's gypsy nose was already twitching.

'Err, Danny, isn't that where Captain Hooker's lot got so badly smacked the other day?'

'Exactly.'

'Excellent. Fucking bring it on.'

'Now we've no idea what's going to come out of the Aj Dayya. Might be an army of them, or might be nothing. That's what we're there to find out. One thing's for sure though – we're guaranteed another grandstand view of the party again.'

We infiltrated as stealthily as we could in the darkness, first down Baghdad Street and then via a series of back alleys we knew. We didn't bother knocking on any doors. We just quietly climbed up the exterior of our chosen tall houses from their back gardens, giving each other a hand as we went up. We didn't want their owners to find out we were there until the morning.

We were spread out over the flat roofs of three houses in an arc facing east across the Tigris that gave us a good view into the estate. We were all on our bellies with our longs and vision aids set up and ready to go.

Set back from the roundabout is a large bronze statue of a horrible great fat ugly woman. She is Al Amarah's most famous resident. During the Iran–Iraq war, she killed a dozen Iranian soldiers by blowing herself into tiny pieces alongside them. Over the years, the myth had perpetuated, and now the locals proudly boasted that she killed 1,000 Iranians. Kids who played around her in the daytime used to look up at her in awe. It summed up the city for us: a place that hero worships fat ugly suicide bombers.

As the minutes slowly ticked down to H hour in the perfect silence of those early morning hours, I got butterflies in my stomach. I wasn't scared; I just really wanted the plan to work. After everything they'd done to us, we were desperate to see the OMS get some payback.

Three minutes after 2 a.m., we heard the first cracks of AK fire to the south.

'Fucking get some of it, you wankers,' whispered Ads to himself beside me. I clearly wasn't alone in my feelings.

The armoured column was entering the city. After being caught napping the last time, the OMS now posted spotters at night. They soon roused the ranks, and within fifteen minutes all hell had broken loose again.

Lines of red tracer and the flashes of RPG rockets poured down on the convoy. But this time, it was taking no prisoners. I followed the convoy's progress by listening in to its lead Challenger's radio reports on my Clansman.

As each junction on the road was approached, enemy positions on or around them were hosed down by the tanks' chain guns first, and then stormed by infantry dismounts in the back of the Warriors. Their job was to clear any remaining RPG nests and remove hidden booby traps the heavy vehicles couldn't see. It was pure mechanized urban warfare, tanks and infantry working side by side to seize a town by its short and curlies.

'Enemy destroyed, Red 6 clear,' reported the tank commander. 'Dismounts loading up now. Proceeding to Red 7.'

And just as the Americans had promised, there circling high above the convoy as it made steady progress north were the two Spectre gunships.

The Spectre crews really earned their pay that night. To the battle group, they were worth their weight in gold. The permanent low pitched drone of their four propeller engines was constantly reassuring. We couldn't see the convoy itself, but we knew exactly where they were from where the Spectres laid down their devastating fire. As long as the OMS men weren't shooting from civilian houses, they would pulverize them as soon as they were stupid enough to show themselves.

Red 11 was soon reached and secured. A tank sat out on each of its four corners, and the twenty-four Warriors panned into an all-round defence behind them.

'Red 11 clear. Now come out, come out wherever you are,' invited the tank commander.

The OMS fell for the trap immediately. Just over 976

tonnes of heavily armed steel in their faces sent them apoplectic, and hundreds of fighters were ordered out to retake the junction. The convoy became a huge magnet, the OMS's troops helpless iron filings.

Ground and air worked in tandem to beat off attack after attack; literally dozens, and they kept on coming. Of course, they stood no chance. The few RPG men that did get their rounds through on to target found their grenades just bounced off the Challenger's ultra thick skins like flimsy arrows. An RPG explosion on a Chally's hull would barely spill its gunner's coffee inside.

Once word spread that it looked like the Brits were going to hang around, we started to get busy too. Carloads of armed men started to leave Aj Dayya. We put rounds into their tyres to make it a little harder for them. Then came the familiar crump of mortar fire, and from very nearby. There was more than one base plate on the go. The OMS had set up a mortar line on five flatbed trucks just 500 metres away from us and were trying to pound Red 11. We could see the rounds launch, but had no direct sight of the base plates so we couldn't engage them ourselves.

We put in a request for Spectre air support. It was just the excuse we had craved.

I passed the coordinates back to the Ops Room in Cimic. Five minutes later, the drone of propellers moved towards us until they were somewhere above our heads.

The VHF beside me crackled into life.

'Alpha One Zero, this is Zero. Be advised Steel Rain is above you.'

Spectre pilots have call signs only the Yanks can get away with. Brit pilots would never be sad enough to call themselves Steel Rain. We loved it anyway.

There was more from the Ops Room.

'Alpha One Zero, Steel Rain has identified a group of armed men on rooftops around Blue 11. Send loc stats.'

Holy moly. The Spectre crews now had us on their little CCTV screens. To avoid a rather painful blue on blue, I didn't hang about telling them exactly where we were. Again via the Ops Room, I guided the Spectre crews on to the flatbed trucks. Then the mortar crews launched another volley, which only sealed their own fate.

Three minutes later, the Ops Room came on again.

'Alpha One Zero, Steel Rain has identified the target. Will use the 105s to neutralize. Steel Rain wants you to be advised that you are within "No Fire" range.'

'Acknowledged Zero. We're cool about that.'

If friendly troops are within blast or ricochet radius of the Spectre's armaments, its crew has to warn you before they fire. Shrapnel could go anywhere with a dirty great cannon firing at an angle out of the sky in the middle of a city at night. Each weapon has its own 'No Fire' range, and for the Spectre's 105mm howitzers it was 700 metres. If you're within 200 metres of its target, it's called Danger Close. It would take the CO himself to sign that off. The threat to us though was slim. We were 500 metres away, at height, and in good cover.

So the OMS mortar crews were going to get the good news from the 105s, were they? Fucking excellent. I passed the news around the platoon over the PRR.

'So keep your swedes down lads,' I was careful to add.

The Spectres didn't disappoint. It was like the gods joining the offensive on our side.

With a deafening boom and echo right above our heads, great balls of pink suddenly streaked down through the night sky towards the first flatbed truck and exploded on it in a rage of yellow flames. Sparks shot up hundreds of feet into the night sky, and bits of metal and wood flew off in every direction. The truck took six shells in a row, and it was like the thing was being hit with a giant hammer – bang bang bang bang bang bang. It pummelled it to pieces.

For Chris, it was all too much. The American blood inside him rushed to his head and he jumped to his feet and punched the air.

'Yeah, brother! Woo woo woo! Give them fucking hell from us!'

The fact that he was supposed to be an undercover sniper clean slipped his mind. But nobody was going to hear him over the sound of the howitzer.

'Shut up, Chris, you silly septic, we're supposed to be covert!'

'Sorry, Danny. Just couldn't resist it.'

Then the aircraft methodically moved on to the next flatbed, and gave it exactly the same treatment. All five of them got five or six shells each, around thirty in total. It was an awesome spectacle, easily the most impressive demonstration of firepower I'd ever seen. It was also a terrific feeling for us up there alone to know we'd got friends like that on our side. If only Spectre was around every time we got mortared.

The whole show lasted ten minutes before the aircraft's drone moved south again. Since each truck had a petrol tank, fires raged on the spot where the trucks once stood for the rest of the night, sending dust clouds high above the area. The smell of gunpowder, burnt wood and singed flesh was overpowering.

A few minutes later, we saw the gunship join its sister craft pounding down shells again around Red 11.

After three hours of furious combat, the OMS's attacks began to dry up. In their stupidity, they had badly worn their ranks down.

At dawn, the CO gave the order we'd all been waiting to hear. It was relayed across all the battle groups' PRRs.

'Advance and storm the OMS headquarters. Let's go and knock on their door.'

This time, all the snipers let off a huge cheer from our rooftops.

With the Challengers leading again, the column advanced over the bridge and on to Tigris Street at Yellow 3. It was met by a barrage of fire from the OMS building's defending force. Fighters were spread out across its garden walls and the park opposite by the river, the place we had codenamed Zinc. Spectre smacked into them too, silencing them in a few minutes.

With no more resistance visible, the OMS building was surrounded. Someone brought out a loudhailer to instruct everyone inside to come out with their hands up. But its occupants had long since fled, leaving their foot soldiers as lambs to the slaughter.

Instead, the Warrior dismounts that stormed it found a giant hoard of weapons of every shape and size. There were enough AKs to equip a battalion, along with mortar tubes, mortar rounds, heavy machine guns, rockets, blast bombs, missiles and mines. Even a Soviet-made AGS 17 automatic grenade launcher. It took three of our great big eight-tonne trucks to take all the stuff away.

A foot patrol sent into Zinc found Spectre's calling card all over the park: dismembered bodies with their rifles and RPGs still beside them.

By 10 a.m., the battle was over. Everyone was jubilant.

Not only had we won a sweet victory overwhelmingly, but it had been a tremendous feeling to have been part of an armoured battle group at war. We were just proud to have been there.

We had to keep up our watch over Aj Dayya for the rest of the day, in case of a counterattack from the estate. Unexpectedly, the five of us on my roof ended up celebrating our success with some very rich homemade Arabic coffee.

Just after the OMS building was stormed, a set of keys went into the padlock on the other side of the sheet metal door that led down into the house whose roof we were on. We all spun round just in time to point our longs at the door. It opened slowly, to reveal a chubby bloke in his forties with a bushy Saddam Hussein moustache. He had a grin on his face from ear to ear, and clasped his hands together as he addressed us in fluent English.

'Not to be afraid. You are most honoured guests in my humble home. We heard you shouting in middle of night after airplane strike. Now we must make you feel welcome. You like Arabic coffee?'

'Err, well . . .'

'I am number one fan of British Army. Mehdi Army are scum. My father in England in 1950s. He was pilot in the Royal Air Force.'

With that, he puffed out his chest in pride. Extraordinary. We had managed to pick the house to sit on that belonged to the one person in Al Amarah who loved our country as much as any of us did. His name was Abdul, and his old man really had been in the RAF. After he invited a few of us down for coffee that was so thick you could stand a spoon up in it, we had to inspect all his father's old squadron photos. He had flown Canberra bombers out of RAF Cottesmore in Rutland. All of a sudden, his two best friends appeared. They too were huge British patriots, and shook our hands incessantly.

After half an hour of glad handing, I got sudden inspiration for a brilliant tactical move.

'Ads, I've got an idea. Come with me. Excuse us for a minute, Abdul, but where's your toilet?'

We found it on the bottom floor of the house.

'Right, Ads. What I'm about to do in there is top secret. It's vital you stand here and cover for me. Understood?'

'Sure, Danny.' He wore a frown of utter concentration. 'I'll follow you anywhere, mate.'

Not in here you won't.

I went inside the toilet and closed the door. Presented with a nice clean porcelain toilet cistern and wooden seat, I pulled down my trousers and pants and sat down in some considerable comfort. It was a tactical bowel move. Having been up on the roof all night, I hadn't been able to manage the morning constitutional. It was a shame to let such a good opportunity go to waste, and who knew when I might get it again? I needed Ads there just in case some mean-spirited OMS man ran in off the street and slotted me on the shitter.

'You sneaky bastard,' he said, shaking his head as I emerged. So I stood guard while he dropped the kids off at the pool too.

The great counterattack from Aj Dayya never came, so we took it in turns for one pair to do a stint on the roof while the other four spent the rest of the day watching TV with Abdul in his nice air-conditioned sitting room.

We were called back to Cimic at sunset. That evening, Operation Waterloo's second phase began. The two armoured Warrior companies and the attached company of Royal Welch Fusiliers had moved into the town's main police stations. At a synchronized time, all four companies in the city pushed out patrols to re-establish law and order on the streets.

The OMS scored an early success with an attack on Sgt Adam Llewellyn. A ten-year-old boy on a rooftop chucked a petrol bomb into his Warrior turret. The top half of his body was engulfed in flames and by the time they had got him out, there was skin hanging off all over him. His burns were awful, but the fact that it was a ten-year-old that had done him was most shocking.

Apart from that, the patrols met little resistance. The few other individual lunatics who took us on were shot dead on the spot. But there weren't many who tried. The OMS had been given a thorough kicking. Dozens of their men lay dead and they had little ability left to fight.

We had proved two important things: we had the bigger stick and we were prepared to use it. It wasn't a trick we could pull every day. The Spectre gunships and A Company's Warriors together were a rare treat that we would be lucky to get again. But the OMS didn't know that, and we weren't going to tell them.

We'd also won the town back for the price of just three serious injuries: Sgt Llewellyn, a corporal shot in the foot, and a private fragged by a grenade hurled from a passing motorbike.

The cherry on the cake for Y Company was found in what was left of a school classroom on the north bank. A muzzle flash had been spotted from a top window in the school during the battle. So a Challenger II put a shell from its main gun straight through it. The body of an OMS sniper was found under the rubble. Next to him was a Draganov sniper rifle. It had been the fucker that shot Baz Bliss.

*

A few days later, it was considered calm enough for the armoured companies to pull out of the police stations and leave it to the local cops to get on with it again. The chief of police was called in by our CO and Molly Phee for a delicate fireside chat.

'Your men have had all the training, we've cleared up the enemy for you, so, with respect sir, is there any reason why they can't start earning their fucking pay now?' the colonel asked him. And for a few days, they even did.

Out on patrols, we learnt what had been happening while we were locked down in Cimic. The OMS had enforced strict Islamic law on Al Amarah's streets. Women who dared to show their ankles underneath their long black veils had been beaten. A man had been shot in the mouth for drinking whisky. Normal people came up to us quite openly to thank us for doing something about it. Many seemed delighted the OMS had been forced to wind their necks in.

It was important to keep up the momentum and build on what we had achieved. Basic security on the streets allowed us to go after a number of smaller targets that we'd wanted to have a crack at for some time. We carried out a series of raids, smashing doors down with a heavy metal thumper. In one house near the OMS building, we found a massive arms stash inside a false wall in the garden. RPGs and boxes of ammo were stacked from the hide's floor to the top of the six-foot wall. The buffoon owner inadvertently put Pikey's well-honed street antennae on to it by standing right in front of it and looking deeply uncomfortable.

Prodding him in the chest with a finger, Pikey demanded: 'Oi jackass, why the fuck is you standing in front of that wall all the time we've been here?'

'What wall mister?'

That sealed it.

14

The success of Waterloo also saw the mortaring on Cimic drop off a little bit to just a strike every couple of days. The OMS had been badly winded, and it took them a few days to get their breath. They were soon back though. Events elsewhere made that a cert.

There was still no sign of any end to the standoff between Moqtada al-Sadr and the Americans. If anything, it was getting worse. Moderate Shia leaders and tribal chiefs were still trying to negotiate a peace between the two sides. But neither seemed particularly interested. There were only two months to go before the CPA was due to hand power back to the Iraqis, and both al-Sadr and the Yanks were desperate for victory before that. Continual fighting in or around Iraq's two holy cities, Najaf and Kerbala, threatened to spread mayhem across the country.

More than 2,000 US soldiers were now encamped on the edge of Najaf. With the threat of an all-out assault ever present, troops made regular incursions into the city's outskirts. As May went on, US tanks were sent for the first time into Kerbala, where a Polish soldier had been killed in the Mehdi Army uprising. The tanks destroyed an al-Sadr office with heavy machine-gun fire and then took up positions just 500 metres from the gold-domed Imam Hussein shrine, the second holiest Shia site of all. In retaliation, Moqtada called for his followers everywhere to launch a new wave of attacks on coalition troops.

The national picture was leapt on afresh by the OMS,

and they used it to renew their rabble rousing in Al Amarah. They were short of new recruits, after folk had seen what mincemeat the Spectre made of the last lot. Instead, they did a bit of thinking and changed their tactics. They came back out in smaller but more lethal packages.

As the battle group had learnt from Op Pimlico, the OMS learnt valuable lessons from Op Waterloo too. To take us on head to head was futile, and the battle proved to be their last big set piece. Until later, of course. From then onwards it was to be high-intensity guerrilla warfare. That meant fewer open assaults and less of a will to hold fixed patches of ground, but more hidden bombs and far cleverer ambushes. Now they'd only confront us on their terms when they knew they had more firepower than us, or could catch us unaware. It became a regular pattern of combat for the next six weeks.

We fought the OMS's new warfare with the usual counter-insurgency tactics: arrest operations, searches, unpredictable patrols, random vehicle checks.

On the streets, we indulged in a new game of cat and mouse. The OMS watched us carefully. When we came back into camp, they would go out and do their own patrols. The kids that had been chatting to us half an hour before were slapped about. Some poor sod who'd been drinking would get shot again.

Half of it was a cold war for the city's hearts and minds. That was just as important as the physical stuff. If we could get the local population on our side, it would deny the OMS friendly territory from which to operate. To do that, the battle group tried to keep Warriors off Al Amarah's streets as much as possible. People hated the Warrior. It was a beast of a thing, it knocked down their buildings, churned up their tarmac and made a hell of a din. I couldn't blame them.

As time went on, it wasn't just the OMS that we were

going up against either. They began to get help from some very dark quarters. With the Najaf standoff well into its second month, the foreign extremists who'd previously concentrated their efforts on Baghdad and the north saw a good opportunity in the south to wreak further havoc. Al-Qaeda had come to town.

Their help came in the form of tactics, expertise and equipment, and a lot of it was highly professional. Al Amarah was too small and poxy to be a major destination for world jihad. But it was the closest city to the Iranian border. That was the transit route into Iraq that most of the holy warriors were using. Al Amarah also had Route 6 running through it which would take them all the way up to Baghdad, so many used the city as a convenient stop-off. The temptation to have a crack at us while they were here proved too strong to resist.

Intelligence briefings revealed that as well as Iranians, now Syrians, Yemenis and Jordanians were all making the trip and were operating for short periods in Al Amarah. They ranged from individual untrained fanatics to large and highly professional groups.

Sadly we never caught any, and it was hard to tell them apart from other religious-looking Arabs at distance. But you could tell if you got into a gunfight with them. They were particularly resilient, and unlike many Iraqis they had been trained to use their rifles properly too. Division HQ in Basra was so worried about their increasing numbers, that Recce Platoon was deployed along the Iranian border for a while to join an operation to catch them. We'd heard that the Americans in western Iraq had even captured some British jihadis from Birmingham. If only the little toerags had come to Al Amarah.

The foreign fighters brought their very own novel brands

of killing with them too. We were told of the increased threat of Vehicle Borne Improvised Explosive Devices (VBIED). That's military speak for car bombs.

Another of the foreigners' tricks was to strap old Soviet-made tank mines underneath road bridges so their shrapnel would come down like lead hailstones on anyone who drove underneath them. We kept a wide berth of bridges for a fair while after hearing that.

A specific warning was made at the end of May that sent a chill down all our spines. Featherstone explained all the information that had come through.

'Guys, we've had some pretty nasty intelligence about which I want you all to be particularly aware. Three cars rigged up with high explosives are going to attack coalition troops or bases on Route 6 somewhere between Al Amarah and Baghdad. They're being driven by three suicide bombers, who are also wearing explosive vests. They'll detonate them if they're stopped.

'Vehicles they are using are . . .' Featherstone looked down at his notes to read off a list. '. . . a black BMW, a white Toyota Christa and a red Toyota Corolla. Each car has a support team of nine or ten fighters travelling alongside it. They will launch an RPG and small arms assault once the cars have exploded. The whole team was trained in Iran for a week before they set off.

'That's all, I'm afraid. Targets and timings unknown.'

In other words, we didn't know where this little package of misery was going, or when they'd get there. But we knew they were on their way.

'The greatest threat to us will obviously be at vehicle checkpoints. Be very careful indeed please, guys, and make sure everybody's wide awake 110 per cent of the time when you're out over the next few days.'

Car bombs we knew all about from Northern Ireland. But suicide bombers was a brand new one on us. We were extra careful when we went out. Beyond that, there's little more you can do.

Suicide killings are the hardest concept for western soldiers in Iraq to deal with. Blokes firing machine guns at you are fine, because you can shoot back at them. But people who are prepared to die to kill you in an everyday situation are almost impossible to prevent. You stop the wrong car at a vehicle checkpoint, you're going to get yourself blown to fucking bits. It's just pure chance.

It took the Slipper City desk jockeys longer than us to clock onto the changing shape of the war. We were up close and personal to them every day, so we could pick up the telltale signs. In one house search we found a couple of mercury tilt switches used to detonate bombs. Now they are smart pieces of kit. As soon as you move the device, the mercury moves, connects the electrical circuit, and boom. So when someone in Abu Napa came up with the bright idea of allowing our Snatch Land Rovers back on the streets, we were more than a little pessimistic.

Major Featherstone told us about the decision in an O Group. The first Snatch patrol would even go out from Cimic that very night. This was going to be interesting. I went back up to the roof and told the five members of the platoon up there.

'Bloody hell. They're mad,' observed Fitz.

Everyone else shook their heads. But Ads had an idea.

'How about this, lads: why don't we do a sweepstake on how long it takes for them Snatches to get smacked? We could all put in a tenner.' The time closest to the inevitable attack on the Snatches after leaving base would win. Ads plumped for 22 minutes. Sam had it at 17, Chris at 31,

Smudge at 25 and I fancied it at 24. Fitz went for the lowest, at 11 minutes. Smudge gave his bet short shrift.

'Don't be silly, Fitzy. It takes just about ten minutes to get out the chicanes and off fucking Tigris Street. That's a wasted orange one.'

Two hours later, two Snatch Land Rovers left Cimic. With the stopwatch running, we watched them go. Just after they turned out of our sight, *bang.* An explosion echoed out over the night sky, followed by a long burst of AK fire. The Snatches came screeching back to Cimic. Nobody was hurt, but one of the vehicles was decorated with long scorch marks on its rear where the roadside bomb had caught it. They had been out for only eight minutes. Fitzy had won by a country mile.

The penny dropped in Abu Naji after that. The Snatch ban was reimposed immediately.

Light-hearted distractions were essential in dealing with the tense atmosphere and helped lighten the mood. But the funny thing about combat is you can never predict how people are going to react until they're in the middle of it. The hardest bloke in the company could become a bag of nerves, and the smallest runt could end up fighting like a possessed banshee. Appearances and reputation count for nothing. Everyone goes through the wringer equally.

Some took a bit of time, like young Sam who had frozen up inside my Snatch during our first and major contact on 18 April. He was full of apologies to me the next day, and felt awful about it.

'There's nothing to apologize for, Sam,' I told him.

'I just wanted to get the fuck out of that vehicle, Danny.'

'I understand. We're through that now, mate. I know you'll come good the next time.' And he did. Sam was a different

157

person in the next scrap we had, and went on to become one of the platoon's most ballsy warriors. I was hoping against hope that the same would happen with Gilly.

There were also a few who just couldn't deal with it at all. One of those was Taff. What happened to him was an awful thing to witness. Taff was a 32-year-old corporal in Recce Platoon, and a bloody good NCO at that. He had a great sense of humour and was very chatty. A typical Welsh taff in an English regiment.

He'd also been in the thick of the fighting on 18 April. That evening, Chris had pointed out to him that he had a lump of sharp shrapnel the size of a pen lid still sticking out of his breast plate. The implication was obvious. If he hadn't been wearing body armour, he'd be brown bread.

Taff didn't like this one little bit, and it had scared the hell out of him. Back in England, his girlfriend was pregnant with his first child. From that night onwards, he started to go downhill. His behaviour changed immediately and he was no longer the same person. He wouldn't leave hardened accommodation unless there was a military reason. Blokes had to bring his meals to him there, because he didn't want to go to the cookhouse. He refused to take his helmet and body armour off ever, even in bed. It meant he couldn't shower either.

For a while, Taff tried to carry on as usual. To begin with people let him be because we didn't want to hurt his pride. He'd been in for years and he had a load of blokes under him. He didn't want to turn around after all of that and announce he hated it there. But it was obvious he did.

All the senior NCOs tried to talk to him quietly. We were his mates, and we wanted to help. I found him sitting in a doorway of the main house one morning staring up at the sky. He was slowly rocking backwards and forwards.

158

'All right, Taff?'

'Hi, Danny. I'm fine.'

'Right shit hole this, isn't it, mate?'

'Yeah.'

'You going out on patrol today?'

'Nah.'

'Yeah, best leave it for a bit, eh, mate. No need to rush things is there?' He didn't reply. Instead, he carried on rocking backwards and forwards on the spot. There was no getting through to him. He was gone.

We felt desperately sorry for him. Neither was it a very good sight for the young toms. Just seeing him had got a few of them thinking, and we didn't need that. It was the OC who eventually told him he had to go.

'Look, Taff, we're going to get you out of here. You're clearly suffering. I'm going to get you back to England for a bit.'

'Right, sir.'

'Don't take it as a slur on your character. You're a good soldier, and you can come back when you feel ready.'

Taff was taken out down the usual chain as a medical casualty. When he got back to the UK, he immediately signed himself out of the army. In three months, he was a civvy. He didn't even want to wait to get a proper medical discharge. We lost a good man. It was very sad for him, and very sad for the company. But nobody thought any worse of him, because it wasn't his fault.

After Taff, the OC set up the trauma diary. It was a good idea and probably saved another ten Taffs in the company. Whenever a patrol had got into a contact, the first thing they'd do when they got back to Cimic was all go into a room with Major Featherstone and Dale. Then they'd talk through every little thing that happened, from the moment they left the front gate to the moment they came back in again. You could say anything you liked in it, from how you felt about killing somebody to how you'd shat your pants. Nobody was exempt, from privates to officers. Everything was aired in fine detail, so nothing could be suppressed.

It has to be said though that Taff was a rare exception. Most of the company became very adept at adjusting to whatever the OMS and their allies threw at us next. As for me, well, I just loved it. War fighting was what I had really wanted to do my whole career, and here I was at last getting a chance to do it in fucking spades. That's how a lot of Sniper Platoon felt too. But that didn't make us better men than Taff. It didn't even make us better soldiers. It's just that everybody is different.

Longy, however, had his own highly individual way of dealing with the rigours of Iraq. He masturbated. And he wanked like there was no tomorrow.

At just five foot four inches tall, Private Sean 'Longy' Long was the smallest bloke in the platoon – despite his surname. Hence the nickname was not a little bit ironic. He got a lot of abuse for his diminutive height, which he took very well. Another soldier aged just twenty, he was one of the platoon's real characters, very popular and likeable. The only thing that let him down was his drinking capacity. He would always be the first to get totally shit-faced, so we had to look after him when we were out on the piss in Tidworth.

Longy got heavily mothered by Ads, who felt that someone so small needed looking after. Most of it was wind-up. Ads's favourite line to Longy when out on patrol was, 'Keep low, move fast.' It had him in stitches every time.

Ads would also tell him, 'Longy, I'm going to marry you. You're so sweet.'

'Fuck off Ads, you poof.' That had Ads in fits every time too.

Longy's masturbatory habits hadn't been an issue in England. When he came to Iraq though, his capacity went through the roof. He would take a porn mag or a DVD player into the loos with him at least five or six times a day. After every patrol, he was straight in there without fail, sometimes without even taking his body armour off. He would emerge fifteen minutes later with a big smile on his face. The lad didn't even have any shame at all. Ads had a regular line for those moments too.

'You complete wanker, Longy!'

'Yeah, fair one,' he could only reply.

Then there was Louey and John Wedlock's way of dealing with the stress.

Over a month had gone by since they went eyeball to eyeball on the front driveway. Word had started to go round the company that they'd even sorted out their differences. Word was wrong.

Major hostilities broke out suddenly one breakfast. Wedlock was in the corner of the cookhouse by the taps filling up half a dozen jerry cans of water. As Louey walked past, he couldn't resist the usual quick dig.

'Orr, hellor, Wedlock. Make sure you fill them all the way up to the top now.'

Perhaps there was something in Louey's laid back Caribbean tones that morning that was particularly provocative. Maybe Wedlock was just having a bad morning. Whatever it was, he quickly stood up and punched Louey hard in the face twice.

Now John Wedlock's punches aren't those of a normal man. A proper connection was more than enough to smash a bloke's jaw into small pieces. Louey swayed, but amazingly he managed to stay on his feet, and punched Wedlock back.

Louey landed one decent blow on him before the two giants locked arms in a furious grapple. At first they pressed each other up against the industrial-sized sink in a bid for one of them to fall into it. Then the wrestle spun them both round and they went careering straight into the long line of tables and chairs where most of the company were tucking into bacon and eggs.

Trays, plastic cups of juice, half-eaten eggs, toast, tables and chairs all went flying in every direction. Blokes desperately dived out of the way of the colossi as they smashed through everything in their way. Chris grabbed my arm and jerked me out of my seat as I had my back to the impending danger.

'Get out the way, Danny, quick. I ain't getting in between the Swede and that brute.'

Soon the cat calls were in full flow too. Soldiers either shouted 'Swede!' or 'Lamp him John', depending on which fighter's platoon they were in.

Louey and Wedlock were in a heap of muscle on the floor in the middle of the room now. As one briefly gained the upper hand, he'd manage to release an arm just long enough to hurl down a horribly hard punch on the other. Then the roles were reversed.

After four minutes of all of us letting them go for it, a sergeant from a neutral platoon decided it was time to step in. He got a few decent right hooks for his trouble. Eventually, a total of sixteen blokes finally pulled them apart.

The whole disengagement process took roughly double the length of time of the actual fight. Louey and Wedlock were not easy men to pin down, and they made furious lunges for each other whenever they could break free of their restrainers. Each already sported huge lumps on their faces and badly cut knuckles.

'I'll fucking crucify you, Wedlock, you fucking scum,' Louey spat at him.

'Fuck you, Louey. I'll fucking kill you first.'

I believed both of them.

Both were sent to see Dale. Instead of fining them as he would have done in Tidworth, he made them shake hands in front of him and told them to fucking well sort it out. If they wanted to take out their aggression on someone, do it on the enemy. They both told Dale it was just about the pressure everyone was under, living in a small confined space and all that. But we all knew the truth. It wouldn't really matter if they were in a five-star spa hotel and retreat. They'd still want to smack seven bells out of each other.

The only other time fisticuffs looked likely at Cimic was between us and the CPA officials' American bodyguards from Triple Canopy. It's funny to think we then ended up becoming best muckers with some of them.

The initial antipathy was only to be expected. It went on for a good month. We didn't just think they were tossers because they all pranced around like they could be straight off a film set, although that was bad enough. Every one of them permanently wore wraparound shades and a silly array of weapons off their belts they probably didn't know how to really use. Worse than that, they acted like they were way above us in the food chain – some kind of elite military force.

Mostly it was just vicious looks at each other. But the tension finally came to a head over the showers.

Being smelly soldiers, we had always been banned from using the CPA and Triple Canopy's ablutions Portakabins which were nicer than ours. Then the only one assigned to the company was put out of bounds because a blind mortar had landed in it. It meant technically the only place left for a hundred of us to wash and crap in were the three showers and three toilets in the prefab accommodation blocks.

Bollocks to that. We'll use what's left. So we started going into the Triple Canopy Portakabin for a shower instead. If they were real soldiers, they wouldn't give a shit. But they did. Petty little notices started appearing on the door that read 'Triple Canopy Only – NOT for Y Company use'. The fucking cheek of it. They were sleeping safe at night because we were out protecting their arses. So if we wanted a shower, we'd fucking have one. We ignored the notices, and ripped them down as we went in for the next shower.

For days they didn't have the bollocks to say anything to our faces. Then one day, Chris was just drying himself down after a particularly nice shower in the Triple Canopy facility, when one of their biggest blokes walked in. He was very thickset, with bright red hair and a goatee beard.

Chris carried on like he hadn't a care in the world.

'Hey, Limey.'

At that, Chris spun round to face the redhead. He was ready for the inevitable punch-up.

'Yes, Yank, I'm in your fucking showers. What are you going to do about it?'

'That tattoo on your leg, man. You a sniper?'

'Yeah. What the fuck's it to you?'

'I used to be a sniper in the US Marine Corps. Recon.'

'Oh, really?'

'Yeah, really. Hold your horses, man, as we say in Texas. We got something in common.'

'Well, my mum lives in Texas, so we've got two things in common. Sorry about your showers.'

'Ah, fuck it. We're mean sons-of-bitches for not letting you use them anyway.'

The redhead stuck out his shovel-sized hand. 'The name's Rob, but everyone calls me Red Rob round here. And you've got a small dick, man.'

Red Rob and Chris bonded right there and then. Once in the sniper brotherhood, forever in it. Within a minute they were discussing the finer points of various sniper rifles the world over. To us, being a sniper transcended anything.

The shower summit broke the ice between our two groups. Once we got talking to them, it turned out most of the Triple Canopy team were pretty good lads. There were a total of three snipers among their team. As well as Red Rob, CK was an ex-SWAT sniper from the Atlanta Police in Georgia, and Harry was a Paddy who'd served as a sniper in the British Army's Royal Irish Regiment.

One night, Chris invited all three of them up onto the roof to have a look at how we did business.

'Have a shot if you want, lads.'

Americans need no encouragement to start shooting at things, and the Triple Canopy lads never went anywhere without their highly customized weapons – which were perfect for the job. The favourite among them was an AK47 with a folding butt, fitted with brand new US-made telescopic sights.

' All three of them were chomping at the bit. That night, it was just the few warning shots that we needed to put down to scare a few shady characters off. But the next night, Red Rob, CK and Harry came up to the roof again, and they got a kill.

It was one of the OMS's most persistent RPG men, who had been floating around on the north bank taking us on whenever he could for the past few days. Of course, being Yanks, the kill led to a whole load of back slapping, high fiving and air pumping.

'Get some! Who's your Daddy?' they bawled out into the darkness.

From then onwards, the boys came up in their free time whenever they could. Not only did we enjoy their company, but they were very welcome extra pairs of hands too when it got busy up there. None of them had lost their aim either.

When it was quiet, we just swapped war stories and obsessed over the pros and cons of our rival weapons systems; the two primary topics of soldiers bonding the world over.

Most of their armoury was Russian- or Chinese-made and had been taken off dead or captured insurgents. They'd even managed to get their hands on a Draganov sniper rifle, which they brought up one night for Chris and I to drool over. In turn, having never seen them before, the Yanks were fascinated by our SA80s.

Unfortunately, their Iraq stories were by and large better than ours, as it turned out most of them had been out for almost a year.

There were thousands of Red Robs all over the country. The fall of Saddam's regime and the arrival of the American one prompted the biggest goldrush in the close protection industry's entire history. Every foreign administrator, engineer or electrician needed protecting, and often by a ratio of at least four to one. They were a whole private army. And because of where their constant travelling took them they often got into more scraps than regular coalition forces. In the old days, they'd be called mercenaries. Now, they were professional security consultants.

The deal the Triple Canopy lads were on was that they'd work six weeks, and then go home to the US for six weeks. Nice life. We had seven months in the sandpit, with a poxy two weeks for our home leave. And they got paid triple our wage. They couldn't say they were serving the Queen though. Just the Queen of Maysan.

On another occasion, Red Rob brought up his laptop to show us his home movie war clips. Many he'd downloaded off the Internet, but an impressive amount were his own. In his time, he'd accrued quite a collection. He'd filmed his pride and joy two weeks before we arrived. It was a thirty-second clip of an OMS man creeping up to Cimic's front gate to throw a blast bomb over the walls. Just as the insurgent sprang up to deliver his package, he was shot dead on the spot with a bullet in the chest.

'That was Jimmy's shot,' Red Rob explained with pride. 'From the roof of the Pink Palace too, on an AK with just iron sights. Not bad for a geriatric.'

Jimmy hair's was entirely grey, along with his beard. Because he also wore blue denim dungarees, we'd nicknamed him Uncle Jesse, like the old fella in *The Dukes of Hazzard*. Of course we were impressed, but I was never going to tell Red Rob that.

'Yeah, right. How old do you couple of Limeys think he is?'

'Uncle Jesse? At least ninety-four,' teased Chris.

'Get outta here, man! He's fifty-nine. Saw active service in Vietnam, US Marine Corps too like me. Even witnessed the final pull-out from Saigon in '75. Yup, fifty-nine and still going strong. Not bad for an old timer, eh? Puts your young pups in their place, don't it?'

Our night sessions led on to all sorts of inter-unit activities. The meat heads in the company were invited to have a 'bench off' with their meat heads; that is, who could bench-press most weight on the machines by the pool. Louey was our star performer, despite professing to never using a weight machine in his life. Having beaten off all the other Triple Canopy competition, he finally lost to an absolute house of a bloke called Jedd, who was almost as wide as he was tall.

Then there were the obligatory photo snaps we'd take posing up with each other, to show to the folks back home. As the two founding fathers of the love-in between our tribes, Chris and Red Rob insisted on posing up together all over the compound. In the daylight, we also gave each other long and detailed lessons in assembling and disassembling our own weapons as well as how best to use them.

It was an off-the-cuff remark from Red Rob though that ended up doing more for our morale than anything else on the tour. He wanted to show his gratitude for a particularly good night's shooting.

'Any extra kit you guys need, you just ask, all right? We get all our stuff via mail order.'

'Oh right, do you? Thanks very much. Can we have a look at your catalogue, then?'

We might have mercilessly taken the piss out of them for it, but the truth is no soldier can ever have too much kit. Our carping was just pure jealousy. For days, we pored over their catalogues like kiddies in a sweet shop.

We sent off for ultra comfy Desert Fox boots, Wiley-X blast-proof sunglasses, sniper's fingerless gloves, Camelback water holders, US Marine Corps webbing, Sure-Fire torches to clip onto our rifle barrels, US Army T-shirts, day sacks, and knee pads. We just couldn't get enough of it.

The item I was particularly chuffed about was a double magazine clip. It held two magazines together, and meant you could pop a fresh one into the rifle once the first was empty without having to fumble around in your webbing. It saved valuable seconds and proved ever handier as time went on.

Soon enough, we began to look just like Red Rob and his mates. With our longs in our hands, only our camouflage trousers still identified us as regular British Army. The RSM would have blown a gasket. Featherstone was pretty relaxed about it all though, and the rest of the battalion too far away to ever know.

It didn't take the OMS long to get back to their daily mortar barrages at us. After a couple of weeks, we weren't far away from the pre-Waterloo rate of incoming. The lunatics had found – or been given by Iran – a few more 82mm mortar tubes too. We knew how to handle mortars now, so our morale was still as strong as ever. But as time went on, they slowly began to degrade our surroundings. They also took away more of our liberties.

A couple more Snatches were consigned to the scrap heap. One was fragged almost out of recognition, and the second's fuel tank exploded after being slit open by a piece of flying shrapnel. As the mortar fire was always the heaviest in the evening, it was decided to stagger the evening meal. Each platoon went to eat at a different hour. That cut down on big queues outside the cookhouse where a lucky round could have taken out ten of us at once.

The God of War was certainly looking down on us at Cimic too, because there were some unbelievable close shaves. The cook had the closest.

A quiet and modest, tall and skinny redhead, he was known to everyone as just 'Chef'. He worked out of a proper little aluminium kitchen trailer full of stainless steel surfaces that had been brought in by the CPA. While preparing the evening meal one night, he left the trailer for thirty seconds to pop to the store room to collect some more veg. While he was outside, an 82mm mortar round came down and tore straight through his trailer's roof and blew the thing up. There was twisted aluminium everywhere. Chef was the hero of Cimic that night, because he didn't sit about complaining. Instead, he cleaned the place up as best as he could and still then managed to get the meal out. The next day a field kitchen under a green tent was brought in from Abu Naji. It offered no protection at all from mortar fire. But without even blinking, Chef moved into it and carried on as normal in there.

Then there was Ray. Private Chris 'Ray' Rayment from Mortar Platoon had the most uncanny knack of getting mortared everywhere he went. So much so, he became known as the Mortar Magnet. Every sangar he did sentry duty in would get a round landing either directly on top of it or just feet away. Ray would always emerge bruised and covered in dust, but otherwise unscathed.

Luckily, he had a great sense of humour about it too. He'd tell everybody to steer clear of him. And whenever he left his barracks room for a sentry shift, he'd say something like: 'Right, that's me off now, lads. If you hear Front Sangar getting mortared, don't worry – it's only me.'

Ray was a gobby little so and so. He never held back on giving you his opinion about what you were doing with a sharp bit of wit. But he had a heart of gold underneath it, and that made him one of the best-loved characters in the company. Ray was also a bit of a ladies' man, and he never gave a hoot if they weren't good looking. 'Any hole's a goal' was his catchphrase. He was the perfect private soldier. You knew he'd always do what you'd ask of him and you never needed to check.

Three other blokes weren't so lucky. They'd crept back into the prefab accommodation block one evening to get a good night's kip away from the sweaty mass. They knew it was out of bounds now, but they risked it anyway. A mortar round came straight through the roof and fragged the lot of them. Only a few deep cuts and some bad bruising, nothing too serious. They didn't get much sympathy though. It was the last time anyone tried that trick.

A political crisis in Maysan at the end of May played in the OMS's favour. Their power thrived off anarchy, whereas ours would only grow with security.

Maysan's governor Riyadh Mahood had got out of town fast after he was heavily implicated in the murder of his own chief of police. The copper ended up with a bullet in his face during a row with the governor and his brother Abu Hatim in a hospital foyer. Styling himself Lord of the Marshes, Abu Hatim was a senior tribal chief and for two decades had led a terrorist resistance force in the province against Saddam.

The brothers were obviously struggling with the whole idea of being statesmen rather than hoods after so long. The rumour was they'd gone to lie low in Baghdad. From then onwards, exactly who the new governor should be was hotly disputed by all and sundry, not least the OMS. Endless rows in the governing council made it harder for Molly Phee to get things done.

Soon afterwards, Route 6 down to Basra was put out of bounds to all routine military traffic. Ever more successful OMS bombs and ambushes made it impossible to pass down the road in any degree of safety. As it was our main supply line, that was a big headache. Everything – men, bombs, beans and bullets – had to come in and out by Hercules aircraft via the landing strip at Sparrowhawk. It was just like living in South Armagh during the worst of the Ulster Troubles. We were surrounded by bandit country in Maysan too.

Were we bothered though? Not a bit of it. For every new obstacle, we'd find a way of dealing with it. The more the OMS tried to fuck us over, the stronger our resolve became. It was the traditional plucky British spirit, and the lads throughout the whole company were always excellent like that.

It wasn't just stubbornness. A newspaper article stuck up on the company noticeboard by some of my platoon typified the mood. Next to a particularly ugly photo of Moqtada al-Sadr, its headline read, 'Rebel leader warns US: I am ready to face martyrdom'.

The lads had drawn crosshairs on Moqtada's forehead and scrawled over it in marker pen, 'British Snipers warn: We will help you get there!'

We grew to *relish* the challenge the OMS laid down. The excitement and the adrenalin rush was like a drug; we were all slowly becoming addicted to it.

15

The only real downer across the battle group, and it wasn't a big one, was that we weren't getting any write-ups back home. Concern had been slowly growing about why there was almost no media coverage in Britain about what we were doing in Al Amarah. At first, we couldn't understand it. We'd been war fighting harder than the invasion force had to a year before, so why was no one interested?

It mattered most to the younger lads. When the newspapers arrived two weeks late (as they always did) for the dates over Pimlico and Waterloo, H was especially put out. Private Andy 'H', Hawkins was a good little soldier and always keen to impress. Like Smudge, he had a bit of an image thing. He came storming up to the roof clutching a brand new pile of papers. He hurled them down in disgust.

'I've been through every single fucking one of these papers, and there's not a fucking word about the PWRR in any of them. Not even a paragraph in the *Sun* and they're always the best at doing squaddies' stuff, aren't they? What the fuck is wrong with them all?'

Lads like H needed to know they were getting respect back home for being in that shit hole. They believed in Queen and Country and they wanted to go home heroes, so everyone in their local pub would want to buy them a drink.

They regularly scanned the Internet and watched Sky News for even the smallest passing reference, when the satellite dish hadn't been blown down. But for months there was nothing.

The older ones among us worked it out soon enough. It was confirmed during a visit from the brigadier who was based down in Basra. The papers weren't writing about us because they hadn't a Scooby any of this was even going on. The MoD was doing an excellent job of simply not telling them. The government had local elections in June. The last thing they needed was pictures of big old tanks on the streets in southern Iraq.

With the kidnappings and beheadings of westerners in Iraq in full swing now, it was also far too dangerous for journalists to make their own way up to Al Amarah. They needed the military's assistance. A TV crew from ITN had been flown up in early April, but the OMS had given their normal warm welcome and thrown a blast bomb at their convoy of Snatches. Nobody was injured, but they caught it all on tape and it made great viewing. That gave the sweaty-palmed media officers at Division thoroughly twisted knickers. No more press came up after that until long after the shooting was over.

We had to thank the MoD and their head-in-the-sand policy for one thing, though. It made calling home a hell of a lot easier. I'd only spoken to my girlfriend Sue once in the almost two months we'd been there. We'd all been so busy, I'd hardly had the chance. Everyone got twenty minutes' free talk time a week on satellite phones. But you had to wait in a long queue and the satellite link was often awful.

I'd barely even given her any thought. Now that I did, it felt very strange. My mind went back to her cosy house in Catterick, the walks we used to take on the moors, the laughs we had in her local boozer. It all seemed a very long way away now. It was more than a few thousand miles away. It was a different world.

Despite that, I did miss her. I was desperate to tell her all about what we'd been up to; the excitement, the amazing highs and the grim lows. 'Guess what I've been doing, love?' and all that. When it actually came to it, I told her absolutely nothing. I just couldn't find any words that she would understand.

'Hiya, Dan. Wow, it's really good to hear you.'

'Yeah, you too. You OK?'

'Yeah, don't worry about me. What about you? Some place called Nafaj is on the news a bit, something about a fat Muslim priest. That anywhere near you?'

'It's Najaf. No, love, it's not that near us.'

'I'm so worried about you, Dan. Are you sure you're nowhere near the fighting? We never hear anything about your regiment. Please tell me everything is OK.'

It felt like talking to someone in a foreign language. If I even began to tell Sue any of it, it would have come out all wrong and scared the hell out of her. How do you even begin to explain what it's like to watch a bloke get his leg torn off and then pick it up and put it under his arm? How do you then say you weren't actually that bothered by seeing it? Yes. Best to just say nothing.

'No, don't worry, love. It's all quiet here, nothing much going on. Tell my mum everything's fine and not to worry either.'

With my kids it was easier, because I just turned the conversation round and asked about them. But I kept the phone calls home to a minimum after that.

Chris was on the satellite phone just after me. He came back up to the roof looking puzzled.

'What did you tell your bird then, mate?'

'Nothing, Danny. I had all my tales lined up, but I didn't tell her a fucking thing. I just didn't think she'd get it.'

*

Towards the end of May, I started to push for more and more freedom for the platoon. We'd proved what we were capable of over many hard weeks of fighting already. All we wanted was the liberty to do the best soldiering we could; it's all good snipers ever want. We'd keep up with all our regular company tasks, but we yearned to take the fight to the OMS whenever we could too. It was far better fun than waiting for them to hit us, and the only way we thought they'd ever be beaten. So we started to do just that.

I'd plan all our own patrols. We went into areas of town where we knew we'd come across the bad boys. That meant an inevitable exchange of rounds for a bit, before they usually lost their bottle and fucked off. We worked as one seamless unit, and we had total confidence in our own abilities. We took the view that if we wanted a fight, we should be allowed to go looking for one. And we got damn good at fighting them too. We began to live for it.

Sooner or later, our enthusiasm was always going to lead us into conflict with the company's two senior officers, Major Featherstone and his 2i/c Redders. The more kills we notched up, the more nervous they got. No matter how legitimate they all were, or how we'd always get back in one piece.

Officers worry a lot about things like that, because they're the ones who get the heat from the politicians when the bullets start to fly. Whitehall always gets very cross whenever it emerges that, bizarrely, Iraq isn't a Garden of Eden. Luckily, as regular soldiers we didn't have to worry about the bigger picture – just doing our jobs. That meant killing the enemy before they killed us.

With Redders, it was always more of an unthinking gut reaction. He was the only one of the two commanders who ever challenged anything we did on the roof.

As a person, Captain Peter 'Redders' Redgrave was a very friendly and sociable guy. He was everyone's mate, and would always call us by our first names; a nice touch from officers. But he had a bit of a nervous disposition, and it came out worst when we were under fire.

This was bad news because he was responsible for running the company's Ops Room. It's not an easy job at all. As well as knowing what all your blokes are up to, it also means you're the link between the company and the battle group Ops Room in Abu Naji. That's like playing two games of chess at once. It's vital to have a cool and calm head at all times. Unfortunately, sometimes Redders flapped. He wasn't a bad bloke, and perhaps any 25-year-old in his highly stressful position would have done the same. It just didn't help much.

One night after I'd left the roof, the lads thought they'd got another fix on a mortar team. Redders heard the rounds go down from the Ops Room and legged it up to the roof to find out what they were shooting at.

'A mortar team, sir. We're putting down some harassing fire, it will get them to move on.'

'Yes, well, that's not the point. From now on, you ask the Ops Room for permission to open fire. Is that clear? Good.'

Chris waited until Redders was halfway down the stairs.

'Don't forget your stick, sir.'

Redders had made an appalling call.

One of the most important principles of sniping is having the ability to take the shot when you can. You might not get another chance. All of my guys were fully qualified, very well versed in the rules of engagement (ROE), and excellent soldiers. It had to be their call, or we'd be no better than the sort of robots that Saddam forced his army to be.

When the boys told me the next day, I was livid.

'Hundred per cent bollocks, lads. We ain't ever going to fucking do that. If you get a legitimate target, then you destroy it. I don't want you ever to ask for permission. If Redders tries to have a go at any of you again for that, you come straight to me and I'll fucking sort it out.'

I was shouting so loudly Redders probably heard. He didn't mention it ever again. It was just typical Redders in an unthinking moment. In fairness, everybody knew he was under a lot of pressure and he probably regretted making the call the moment he said it.

My problems with Major Featherstone were different. The tension was slow boil. It wasn't just an enemy bodycount thing with him. It was the fear of ours too. As the boss, a lot of casualties would – rightly or wrongly – look very bad for him. I was convinced that's what dictated his cautious calls. That way he could remain in control.

Sometimes he was right. Even I knew I could be a bit gung-ho at times. But at the same time I was convinced that our cautiousness was starting to seriously hinder the effect we were having on the enemy.

One night, we went out on a patrol to the bus depot on the north bank. It was a popular spot for OMS fighters to gather. They'd chat there, plan an attack and move off.

We set up a covert OP (observation post) nearby in some rough ground to monitor any activity that there might be there. Around midnight, about a dozen shady-looking characters with weapons turned up. Unfortunately, right at that moment some idiot on the Cimic roof decided to throw up some 51mm mortar illume. The OMS men spotted us immediately and opened fire.

We were in good enough cover to hide until the illume went out. Then I threw together a quick plan for a snap ambush on the fighters. If half the patrol dog-legged round to the left quickly, we'd catch them on their flank and kill them.

I told the Ops Room my intention. After a short pause, Featherstone came on the net.

'The answer is no, Dan. I want you to come back to camp.'

I couldn't believe it. We had to sit there and wait for a Warrior to come and extract us instead.

A week later, I had taken a multiple of about ten blokes over to the north bank again one morning to investigate three large Katyusha rockets that were all wired up and ready to fire at Cimic. We were about to destroy them with a 30 mil round from a Warrior.

Suddenly, peels of gunfire erupted from the big road junction at Green 5. It was one of the boys in black's favourite ambush points. A look through the binos revealed one of our fuel convoys in the shit. Three Snatches driven by Royal Fusiliers had been escorting a couple of petrol tankers down Route 6. The tankers had managed to drive through it, but one of the Snatches had been disabled so the other two stopped to help it out.

It was some distance from us, but the Fusiliers were clearly in a lot of trouble. And anyway, it was a good chance for us to get involved in something.

We ended up having to run across 900 metres of waste ground to get there. As we jogged, I got on the radio.

'Hello Zero, Alpha One Zero Alpha. Contact Green 5. Wait out.'

Featherstone was on to me immediately.

'Danny, you're not to get involved in that contact.'

'Too late sir, we're here now,' I replied, with still 500 metres to go. Bollocks to that. We weren't going to run away from the enemy.

'Danny, for fuck's sake. I've told you you're not to get involved in that contact. I'm sending the Warriors round to pick you up.'

We reached a long three-foot wall 150 metres from Green 5 that gave us a strong position to start engaging the enemy from. They were in clumps on the junction's single- and two-storey rooftops. The weight of our suppressing fire gave the Fusiliers time to rig up a tow rope to the crippled Snatch, and within a few minutes they were all out of there.

Then the Warriors turned up. Sgt Chris Adkins was their commander, a mate of mine. He understood what was going on.

'Come on, Danny, get on the back. We've been told to get you out of here. Please, mate.'

I felt like a naughty schoolboy. As we trundled off, I saw through the Warrior's back window an RPG man running across the junction in broad daylight waving his weapon in the air. We'd let the enemy feel they'd won again.

This time I was furious. What were we wearing the uniform for? Why did Featherstone let us carry rifles if we're not allowed to use them?

It all came to a head between the OC and me one particularly hot evening thanks to a drunken Iraqi policeman.

We were patrolling in the souks off Baghdad Street when gunfire broke out just around the corner. We sprinted back to the main road to find a fat old police sergeant on a motorbike wobbling all over the place, and blasting rounds from a pistol in the general direction of anybody he saw. He was pissed out of his head.

Chris, Ads, Pikey and I waited until he'd wobbled just past our corner before we jumped out with rifles raised.

'Kif! Kif!' we shouted, which is 'stop' in Arabic. 'Assila,' we said, which is 'weapon', and pointed to the floor.

We got him off the bike and tore strips off the fat fool. He looked very sheepish. I explained to him we were taking his pistol and the keys to his bike, and he could come and pick them up the next morning from Cimic House when he'd sobered up.

As we set off back to Cimic, I relayed the information back to the Ops Room and explained the reason for the gunfire.

'Happy with that, Danny,' Redders said.

Five hundred metres down the road, Redders came back on again.

'Alpha One Zero Alpha, this is Zero. Ignore my last. Can you go back to the policeman and give him his weapons and keys back, please? Sorry, new orders. We can't be seen to be undermining the IPS.'

There was no point arguing the toss with Redders. I knew exactly whose orders they were. It was Featherstone's worst call yet. I was seething.

The cop was still sitting on his bike feeling sorry for himself. He got his pistol and keys, but I had unloaded the magazine and put the ammunition in my pocket. The cop began to giggle as we walked off. We had lost a huge amount of face with the crowd that had now gathered to watch the whole ludicrous charade.

Within ten minutes, I was on the stairs up to the Ops Room on Cimic House's first floor. I hadn't even bothered to take off my webbing or body armour. The place was very busy.

Confronted with the sea of people, I boomed: 'So what fucking dickhead made that stupid jackshit call then?'

There was total silence. Slowly, all the men in the room parted to reveal Major Featherstone leaning back in a large office chair.

'Well, actually Danny, it was mine.'

'Well that was a fucking good call wasn't it, sir? Top fucking marks.'

Total silence. Featherstone bolted up, red in the face.

'Right, Sergeant, we'd better take this outside.'

'Fucking fine with me.'

On the first floor balcony, overlooking the Tigris, we had the mother of all screaming matches. The entirety of Cimic House must have been listening to it. It would have been hard not to.

Featherstone was proper angry too now that I'd embarrassed him so badly. He was right to be. I was way out of line. But with the temper I had on, I wasn't going to admit it.

'What the fuck do you think you're doing, Sgt Mills? How dare you talk to me like that?'

'Sir, I don't want to fucking fall out with you, but that was a piss awful call. You were in the wrong.'

'Oh, you fucking think so, do you?'

'Yes I do. One, the copper was in uniform and that brings the police into disrepute. Two, he's drunk as a fart. Three, there was a good chance he was going to kill somebody. How does it look to the terrified locals if we're there and just walk on by? And how would it look if the newspapers found out that Private Smith, Y Company, was killed after Major Featherstone, Y Company, had just rearmed the drunken twat who did it? Not to mention our complete loss of face in front of the locals. He's lucky I didn't blow his fucking head off then and there.'

'Tough shit. Look at the big picture will you? We are not judge and jury in this town. We're here to help the local security forces. That doesn't mean publicly undermining them, no matter what they're doing.'

'He's already undermining himself by his actions. He's minging in uniform with a gun in his hand!'

'Well, it was my call. You've had your say now, Dan. Don't ever do that again in my Ops Room.'

The whole row was in code. It wasn't really about the copper, and we both knew it. But we also both knew it was better to have a shouting match about something minor like that than something major, like what to do when presented with the enemy. That was a row that it would have been very hard to come back from. I knew he thought Chris and I were dangerous and too aggressive. But he never once told me I was taking too many risks. And I never told him that he was overcautious and too Politically Correct.

The following morning, he came to find me.

'Danny, can I have a word? About last night, I've been thinking about it. It was a shit call, and you were right. I apologize.'

'Right, fair enough, sir. It was wrong of me to lose it at you in the Ops Room as well.'

Letting off steam relieved a bit of the tension between us. Featherstone had said sorry, and I respected him for that. He wasn't a bad bloke either, and he had a job to do too. In the cold light of day, he did have a fair point about demeaning the coppers, and I felt a bit embarrassed at exploding on him like that. Ultimately, the buck stopped with him. He was the one getting the abuse from the CPA sorts for us being too warlike, and he'd be the one who would have to write to the mothers and fathers of anyone killed. That's why they pay officers more than the rest of us.

After that, I tried to understand the OC's way of thinking a little more, and he gave me a bit more rope. There was already more than enough fighting to be done outside of camp to bring it indoors as well.

It has to be said that the heat also wasn't really helping anyone's temper.

Just when we thought it couldn't get any hotter, it did. It was the end of the first week of June, and the temperature was already hitting 50 degrees centigrade. It was silly heat. It made every task harder, every day longer. And it was relentless.

Sentries manning Front and Rear Sangars in the middle of the day would often collapse from heatstroke. They were in the shade too. It was decided that no foot patrols would go out between 11 a.m. and 3 p.m. when the sun was at its hottest. Al Amarah looked like a ghost town between those hours anyway. Even the OMS locked themselves up inside. When you did go out, you'd always take care to get the lads in the shade every half an hour or so for a quick five-minute cool-off and a water break.

The worst place of all to be during an Iraqi summer was in the back of a Warrior. Built to repel a Soviet invasion of Germany, they had no air conditioning and little ventilation. Just a heater. As soon as you got in the back of one, bodily fluids would start running straight out of the bottom of your trouser legs like a tap. Blokes cooped up together for long periods of time in a battle would often be reduced to vomiting on each other as the temperature inside got up to 80°C. Regular checks would also have to be made on the Warrior drivers on guard at Cimic's gates. They'd pass out having to sit in the front compartment next to the hot engine block.

Generally speaking, the lads will put up with anything as long as you've got a nice cool room to come back to at the end of the day. But with the accommodation blocks still out of bounds, we didn't even have that. It was still dozens of blokes crammed into every Cimic room, hot-bedding, tripping over each other, and with the place permanently shrouded in a smelly thick cloud of body odour and sweaty socks.

Sleep became ever harder at night. No matter how knackered you were, you'd always wake up in a pool of sweat after no more than an hour or two – even wearing just your jockeys on top of your sleeping bag. It was hard to believe we had July and August – traditionally Iraq's hottest months – still to come.

News came through that there had been two weeks of nonstop rain in Hampshire. We marvelled at what that must feel like. It hadn't rained since we'd stepped off the plane.

Great little morale boosts came along from time to time that would make the heat bearable.

'Front Sangar to Ops Room,' came the excited message one day over the PRRs. 'Anyone for a jolly little punt?'

An eight-tonne truck had just turned up among a resupply convoy loaded with two brand new Mark 5 rigid raider patrol boats on the back of it. The OC had put a request in for them, but nobody believed they would ever arrive. The Mark 5s are the small flat things the Royal Marines use. Every time we wanted to go over to the north bank, we'd have to cross Yugoslav Bridge. The only other alternative was going through Aj Dayya and that wasn't sensible. Our enemy had realized that, so the bridge became their shooting alley with us as the tin ducks. The boats were great, because they allowed us another discreet infiltration over the Tigris from Cimic without even having to step out of the front gate.

We heard that, by the beginning of June, the battle group had killed a total of 280 enemy fighters in Al Amarah since our arrival. That was an average of almost five a day. Of course, it was a tiny fraction compared to the final sum. Not bad for a couple of months' work though.

At another O Group, it was also announced that Bravo One had taken a bullet in the kidney. That got a particularly big cheer. Bravo One was the codename we had given to the head of the Al Amarah OMS. His name was Saad e Mar. He was in his forties, had a big black beard, big eyes and big ears. He carried a grenade and pistol on him at all times, even in bed. He was wanted by the coalition for all sorts, and we'd been told to kill or capture him if we ever got the opportunity.

He was also a big figure in the Mehdi Army nationally, and had been at some hoods' meeting in Najaf when they had got into a gunfight with the Americans. Sadly, he was still living to tell the tale. Patrols were all cancelled for a day as we kicked in the doors of three different houses to nick him on his sickbed. He was nowhere to be seen. We just missed him at one, and he'd escaped by vaulting a back fence. I only hoped that opened up his stitches again.

The best morale boost of all came thanks to a full colonel's arrival one day in Cimic. He'd been sent out to see us all the way from Permanent Joint Headquarters in Northwood. As more and more contact reports filtered back to them, the generals back in London had begun to appreciate the level of combat intensity we were engaged in. They thought it was time to give us a bit more of a level playing field against the OMS.

All the patrol commanders were told to report to Cimic's briefing room in the main building. The OC and Dale were there too. Sitting crosslegged on a chair was the colonel. Tall, with greying hair and cold blue eyes, he had a huge natural air of authority. Not someone you'd fuck with in a hurry. He addressed all of us.

'First of all chaps, well done. What you've been doing out here hasn't gone unnoticed, I assure you. It's not what any of us had expected, admittedly. However, you've responded terrifically. The chiefs have huge admiration for you, and I have been asked to pass that on.

'The real reason I'm here though is to talk about the rules of engagement. Let's cut to the chase. You're war fighting out here, without anyone saying it's war fighting. What we need to know is whether you feel you can still get the job done under the existing rules. Do you have any questions about them?'

We discussed a series of different scenarios. In a normal gunman-versus-soldier situation, we told him we felt no restrictions. They were clearly endangering life so we could kill them. Other areas were a lot greyer. The OMS knew our rules as well as we did. They exploited that knowledge mercilessly, as Ads's experience with the mortar teams crossing Yugoslav Bridge showed.

The tactic that really wound us up was their regular use of unarmed men to guide mortar or RPG fire on to us in Cimic. The fuckers would stand right out in the open within easy range, knowing we couldn't shoot them. They were clearly men of authority. They'd use their position to openly orchestrate the battle and work out exactly where we were so their fire would be more accurate. We'd given them the Northern Ireland name for the scrotes who did the same thing for the IRA – dickers.

I put one scenario to the colonel that I'd witnessed on May Day while over watching Private Beharry's abandoned Warrior.

'How about this one, sir? An unarmed dicker in normal

civvies popped out of an alleyway in front of Cimic, kneeled down in an RPG firing position, and pretended to pull the imaginary launcher's trigger while pointing at the Warrior. A couple of seconds later, a couple of RPG warheads came flying down into the thing from out of our view. The unarmed bloke gave a thumbs-up to his mates, and fucked off. What should we do about that?'

'Shoot him.'

'Really?'

'Yes. He is showing just as much intent to endanger life as the RPG man himself. He is just as guilty of the action. A dicker can be a legitimate threat, so he can be a legitimate target too.'

'What, even if he's unarmed?'

'I'm not encouraging wanton killing and recklessness, Sergeant. Threat to life is still the governing principle, and that must be very clear.'

The colonel smiled. 'But nowhere in the ROE does it say you can't shoot unarmed people.'

Something very interesting happened in that room. Without actually openly saying so, the colonel had completely rewritten our rules of engagement. He had given us tacit permission to shoot unarmed civilians if and when we felt it necessary. That was proper war fighting ROE, and it was unheard of for the sort of tour we were supposed to be on. It also had been done without ministers having to tell parliament and cause a big hullabaloo across the liberal sections of the media. The colonel was a pretty senior guy, but it wouldn't have been his call. That would have had to come all the way down from the top.

The date of his visit was 6 June, the sixtieth anniversary of the D Day landings. It was fitting, because what he said was a liberation for us too. It was exactly what we had needed. Of course, the relaxation didn't mean that we went straight out to drop a load of twelve-year-olds for chucking stones at us. But it did give us the ability to blunt a few of the enemy's subsequent attacks; attacks after all that had only one intention, to kill us.

The next unarmed dicker the lads managed to get a bead on got quite a surprise.

He was spotted a few days later, in the middle of a series of concerted mortar strikes. The base plate was well out of our view from Cimic. Five mortar rounds were launched during the first volley, landing in and around the compound. Longy and Des were spotting for Oost. They'd already seen a shady-looking character watching us from a wall on the other side of the dam to the west. In his late twenties, with short wavy black hair and a neat goatee beard, he was carrying binoculars and a radio.

Longy brought Oost on to the wall 600 metres away, and the South African calmly waited for the second mortar volley to start. Sure enough, when the dicker popped up again to have a good look and radio in where the new rounds were landing, they knew they'd got their man. He was leaning out from behind the wall with the top half of his body and his right leg exposed. Oost pumped a 7.62mm green spot straight into the right side of his ribcage. It tore his insides out, and he dropped like a stone.

'That'll teach him,' said Oost as he looked up from his L96's sight. 'You should have seen the look on that twat's face.'

The kill had a substantial effect on the dicking. The OMS spotters wound their necks in pretty sharpish. Word spread that if you tried it on now, you were going to get your head blown off. It made their mortar aiming harder which meant more fell off target. They soon compensated by upping the rate of rounds to increase the probability of landing some in the right place.

The other visit we got from the UK at that time was a delegation from OPTAG. Two of their senior sergeants came out to do a routine inspection of the company to see if their teaching back in Kent needed any updating. Being the arrogant sods that they were, the two sergeants didn't initially believe it did. They soon changed their minds.

16

Sniper Platoon was landed with taking the OPTAG sergeants out on our patrols for a day. Between us, we nicknamed them Pinky and Perky because after a morning in the hot sun, they looked like two little burnt red sausages.

Pinky and Perky were very gung-ho. They'd escaped their dull jobs in England for a few days and they wanted to see a bit of the enemy. That afternoon, we took them out on a long patrol right through the north bank. We walked bloody miles, it was bloody hot, but all we were attacked by was a pack of rabid dogs. Pinky and Perky were not very impressed. They also knew how to wind us up.

'Come on, Danny, I thought you lot were supposed to be in the thick of it out here?' goaded Pinky, who came from a posh Guards regiment. 'Can't you get us some action, war boy?'

They came out with us that night too. We were tasked with a joint patrol along with a multiple from Recce Platoon to show a presence around the houses of two local civilian workers in camp who had been threatened by the OMS. We set off in different directions on one loop of the town centre, and agreed to meet up in the middle.

Our very own Glasgow TA action man Major Ken Tait asked if he could come along too. Ken always jumped at any opportunity to get away from his desk. His experience with us during our first contact always made him a welcome addition.

On the streets, there were a lot of people out drinking

and making merry. That was unusual, but we were told it was because a big wedding was going on in the direction we were heading. We turned west on to Nasiriyah Street, which links the Blue route with the Yellow route, and then south into a smaller less well lit road that led down alongside an old cemetery to the left.

I was looking forward to catching a glimpse of the dirty great big Iraqi bride. Instead, the road was totally empty and silent. The worst of all combat indicators. Somewhere ahead in the darkness at the end of the street, we heard a group of men run across our path, exchanging urgent whispers.

'Standby, standb—'

I had just about enough time to get a quick warning out before the whole fucking world erupted.

A terrifying low-pitched pounding noise opened up to our left. At the same time, the top of the high brick wall next to our right shoulders began to disintegrate. A long burst of heavy machine-gun fire was ripping just over our heads and turning the wall's upper brickwork to dust. Then, another similar hellish din opened up from a rooftop directly to our right.

They were Dshkes, a Russian-made beast of a thing that fires half-inch calibre rounds and was designed to bring down helicopters. If one of them hit your arm, it would take it right off. If it hit your body, you'd have an entry and exit hole the size of a dinner plate. And if the gunner had aimed just a fraction lower, he would have blown Pikey and my heads off. I'd never seen anything like it.

The whole patrol cowered down as the lefthand Dshke demolished a 20-metre-long strip of the wall. A flying chip of brick lodged in OPTAG Perky's cheekbone, opening up a little cut. The gun was positioned 200 metres away on the roof of a big white house that adjoined a mosque. Between the mosque and us was the cemetery.

Though the Dshke gunner on the rooftop to our right was far closer, his fire was slapping into the road further away from us as he struggled to traverse the huge tripod-mounted weapon's arcs into a tighter angle onto us.

I made a split-second call, and decided the most dangerous fire was coming from the mosque.

'Everybody to the left side of the road. Take cover behind the cemetery wall!'

We sprinted over as one. Without me saying a word, Ads stopped and turned around in the middle of the road. With balls of steel, he raised his SA80 to his shoulder and lined up the Dshke gunner just above us in his sights. Five seconds later, as the gunner desperately tried to bring his rounds on to Ads, he was dropped with two single shots.

'Target down,' Ads announced, as he joined the rest of us, cool as a cucumber.

It was the most professional enemy ambush we had yet encountered. And it damn near worked. But half the immediate threat had been neutralized, thanks to Ads, and we could now take these bastards on. Half a dozen AKs also opened up on us from the mosque area. The drills were well practised by this stage and I didn't need to say a word. Calmly, the lads started peering over the cemetery wall and putting rounds back at the muzzle flashes.

We could hear OMS men on the far side of the cemetery cutting about, so I found the entrance along our wall and kicked the sheet-metal gate open.

'Two Minimis on the ground in here!'

That set up a proper stable firing position to stop any of the fuckers creeping up on us through the gravestones. We also started slamming UGL rounds at the remaining Dshke.

193

Sam eventually silenced it with a fantastically well-aimed grenade that exploded just a few feet from it. The boys whooped with delight.

'Gunman on the rooftop to the south,' screamed Des. As he spoke he spun around, engaged and dropped the enemy fighter at the far end of the street who was trying to outflank us. *Hmm, these bad boys are good. Good job we're better.* Several more appeared where the dropped fighter had come from, as well as a taxi full of nutters blazing away too, so a couple more blokes joined Des to take them on.

I jogged back up the wall to the cemetery gate. As I'd ducked down to peer into it again to assess the scene, some very loud automatic fire opened up from right behind me.

Where the fuck's that coming from? Hang on, if there's someone right behind me . . .

Everything suddenly slowed down. To my immediate right, a patch of the wall was getting eaten. Holes in the brickwork were rapidly appearing amid little puffs of dust. They were getting closer to me. That's when I realized.

Fuck. I'm going to get some of this.

My anti-clockwise swivel to face the loud noise only got halfway. Instead, I was instantaneously picked up and hurled through the air, landing in a heap ten feet into the cemetery past the Minimi line, with a searing pain in my left shoulder.

The best analogy to getting shot is being kicked hard by a well-built mule. Forget all that crap about forgetting to feel pain. It really fucking hurts. By the time I'd worked out what had happened and managed to scramble into cover, my whole shoulder had begun to numb up.

'Danny's down, Danny's hit,' the frantic shout went down the gun line.

Fuck and shit. This is going to change everything. Had the round gone right through or not? No exit wound I could see, so looks like not. Even worse. Now someone's going to have to dig that out, if I got as far as a medic of course. I put my right fingers under my shirt collar to feel for the hot blood.

Nothing. What the bollocks? All I felt was my intact skin and the bone underneath it, and a lump the size of a golf ball rapidly growing. Mighty bizarre. Doesn't matter, no time to think about it now. What was more important was that we now had enemy on three of our four sides.

As I crawled out of the cemetery and ducked down next to him, Longy was busy engaging the bloke who shot me. I was still confused, but my savvy was returning.

'I thought you was dead, you fucker.'

'So did I, Longy. Fuck knows what happened there.'

'Some peacekeeping tour, eh.'

Redders came on the radio from the Ops Room insisting to talk. Unfortunately, he wasn't winning the three-dimensional chess game that night.

'Alpha One Zero Alpha, this is Zero. I've looked at the map. You mustn't proceed any further in the direction of the mosque. That area is out of bounds.'

Yes, as well as full of enemy trying to kill us.

'Please extract to the south, Dan.'

Excellent. To the south, Des and the others were locked in a full-pitched gunfight with an ever growing number of OMS men. It was typical Ops Room stuff. I couldn't blame Redders though. It was proving hard enough for me to keep up with the battle with the speed it was changing, let alone someone miles away with just the odd radio message and map to go on.

'Yes, thanks for that Zero. I will extract south once the three fucking machine-gun posts there have been destroyed. Sorry if we didn't have time to mention that.'

Another voice over the net. It was Captain Simon Doyle, commander of Recce Platoon who was out leading our sister patrol that night. When he first heard the Dshkes open up, he was over a mile away at the other end of town. He had immediately got on the radio to me to say he was coming down to help us.

'Danny, this is Alpha Two Zero. We're getting pretty close to you now. Sorry, mate. Had a fairly big enemy contact on our way. If you can extract back up the street the way you came into it, we'll cover you from the main road a bit further down it to the west.'

Top news. Captain Doyle was ready and waiting to clear our escape route to the north. Simon was the total opposite of Redders – a quiet but highly confident officer, and a very good commander. He's just the sort of person you want with you in the shit. So when he said he was there to cover our arse, I believed him.

It was time to go.

'Prepare to move!'

The lads slipped into pairs ready to fire and manoeuvre up the street. Then, a terrified little whiney voice came over the PRRs.

'Danny, Danny? Danny, where are you?' It was OPTAG Pinky.

'I'm here, you muppet.' I looked around. He and Perky were nowhere to be seen. 'Hang on, where the fuck are you?'

'Danny, don't leave us. We've got to get the fuck out of here.'

I had totally forgotten about Pinky and Perky. Come to think of it, I hadn't seen them since the start of the contact. Then, a door in the wall on the opposite side of the street to the cemetery opened up, and Pinky and Perky crawled out of it. They completely disregarded my orders to get behind the cemetery wall and ducked into the nearest hiding place instead. They'd been lying in the shrubs of the garden ever since, trying to pretend they were geraniums.

I gaped in disbelief at the sorry sight as they crawled up next to me.

'Jesus Christ, Danny. How long's it been like this for?'

Chris answered before I could. 'Since we got off the fucking plane. You can get up off your knees now.'

They'd got the contact they said they really wanted all right. After all their banter, they hadn't even fired a single shot.

We set off for the rendezvous point with Captain Doyle just under a mile away, putting rounds down at flash targets on rooftops or around street corners that tried to open up on us. As we ran, I told Major Tait to take out the street lights to obscure our movement from the enemy fire. With another Benson and Hedges smouldering away through his schoolboy grin, he took to the task with relish and barely missed a single one. The irony that his day job in Al Amarah was to supervise its rebuilding wasn't lost on him.

An OMS bullet passed through H's trouser leg opening up a small cut. Other than that, we reached Captain Doyle unscathed. Both patrols then tracked the rest of the way down Nasiriyah Street together to meet two Warriors sent out to pick us up waiting at a prearranged junction.

Unfortunately, the Warriors were parked up under some street lights. Major Tait frightened the hell out of their crews by dashing straight up to the vehicles and hosing down the street lights with an extra long burst of automatic SA8o. His blood was still up and he was loving it.

'OK, Mr Tait, no more street lights, thanks. I think we've done enough now.'

197

'Nae fuckin' bother, Danny. Wha'er you say.'

As we mounted up, we could already hear the whine of ambulance sirens coming from the direction of the cemetery. At least we'd done them a bit of damage too.

Back at Cimic, Captain Doyle and I went up to the Ops Room to check in. Among other things, I had to report that my twelve-man patrol had fired 512 rounds from SA80s, 330 Minimi rounds, and five UGLs. When we walked in, Redders was nowhere to be seen. Puzzled, we asked one of the company signallers reclining on a swing chair for his whereabouts. He just smiled.

'I'm under here, chaps,' Redders himself replied. And there he was, with helmet and full body armour on, crouching under his desk with the radio handset in his hand. The odd mortar had fallen outside, but he was rigged up for a full-on nuclear strike. The poor sod was stuck in that room with nowhere else to go all day long; it was obviously beginning to get to him.

I took off my body armour and shirt to show Dale the bruise where I'd been shot. The golf ball bit had gone down, but it was now the size of a grapefruit and full of deep pinks and purple.

Dale and I inspected my kit to work out the mystery of what had happened. The round had torn up the strap of my brand new day sack I'd got from the Triple Canopy mail order catalogues. It had only just arrived, and at the cost of $70 too. I forgot all that once I realized it could also have saved my life. The thick rubber strap had slowed down the bullet considerably, before it then passed through the thin cotton cover of my body armour, its rubber interior, out again, and then through my shirt. Then, as Dale discovered, that's where it had lodged, in the inside of my body armour with just its sharp lead nose poking through.

I was dumbstruck.

'Faarkin' 'ell, Danny. How did you escape that one, eh?'

He worked the round out with his thumb and finger tip. 'You want to keep that, Danny. Show it to the grandchildren one day.'

I popped it in my pocket as a good luck charm, chuffed to bits with the best tour souvenir out of everyone so far.

'Anyone got a camera?'

The next day, Ken Tait was summoned to see Major Featherstone. The OC had heard about his street light antics and wasn't hugely impressed. Poor old Ken got a major bollocking and was banned from going out on any more foot patrols. He was heartbroken.

Pinky and Perky were strangely quiet. Nor did they ask to come out on any more patrols with Sniper Platoon. They left a couple of days later with a pair of badly damaged egos, but some very full notebooks.

After most large contacts, the boys and I would always be keen for a battle damage assessment to see how well we'd faired against the OMS. The run-in with the Dshkes was no exception, so we did our normal trick of skirting by the city's main hospital on our next daylight patrol.

The Victoria Hospital (more of our colonial heritage) was just before Yugoslav Bridge on the south side of the Tigris. It was where all the OMS casualties were taken, dead or alive. Whenever they had a few men in there, the OMS leadership would post an armed guard on the hospital gate. They were sure we'd try to pop over to finish them off. We never went inside the hospital, because we could always get what we needed off the guard. It was also terrific fun winding him up.

'Hello, knobhead,' Pikey announced, after we crept up on him. Terrified, he tried to unsling his AK from his shoulder but just ended up dropping it. He was a scrawny looking little scumbag in his early twenties. A nobody foot soldier.

'Don't worry, we're not going to shoot you. Just come for a chat. How many OMS men in today?'

The guard scowled at us from behind the bars of the metal gate. We'd seen this one before here and we knew he spoke just enough crappy English to understand us. Pikey gave it another go.

'Sadr men. Britani jundi shoot how many?'

Conspiratorially, he looked over his shoulder to make sure nobody was watching, before replying in hushed tones, 'Seventeen. Eleven wounded, six dead.'

Excellent. It had been a good night's work after all. A look behind the guard at the hospital's emergency entrance confirmed what he told us. The ground was littered with fresh blood-soaked dressings and discarded IV drips that none of the staff had had a chance to clear up yet.

'Ooh. Oh dear, knobhead. Looks like we smacked your arse again,' Pikey continued.

'But we kill Britani jundi commander.'

'No, you didn't. He's right here,' pointing to me.

That really confused him. The OMS guy had obviously seen me talking on the radio or giving orders, and then when I went down. Obviously he hadn't seen me get back up again though.

'Bad luck, knobhead. See you tonight then, hopefully, eh? We'll look forward to it.'

He managed a nervous smile.

17

Going out on fighting foot patrols was a real adrenalin rush, and every sniper in the platoon relished the challenge. But there was also nothing quite like the few chances we got on the tour to get out in the field and set up a proper desert observation post.

Not knowing we'd be based in a town then, we'd done masses of training for desert OPs back in Tidworth, and we'd brought all our proper kit out with us too. They only came up when we got pinged for Operation Bayswater, a permanent and rolling task to catch out mortar teams having a go at Camp Abu Naji.

Not that we liked to admit it, but Slipper City got a fair few mortar rounds and rockets chucked at it too. On the few occasions Y Company could spare us, we went down to the marshland between the camp and the city and put in a reactive OP. The most popular site for base plates was at the very southern end of the Kadeem al Muallimin estate. After Aj Dayya, it was the city's most pro-OMS estate and several of their mortar crews were known to live within it. A reactive OP meant we'd just sit and wait for them to turn up. If they did, we'd kill them.

We'd tab for three kilometres to our chosen location as a team of eight. A rear protection force of four was left about a klick behind us to watch our arses. Then the final four would creep up on our bellies for the last couple of hundred metres so we weren't seen. It was a pretty exposed area, and the only place for a hide was the dried-up river beds. We dug ourselves covertly into the dried shale and slate, and that was us for the night.

One night in mid-June, we inserted at 7 p.m. just as the sun was setting. The plan was to extract at 3 a.m. after any mortar crews who fancied some action would have gone to bed.

On our maps, we were set back around 500 metres from Purple 8, a road junction at the south-west corner of the estate not far from the town prison. Ever since the NGOs left in a hurry, the prison had been heavily fortified and then occupied by the Royal Welch Fusiliers company.

It was very much enemy territory, so it was exciting work. The challenge of not being compromised coupled with the thrill of the hunt. We were good at this, and they weren't going to spot us in a hurry. We wore our sniper smocks as camouflage. They are big baggy canvas tops with a hood and plenty of pockets. You spray them the colour of the terrain you're going to be in before you go out. Elsewhere we'd use our head-to-toe Ghillie suits, but Iraq was too hot for that. The smocks' pockets and pouches are in its sides, arms or at the back. That way when you're on your belly in the prone position, you can just reach round with a hand and grab what you want. They'd be stuffed with food, a camouflage net, secateurs, a calculator, trowels, our sling set-ups, maps and water.

Our drag bags were also laid up beside us, with the heavier stuff such as scopes and ammunition. We never went out with less than six mags for each rifle. Then of course there were our longs, set up on bipod legs.

Keeping body movement in an OP to a minimum is absolutely crucial. Movement just attracts the eye to you. If you're a fidgeter, you're no good to a sniper platoon. If you've got a problem with insects, tough shit. You learn to live with all sorts of things crawling over you. Luckily, it's too hot in Iraq at that time of year for mosquitoes. They've all been killed off by the start of May.

Lying up means controlling your bodily functions too. Sooner or later, they are going to be issues if you're in an OP for any length of time. If it's a piss you need, then you slowly roll onto your side and piss in an empty water bottle. Otherwise you or your spotter will have to lie in it for the rest of the night. If it's something else you need to do, then you reach for your clingfilm, turn over, trousers down, and off you go. It's not the most enjoyable experience for your oppo, but needs must. Once you're done, you wrap it up and pop it in your Bergen so your hide isn't detected when you leave it. A regular snipers' wind-up is to put your poo in someone else's Bergen. When they're back in camp unpacking, you can normally hear the shout for miles.

'Wharr, who's shit is this?'

If you didn't like the platoon commander, you'd shove it in his Bergen instead.

On my sniping course, I put my Number Two through even worse. We'd been in a hide on the edge of a wood in Salisbury Plain for two days waiting for a target to turn up. I'd managed to suppress the urge for the whole time, right up to the moment the target's car turned up. I couldn't believe it, it was coming and he was coming, and there was nothing either of us could do about it.

There was only one option available, so I slung a quick tree hook and got into a squat. While still marking the target through the sight, I pulled my trousers down. My Number Two got out the clingfilm and held it under my arse. While semi-retching from the pong, he still managed to catch all my warm faeces, and ten seconds later I got the kill. I had to buy him a fair few pints that night just to get him to stop whinging.

Sometimes we would have to wait in the river beds until pretty late for any action. It wasn't until just before 2 a.m. that things began to stir that night.

Without any warning, the whoosh of two RPGs fired almost simultaneously about a kilometre away from us broke the night's perfect silence. They impacted with big bangs and flashes on the prison's walls. The firing point was out of our sight on the other side of the long low building so we couldn't return fire. I got on the radio to Abu Naji's Ops Room to report the contact.

'Zero, Alpha One Zero. RPG contact on Broadmoor. Firing point from around Red 8, judging by their nine-second flight time. Do you want me to collapse my current task and pursue the enemy?'

We could have a good fight on here.

'Alpha One Zero, roger your last. No, hold your current position. Two Whiskies being dispatched as QRF to Red 8.'

Bugger. Whiskies was radio code for Warriors. Five minutes later, we heard the two Warriors trundle by past us to our east up the main road into Al Amarah towards Red 8. Then the inevitable and the Warriors were engaged too. More sounds of whooshing RPGs, then a long burst of SA80, followed by the clatter of Warrior chain guns. It was a big old exchange, but, infuriatingly for us, totally out of our view so we couldn't help them out.

Then, the all too frequent message over the net.

'Contact casualty. Wait out. Two men down.'

More Warriors turned up and extracted the injured men, finally ending the battle. Later, we found out exactly what had happened.

As the leading Warrior approached Red 8, the same team that had hit Broadmoor put a well-aimed RPG warhead right on to its driver's hatch. Just inside that hatch was none other than Private Johnson Beharry again, the very same poor sod who had undergone all the heroics on May Day.

The grenade exploded on impact six inches away from his head. It did appalling damage to him, blowing dozens of tiny shrapnel fragments into his face and brain.

The vehicle's commander, a lieutenant, then slotted all three RPG men with a fine bit of firing from his SA80 out of the turret. Without having any idea of Beharry's injuries, the lieutenant ordered him to get them the fuck out of there. In another show of superhuman endurance, Beharry fought through immense pain and bleeding to regain control of the fucked Warrior and reverse it 200 metres out of the kill zone. It smacked into a wall after he finally passed out.

That looked like good night for Beharry. He went into a coma, was listed as VSI (very seriously ill) and flown back to the UK for extensive brain surgery. The doctors said he didn't have much of a chance. They told the CO to pray.

We were well pissed off when we heard exactly how bad he was. It was just sod's law. If only the RPG team had come out for their fun and games 200 metres closer to us, we would have had them in our sights and done them. By total chance, they didn't; so they did Beharry instead.

Unlike the bullet in my pocket, that RPG warhead had Beharry's name written all over it. Sometimes, that's just the way it goes.

We heard the first whisperings of a ceasefire a week later in an intelligence report passed down from Division.

Moqtada al-Sadr was going to do a deal with the Americans, said the Int boys. He was going to call a halt to all the violence across the south.

Bollocks he was. None of us believed a word of it. If there was one thing the fat ass was good at it was talking shit, and we'd heard that particular pile of it several times before. Neither did we have any interest in believing there might be a ceasefire. After a two-month slog, we really thought we were getting the upper hand over the OMS. Especially after that very night too, when we caught our first live terrorists in the act. It was a terrific result because we'd normally only be able to pick OMS men up off a mortuary slab. They weren't too talkative then.

Again, Sniper Platoon was in the thick of it. Showing more balls now thanks to the ROE colonel's visit, Featherstone had ordered fifty men out on a big ambush to try and trap any mortar teams at work that evening. He'd even come along too. We panned out over a 500-metre line across the north bank among the Iraqi Army camp ruins, and laid low waiting for something to happen.

When a volley of mortars was launched at Cimic a couple of miles to our east just after midnight, we thought we'd blown it for the night. Then, a wonderful stroke of luck. The mortar crew of three drove back from the job right into our line. With no idea we were there, the idiots even stopped 100 metres away to get out for a fag and a chinwag. They'd obviously pulled away from the launch site to a point of safety, and were now on a debrief.

We were on them in seconds. A pathetic lot of scrawny toerags they were too, unkempt with stubbly beards and dirty clothes. Not the OMS's shock troops exactly, but crucially alive. One froze on the spot, the other two legged it, and so my boys went straight after them and cornered them in a house. Outnumbered and surrounded they gave up without a fight.

In the boot of their battered old red saloon car was a 6omm mortar tube, twenty mortar rounds and a dirty great big bag full of US dollars. They had just been paid.

An hour later back in an Abu Napa cell, they were singing like canaries. They were grassing up everyone they knew in the hope of shortening their jail sentence. The next morning we were all pumped up. After the frustration of the Beharry ambush, the arrest had given the whole company a massive boost. By 9 a.m., we were making the final preparations to go out and kick in a special party-size pack of doors.

That's when the Abu Naji Ops Room dropped the bombshell. A ceasefire really had been called in Najaf. Everyone crammed in front of the cookhouse TV to watch it unfold on CNN.

After two and a half months of duelling, Moqtada al-Sadr had made his move. There were less than two weeks to go until the American-led CPA was due to hand power over to a new Iraqi government. The Yanks were desperate to make it a success, and that meant doing it in peace. Moqtada knew that too. He reckoned that all he had to do was wait for the Yanks to come up with the right terms and then benevolently accept them.

He was right. The Yanks buckled, and intermediaries thrashed out the deal.

The Americans would drop the murder charges against him and pull all troops out of Najaf. In return, he would disband the Mehdi Army and renounce violence as a way of getting what he wanted. There was no doubt who the real winner was. Moqtada had broken the will of a superpower, and it made him all the more powerful in the eyes of his fanatical followers.

Amid frenzied scenes in central Najaf, he read out a statement calling on all resistance fighters to go home and stop attacking coalition security forces. Meanwhile, he was going to set up a political party and contest the elections next year.

CNN showed filmed footage of jubilant Mehdi Army fighters streaming out of Najaf's giant Imam Ali mosque and laying down their AKs in a pile. It was an astonishing thing to see, and we were all captivated. All of us, apart from Des.

'Oh no, please don't do that!' he appealed to the TV screen. 'Pick 'em up, you great big fucking chicken shits. Who the hell else is there for us to scrap with? Jack bastards.'

Yet again, events on the national picture dictated the next major turn on our rollercoaster tour. In Al Amarah, the OMS asked for an urgent meeting with our CO Colonel Maer that afternoon. All operations were suspended with immediate effect until we knew how this one was going to play out. Including our raids. Typical.

The OMS and Colonel Maer swiftly thrashed out their own mini deal and signed a ceasefire agreement. They too had to make a public statement urging no further attacks on the Iraqi security forces or us. They also promised not to hoard weapons in mosques any more, which were out of bounds to us. On our side, no more OMS men would be arrested and all outstanding warrants dropped. We would agree to respect them as an institution. In a clever political move, the OMS also got us to promise to send no more Warriors into the city.

Des and his limitless bloodlust aside, most of the company's first reaction to the shock development was one of honest relief. No matter how much we enjoyed the fight, it had to be said we were all completely knackered. Physically and mentally. It's hard to keep up that tempo of operations for any decent period of time without it wearing you down. The Cimic compound was also in a shabby state and our kit was ragged.

That afternoon, the ceasefire terms were read out over the city mosques' loudspeakers. All of a sudden, it was bizarrely quiet. The livewire tension that we'd been living under for so long evaporated in an instant.

As a mark of our respect to the ceasefire, all combat troops were confined to Cimic and Abu Naji for a full forty-eight hours. That really brought it home to us that the war was over.

It was great to have a couple of days to sit down and have a cup of tea for once. The ceasefire also meant we could move out of overcrowded Cimic and back into the more comfortable prefab accommodation blocks. The ban on Snatch Land Rover movement was also lifted and Route 6 to Basra was reopened. That meant we could move more people in and out for their two weeks' R&R home leave, and resupply at our leisure.

Catching up on so much missed sleep was what I most enjoyed. Nights were lovely and quiet without the random explosions incoming, or the frequent mortar horn blasts to warn people not to step outside for a smoke or a pee.

But the novelty of peace wore off soon enough.

By the end of its first week, we were bored out of our skulls. Des had been right after all. We had come to understand the fighting as normal everyday life. It was anything but that, yet we had grown to love it all the same.

Our routine changed dramatically. To propel the peace, orders came down from Slipper City for us to 'decrease the military footprint'. A wonderful bit of officers' speak meaning we had to do our best at pretending we weren't really there. We were told to try to support the police and their authority as much as possible – the same fuckers who enjoyed watching the OMS shooting at us only a few days ago. Everywhere we went, we had to wear our soft hats and berets, and it was back to endless smiling.

Broadmoor was closed down as a base and the Royal Welch Fusiliers went back to Abu Napa. Recce Platoon got sent away to patrol the Iranian border again. We were desperately jealous. They weren't scrapping with Iranian border guards or anything as good as that, but they were out and about doing something. We were sitting in Al Amarah with big false smiles on our faces and our thumbs up our arses.

Chris summed it up perfectly.

'You know what, Danny? This place fucking sucks now. There's no fun any more. It might just as well be Bosnia.'

He was right. It was Bosnia in the desert, just like any other British Army peacekeeping tour. That's fine if Bosnia is all you're expecting. But after the rush of what we'd been through, it was hard for us to swallow. .

Of course, it was the OMS's definition of ceasefire. That didn't mean a total cessation of mortar strikes. Instead, they politely limited themselves to only lobbing a couple of volleys a week, to remind us they were still there. The OMS would always deny it was them, and for all we knew it might have been some tribe cross about something else instead. But old habits die hard.

After what we'd got used to, a few mortar rounds a week wasn't going to get the blood pumping again. As they came in, we tried hard to stifle our yawns.

The highlight of the day was if we went out for a boat patrol along the Tigris. At least you could see a bit of nature on its vast and timeless banks. After we'd seen all there was to see fifteen times on the boats, that bored the arses off us too.

Then, life got even more tedious. We didn't think that was possible, but with the handover of power we realized that the start of the ceasefire was actually the good days.

Chris woke me up early on the morning of 26 June. He was furious.

'Oi, Danny, wake up, mate. I can't believe it. The Triple Canopy lads have all fucked off. Molly Phee's gone and all.'

'What? Sorry, mate, you've lost me.'

'They've gone, Danny. The CPA officials, the close protection teams, the lot of them. They all bugged out in the middle of the night without telling anyone. We're in Cimic on our own from now on.'

'Oh, right.'

'Guess what. Fucking Red Rob didn't even say goodbye. Some mate.'

It wasn't Red Rob's fault. To prevent any triumphal terrorist attack on them, Molly Phee and her entire entourage had pulled out of Al Amarah back to Baghdad in the small hours in total secrecy a few days before the official handover date. Only the CO knew.

Since the CPA was being disbanded to be replaced by Iraqi politicians, its job was done. It was a blow to us because we lost some good mates who we'd spent a lot of hours with on the roof. More importantly, the supply source of all our new sexy kit had been cut off, and that was a real bummer. From then on, we'd have to make do with the British Army routine issue. With Triple Canopy's twenty men gone we also had to fill their places. That meant more of us on guard duty and in the sangars, where they'd always have a couple of men too.

Later on when Chris went up to the roof, he discovered Red Rob had said goodbye after all. He'd left a business card along with a little note in the sleeve of Chris's long. It read:

Seeya Limey. Sorry couldn't tell you we were leaving. 'Secret squirrel shit,' as you'd say. If you're ever in Texas visiting with your Mom, look me up.
PS you've still got a small wiener.

18

Molly Phee's disappearance was a precursor of the big event itself. To foil any nationwide terrorist spectacular, it too went ahead two days earlier than planned. In a secret Baghdad ceremony, power was handed over to the provisional Iraq government led by new Prime Minister Iyad Allawi on 28 June, at 10.26 a.m. The battle group only found out about it when it popped up on Sky News.

A public holiday was declared, and all the shops were closed.

It was another very bizarre feeling for us. From being the all-powerful invaders and conquerors of Iraq, we were now just its guests and obedient servants.

We watched city people's reaction closely in case it sparked fresh trouble against us. In fact, they seemed to be pretty happy about it all. Like us, they were also a little bemused. Iraqi people had had no say in running their own country for decades, and most of them really didn't know what to do about it. They and us wondered how the brave new world would look.

We soon found out. For us, it meant an onslaught of a million tedious rules and regulations. Our wings were well and truly clipped.

After 28 June, we lost all our powers of arrest. That was now the Iraqi police's job. We couldn't even go out on patrol in the city any more without the cops and an interpreter having to accompany us, which in itself was a massive extra ball ache. The cops often wouldn't turn up at our agreed rendezvous. So we had to get in our vehicles, go over to the police stations, and try and persuade them to come out with us. Half the time would be spent trying to organize them, and working out again what had happened to their latest batch of weapons. When we did finally get out, they'd do all the talking at any vehicle checkpoint. We'd just sit there as back-up.

If we ever wanted to search someone's car, we had to give them special new flyers printed in Arabic and make sure they'd read it first: Stop. Turn off your engine please. Thank you. We're here to make Iraq a safer place, you know. One of our men wants to look in your boot. Do you mind? Thanks awfully, so kind of you.

It was all deeply painful. God only knows what we were supposed to do with the people who couldn't read. The locals didn't seem to give a toss about the new regulations, and they didn't bother to read the flyers either. To them, we were soldiers who wanted to look in their boot. In Iraq, when an armed man wants to look in your boot, you let him.

The peace also gave Major Featherstone a chance to kick-start his nation-building projects again, all the real Cimic stuff. He seemed a lot more comfortable with that than with combat. For us, it meant escorting the Cimic guys out to do a job, and back again when they'd finished.

As we were loading up for another escort trip, Oost told Des: 'You know what, man, if I only wanted my life to be about helping out the locals, I'd have fucking joined Oxfam.'

Chris put it another way: 'You know what, mate? This place ain't like Bosnia now. It's *worse* than Bosnia.'

Newly trained soldiers from the fledgling Iraqi Defence Force also came to man our gates at Cimic House. The place was no longer coalition property, it was Iraqi. Iraqis therefore had to be seen from the outside world to be in charge of it. Our experience in Al Amarah had taught us never to trust any of them in uniform. The IDF's reliability proved that to be true. Some days, the soldiers didn't even bother turning up at all. On others, they'd just fuck off home early and leave the gates unmanned. They only worked when they felt like it. Nice life.

Then there was the OMS. They thrived off the handover, and made a big song and dance about what good and responsible politicians they were going to be. It was all rubbish though, and we knew Moqtada had no intention of disarming any of his followers, despite his solemn promises. On the contrary, we got regular reports that the OMS were building up another sizeable arsenal inside their HQ. There was not a damn thing we could do about it either. We were no longer the law.

The cheeky sods got so full of themselves that one day they even had the audacity to complain about the amount of patrols we were doing with the police. They wanted us off the streets altogether. We told them where they could go on that one.

Try as hard as we did not to think about it, there was also the niggling irritation that we couldn't actually say we'd fully beaten our enemy. We fought like men possessed for more than two months and after all that we still weren't able to declare a categorical military victory against the OMS. It was unfinished business, but that's the way we had to leave it.

We even started to get necky comments from some of the more politicized sorts who worked at Cimic. Then there was the assault on Longy's hobbies. A week after the handover, the compound's caretaker, a heavily religious man, came across a cleaner flicking through an old porn mag that he had found while emptying the bins.

'This is disgusting Western sin,' he complained to Featherstone. 'This is our country now. I am disgusted that good Muslims are subjected to this un-Islamic filth while they have to do their jobs.'

'Yes, I'm sorry, it won't happen again,' Featherstone had to promise. I had to tell the boys not to put porn in the bins after that. Which was ironic, since another cleaner, Rasheed, was a massive supplier of hardcore porn to Ads, the company's resident porn king. Ads prided himself on the title, and would always loan his porn out free of charge, which was very generous of him. He wouldn't even charge Longy, who got far more use of it than his fair share.

Ads originally came out with about twenty DVDs and fifty magazines, but that had mushroomed considerably on the tour thanks to Rasheed. There was no chance Ads would be able to take it all home with him, unless he was happy to leave everything else he owned behind, so he did a deal where Rasheed would get it all back when we left. Porn was a habit Ads said he'd picked up from his City trader days. Then, when he made his bosses money, they would take him to lap dancing clubs and pay for all his table dances.

Rasheed didn't just supply the normal stuff either.

'You like real dirty dirty movie too, Mister Ads?' he asked, after a couple of successful porn deals had gone down.

'Yeah, course we do, Rasheed. What you got?'

'Not shocking you?'

'Fuck off, Rasheed. We're soldiers. You couldn't shock us if you tried.'

He could shock us, and he did. It was astonishingly hard core, and really tested the imagination. A lot of it also looked like it was homemade, possibly locally. There were midgets, fat women, old women, gorgeous women, ugly women, pregnant women (particularly sick), veiled women; every imaginable sort of women, getting pretty much everything done to them. Animals always seemed to feature strongly too in Rasheed's movies: dogs, horses and particularly donkeys (an Iraqi favourite).

Thank God the caretaker never saw any of those. He would have had a heart attack on the spot.

After the mother of all adrenalin hangovers that lasted at least two weeks, we slowly accepted our plight. It wasn't as if we had any choice. Our job was to just get on with it, like we did everywhere else. Look on the bright side too; in fairness, we'd had two good months of unadulterated fun so we couldn't really complain about four months of tedium.

Peace was obviously good for Iraq, and battle-scarred Maysan province in particular. The more the place moved forward, the sooner all British troops would all be able to sod off home. Our strategic aim had always been to bore ourselves out of a reason for being there. No need for fighting, no need for soldiers.

The long and blisteringly hot weeks slowly passed by. The days took on a depressingly repetitive routine. Bed, cookhouse, work, freetime; cookhouse, work, freetime, cookhouse, bed.

Work took more concentration, because our patrols were so much more mundane. Tasks seemed to last twice as long as they did before.

Meals became a high point. We lingered over them now, rather than throwing the scoff down as quickly as possible to get back to the fighting. Mealtime chat was always about the menu. The food wasn't bad and Chef would try his best with whatever he was given, but it was always the same dishes. Fish and chips, beans, beef curry, ham with pineapple pizza, pies, spaghetti bolognese. The army, prides itself on being able to give you almost the same grub whether you're in Torquay or Timbuctoo. It's great if you're in the middle of a desert; not so when the odours of an Arabic feast sizzling away in Tigris Street's cafes and kebab stalls were constantly drifting over our walls.

Nobody said anything to Chef, because we didn't want to hurt his feelings. He worked like an ox, and had won massive respect for cooking every day under just his shitty green tent for several weeks of mortar strikes after his trailer had been blown up. But he could start to see it on our faces.

'I'm really sorry, guys, I wish I could do something else for you,' he'd apologize as we trooped in.

'Rubbish, Chef. It's fucking cordon bleu, mate. Keep it up,' we'd always reply.

Sleep was now almost impossible during the day because of the heat, even after the many mortar-damaged aircon units were replaced by the engineers. During the afternoons, they would blare away on ultra cold making almost no difference whatsoever. If you got a night shift, it was just tough shit.

But what was hardest was how to fill the long hours of spare time we now had on our hands. Every single minute of it had to be spent in Cimic. There were no bars or night-clubs to go too, and certainly fuck all to see, even if we were allowed out on the town – which we weren't.

To start with, that largely meant watching a shedload of DVDs. A lot of the boys had mini-DVD players or laptops, so you'd plug in a pair of speakers and a few of you could watch together. After a while, we'd watched them all, and any new arrivals were devoured within hours by the whole company.

No matter how desperate anyone got though, they'd never sink as low as to watch a *Blackadder* DVD with Chris, no matter how many invites he'd issue. Within a week, he'd already driven the whole platoon mad by saying all the punchlines a second before Rowan Atkinson did.

Saved from the truth so as not to hurt his feelings, Chris couldn't understand it.

'What's wrong with you fellas? *Blackadder* is a comic legend. None of you got a sense of humour?' he'd ask.

Fresh newspapers too along with any other whiff of the outside world were also ravished in a frenzy. Top of the list of most desired articles after the ceasefire were brand new copies of lads' mags like *FHM* or *Loaded*. The blokes who had them sent out guarded them zealously. The rule was they'd only have to pass them on after they'd had a chance to read them cover to cover first.

Not understanding the importance of this rule, our little hairy companion Tigris wreaked havoc. Like every other dog, she had a habit of picking up newspapers and magazines and depositing them in different rooms. Unfortunately, it took weeks for anyone to work this out. So when someone's most cherished possession went missing and he'd eventually track it down to the floor of some other bloke's room, false accusations would frequently fly.

Thanks to Tigris, two lads from Mortars once ended up eyeball to eyeball after one accused the other of heinous *FHM* theft for the third time.

'Of course you fucking lifted it, it was under your fucking bed!' screamed one.

'You call me a tea leaf one more time, and I'll smash your face in,' the other replied.

'You fucking deny you pinched my *FHM* again, and I'll do you first.'

Sensing peace needed to be made, Tigris solved the riddle immediately by picking up the disputed copy of *FHM* right in front of both of them and trotting off to deposit it in another room altogether. Fisticuffs averted.

With Molly Phee's departure, we became Tigris's new owners – all 106 of us. She'd earned our full respect by then so we adopted her with pride. All the incoming rocket, mortar and sniper fire that Cimic House had attracted during the fighting had made the compound about the most dangerous place in the city for the dog to live. But she never left, despite ample opportunity. It was good loyalty, and soldiers like that.

Tigris was no fool. Now that we'd been able to move back into some of the less destroyed accommodation buildings, she plumped for Major Featherstone's bed as her sleeping quarters every night. It was the most comfortable billet in the compound by some distance. The OC never once kicked her out. He couldn't; he was the biggest sop for her out of the lot of us.

A few of the lads had also brought out PlayStation consoles. Suddenly their popularity doubled overnight. The car racing game *Gran Turismo* was the most popular. A lot of money used to change hands with the lads' eyes glued to the box and their thumbs working overdrive. Oost was the undisputed video game king. He had incredible reaction times.

There was also hefty competition on who could compile the best tour home movie.

Almost everyone could record moving images on his camera or mobile. During the fighting days, nobody had held back. We got some great scrapping shots from our roof too. Since you could edit all that on a laptop by then and even bang a good soundtrack on top of it (always heavy rock or thrash), there were some really brilliant montages put together. It's a shame the TV news boys never made it out to us, because it was the best combat footage I'd ever seen.

One major salvation was the engineers getting the Internet up and running again in Cimic. A mortar round right on top of the satellite dish had put an end to it pretty early on. Once the CPA left and we had more space, a small room was specially set aside in Cimic for a few computer terminals. The sappers also rigged up a wireless connection, so if you had your own laptop, you could do it from your bunk. Not bad for an outpost in the middle of a war zone. I used it for sending e-mails home and keeping up with Euro 2004. Until England got knocked out in the quarter-finals again . . .

The young single lads in the platoon loved the Internet for a different reason. They spent hours on end exercising their hormonal frustrations on it. Smudge, H, Sam and Longy (when he wasn't in the toilets) all got addicted to a site called Hot or Not. On it, photos people had posted of themselves would pop up and the viewer would be asked to grade them in terms of looks from one to ten.

Cimic House would constantly echo with shouts of abuse or disbelief at the various choices the boys were asked to make.

'You're joking, Ads, she's a total minger!'

'Not as much of a pig as that last bird you gave a nine to.'

'Now she's a real honey.'

'Shut up, H. She looks like your gran.'

Then the boys discovered dating sites as well. After that, they hardly did anything else – night or day. It became an utter obsession.

The self-declared king of the electronic chat-up lines was pretty boy Smudge.

'Fucking Iraq. I'd be getting laid twice a night if I wasn't stuck out here with you losers,' he bragged.

Foolish words. Such unchecked vanity was a red rag to a bull for soldiers. Chris and Fitz were quick to meet the challenge.

Unknown to Smudge, they too joined his favourite dating site, but from Chris's laptop on the broadband connection in the Quick Reaction Force room. They signed up under the name of Natalie, aged nineteen. Natalie had measurements of 34-24-34, and a DD cup size. Then they cut out an extra busty photo of Abi Titmuss from *FHM*, uploaded it as Natalie's mugshot, and under it posted the message:

'Hi, boys, I'm Nat. I want to meet a hunky soldier serving his country abroad. Fair hair action men please. Blond on blonde action only for this little bazooka.'

It was hilarious, if a little unsubtle.

'He'll never go for it, it's too obvious,' said Fitz, as he and Chris guffawed their way through the delicate enterprise.

'Of course he will. He's Smudger, isn't he? You wait and see.'

He did go for it. Like a rat up a drainpipe. Smudge couldn't wait to tell the other lads about his find, and to warn them off her too. Natalie was his.

'Fucking 'ell, boys, there is the hottest chick you've ever seen who's just come up on the site. She's after squaddies on Ops too. She looks like a model, fucking unbelievable. Her name is Natalie. Lovely name too, don't you think? I've already messaged her, so none of you bother, OK? Anyway, she only likes blonds, and you're all too ugly.'

How he didn't recognize it was Abi Titmuss we had no idea, especially since she was on the front cover of every lads' magazine around at that time. The reality was he didn't want to. Natalie was his dream come true.

Sure enough, the next day Natalie messaged Smudge back, with no small amount of giggling coming from the QRF room. In no time at all, they were getting on like a house on fire.

Natalie was keen to know what Smudge had been up to, and what a big brave boy he'd been. Smudge knew he couldn't give away too many operational details on an open Internet line, but he couldn't disappoint the poor woman either.

His reply: 'let's just say baby that i've seen a few things, you know what i mean? of course, i can't talk about it because it's top secret. apparently i'm going to get a big bravery medal, and the SAS want to see me too. but i don't do it for the glory. i do it because someone's got to keep the world safe haven't they?'

That had Chris and Fitz rolling around on the floor crying their eyes out.

It was only a matter of time before the messages went dirty. Smudge initiated it, and Natalie was more than happy to take it even dirtier. They discussed their various sexual preferences, with Smudge particularly keen to learn Natalie's views on one certain position that I thought was still illegal.

Worst of all, he even confessed to wishing he could give himself a blowjob so he could keep himself happy when away on tour.

It went on for a good couple of weeks. Smudge was coming up to his allotted two weeks of R&R. He had an announcement for the platoon.

'Guess what, lads, Nat's agreed to spend the whole of my R&R with me. We're going down to the seaside and we're going to have two weeks of nonstop perfect sex. Can you fucking believe it! It's more than just sex though, guys, OK? I'm really falling for her, and she really likes me too. Do you think I should introduce her to my parents yet, or is it too early, Danny?'

'Oh, er, no, I wouldn't do that just yet, Smudger. Don't you want to see your mates instead?'

'Fuck them. This is the real thing. Look, I'm not going to cut my hair down to the bone any more so I can grow it a bit longer for Nat. She loves it like that. That's OK with you, isn't it?'

It was awful. He was head over heels in love with Natalie. He had planned to spend his entire R&R with a stunning woman that only existed inside Chris and Fitz's heads. Not in their wildest dreams did they ever think they'd get him that badly. Word spread around the whole platoon about Natalie's real identity, so everyone was now having a good laugh behind poor old Smudge's back.

As the platoon commander, I did my best to stay aloof from the wind-up. It was going to end in tears sooner or later, and as the responsible one it was best I stayed out of it. But I couldn't resist having a peek in every now and then.

As his R&R date got closer, Smudge spent more and more time in the washing block perfecting the best look for Natalie. At last the day itself came, and he sorted out his best civvies for the occasion. Nat had even offered to meet him off the plane at Brize Norton.

A few of us made a deputation to Chris and Fitz.

'Look, you two, you've got to fucking tell him before he leaves. What happens when he turns up at Brize and she's not there? Chris?'

'I know, I know, Dan. We have to. I just can't think how the fuck we're going to do it.'

They decided there was no point in beating around the bush with it. In what was supposed to be Smudge's very last online conversation with Natalie before they were due to meet, Chris and Fitz chucked in the hand grenade.

This is how their last messaging went.

Smudge: 'can't wait to see you tomorrow baby. you got the instructions through from me on how to get there ok yeah?'

Natalie: 'yes i did, my little warrior. but there's just one problem.'

Smudge: 'what's that baby?'

Natalie: 'i'm not going to be there darling.'

Smudge: 'why not??'

Natalie: 'because i don't exist. this is chris and fitz in the QRF room, and it has been all along, YOU FUCKING KNOB!!!!!'

I was in the QRF room with them. Smudge was in the Internet room alone. There was silence from it for a good thirty seconds. It took a little time for what he had just read to actually sink in. Then we heard a chair hurled on the floor, a couple of screamed expletives, and the rapid thump of boots down the corridor.

Smudge kicked the QRF room's door open so hard it practically came off its hinges. His face was puce with rage. Not only had the woman of his dreams just disappeared in a puff of electronic smoke, but he'd got nothing planned for his R&R any more – and he was the laughing stock of the whole platoon. He went crazy.

'You fucking *cunts*! I can't fucking believe you fucking did that to me! You *fucking mean bastards*. That's sick, that is. I really fucking liked her, you know!'

'Er, yeah, we know, Smudge. We were on the other end, remember. Look, relax. It was only a joke . . .'

But Smudge was gone. He kicked the iron bunk beds, stamped a wooden chair to bits and repeatedly punched the walls. Then he ran out into Cimic's garden, where he sat for an awful long time, until his transport arrived to Slipper City and the flight home. He was truly heartbroken.

19

When Smudge came back from R&R two weeks later, he'd relaxed a bit. He never really saw the funny side of the joke, but at least he'd stopped breaking things whenever Natalie was mentioned. It also helped considerably that, despite his terrible grief, he'd also managed to pull a half-decent bird while he was on leave.

More importantly, he brought back with him an update from the hospitals in the UK on all the serious casualties we had suffered.

Private Beharry had been downgraded from VSI (very seriously ill) to just SI. That meant there was a decent chance he'd live, but nobody knew in what state yet.

Adam Llewellyn, who got petrol bombed, was going to be OK too. He was having skin grafts. Baz Bliss, who took a slug in the lung, had lost a lot of weight but was doing well too, and Kev Phillips, who got shot in the neck with the CO on 18 April, was shaping up the best of all. The nutter had even already got a tattoo of the words 'entry' by the scar on his neck where the bullet went in, and 'exit' over the scar on his shoulder where the round had left his body.

Pikey also went away for R&R around the same time. He hadn't pulled, but he was just as chuffed because he'd had a decent pub fight instead. True to form, he'd also managed to lug back with him seventy-five trendy shirts, the sort of things you'd wear to a glitzy party. He just couldn't help himself.

'What are you going to do with that lot, Pikey?' I asked. 'This is the desert you know. There isn't a nightclub in 500 miles. Nobody's going to buy them here, you fool!'

Pikey knew better. 'Ah, well, we'll see about that, Danny. You want one yourself? Lovely quality, look, just feel that will ya?'

He'd correctly worked out that here we were, a lot of very bored blokes in the middle of nowhere, with not a bloody thing to spend our money on. Given a chance at a bit of consumerism, we'd all tear his arm off. We did. He'd flogged the lot within two days. To my utter shame, I ended up buying one too.

We'd do literally anything to relieve the boredom. Sam even proposed a day-long wank-athon competition against Longy. Sam never got close. He readily conceded at lunchtime when Longy was already four ahead.

A better idea someone else had was to get the compound's swimming pool up and running again. It had taken a fair few bits of shrapnel but no direct hits, so the lining was sealed up pretty quickly. A hose was found, the pump was fixed, and it was filled full of river water treated by the onsite plant.

By mid-July, four weeks into the ceasefire, it was ready for use again.

A rare day off was declared to celebrate its opening day, a Friday. Almost the whole company flocked to it for a cooling dip and a bit of sunbathing. Its reappearance spread a coltish, holiday atmosphere around the camp. It was a novelty, something different to break up the routine. The only important thing was not to look too closely at the colour of the water.

'Faarkin' 'ell, Danny, this could be the Algarve,' said Dale,

Best buddies: Chris Mulrine and
US bodyguard 'Red Rob'

Chris supports his L96 in a tripod on the
roof of the Pink Palace

The platoon's accommodation block after a mortar direct hit

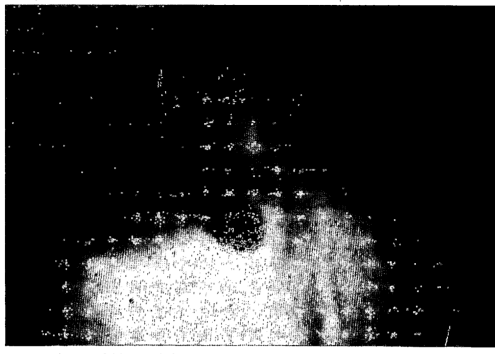

The painful bruise left on my shoulder by an AK47 round during the
OPTAG patrol

The hole left by the bullet in my
body armour

Pte Daniel Crucefix, who got stuck
at Cimic House for three days with
a piece of shrapnel the size of a
credit card in his nose

Pte Johnson Beharry VC poses with a belt of 7.62 mm rounds, a few days before he was critically injured

Pte Johnson Beharry's badly shot-up Warrior the day after his Victoria Cross action

Chris with an L96 and Oost with an SA80 and underslung grenade launcher outside the Pink Palace

Concealed sniping. Chris is Number 1 and Des is Number 2, during a raid on an enemy house

Heavy metal. A Challenger II Main Battle Tank from the Queen's Royal Lancers

Mortar-damaged roof sangar. I left with Oost just ten seconds
before a round came through the roof and exploded inside it

A US engineers' convoy burns after its
huge ambush on 1 May

Bored snipers watch a DVD during the July ceasefire. *Left to right*: Smudge,
Harry, Ads, Longy and Pikey

Snipers in the roof-top sangar, with the 'Royal Marine' team hard at work on the right

The 'Royal Marine' sniper team. Buzz, *left*, and John, *right*, at work in the roof-top sangar

Dan receives his Mention in Despatches silver oak leaf from Brigadier Iain Cholerton, the Army's most senior officer in Wales

MENTION IN DESPATCHES

By The Queen's Order the name of

Sergeant Daniel Mills
The Princess of Wales's Royal Regiment

was published in the London Gazette on

Friday, 18th March 2005

as Mentioned in a Despatch for Gallantry

I am charged to record Her Majesty's high appreciation

Secretary of State for Defence

Dan's Mention in
Despatches certificate

as he spread his not inconsiderable girth down on his towel. 'Fetch us a Pina Colada will you, mate?'

'More like Butlins from the 1950s, I'd say. We all look the bleeding same!'

Swimming trunks hadn't been on the official kit lists. All we had to sunbathe in were our identical dark blue, tight-fitting regimental running shorts. Pants were banned for hygiene reasons.

'Yeah, check out the T-shirt tans too, Danny. Good job there's no birds here, we'd all get dumped on the spot.'

All around the pool was a mass of dark brown faces and arms with lilywhite legs and torsos. Dale was right, it wasn't pretty.

Then suddenly a commotion in the deep end.

'Oh, Jesus! You horrible little beast,' someone hollered.

The spectacle was a novelty for Tigris too. In her uncontrollable excitement, she'd taken a long run up and hurled herself in, peeing wildly as she flew through the air.

I tried to use some of the long days of inactivity to catch up on my platoon commander's paperwork. There was a mountain of admin I had to go through, that stemmed all the way back to April when we'd first arrived, almost four months before.

I had to write an annual review report for every platoon member, which meant interviewing them all. How were they finding life? What courses did they want to do? All that sort of stuff. It felt a bit demeaning having to put them all through that, when we'd been through so much together and I knew them all inside out anyway.

The only personnel problem the platoon really had was Gilly. Before the ceasefire, I'd hoped in vain that he'd find his fighting feet sooner or later. He never did. He hadn't got any worse, which quite frankly would have been hard anyway. He was just Gilly, a completely useless bastard.

A few of the NCOs had come up to me to say he wasn't very comfortable with his weapon, and wasn't backing people up enough during contacts.

Now I had the chance to actually go through the ammo lists to see how bad he was. When I did, I was gobsmacked. There it was in black and white for every single week: rounds redistributed to Gilly, zero. We'd been through all of that, and he hadn't fired a single solitary shot.

That was it. I resolved to get rid of him as soon as I could. He was one giant waste of space. Worse than that, he was a fucking liability. If the man next to you isn't covering your arse when you ask him to because he's too concerned about keeping his own head down, you're going to get killed.

The perfect opportunity arose a couple of weeks later. During an O Group, Major Featherstone read out a request the company had received to provide two soldiers to escort the Ammunition Technical Officer (ATO) about the desert to blow up old ordnance. In civvy speak, that means the bomb squad to get rid of old artillery shells and the like.

Before the OC had even finishing speaking, I had my hand up.

'It'll be hard, sir, but Sniper Platoon can volunteer one.'

It was also a good way of getting rid of Gilly without causing too much of a stir, and he didn't lose any face with it either. He wasn't a bad person and I didn't want to shred what little confidence he had left if I didn't have to. I took him aside that night.

'Gilly, I've got some good news for you, mate.'

'OK, Sarge.'

'You've been selected for a good job away from the

platoon and the company. It's based back in Abu Napa, and I think you'll like that too. You're going to be escorting the ATO on all his duties.'

'Right, Sarge.'

It wasn't the reaction I'd been expecting. ATO meant big bangs, and Gilly didn't like those either. I tried another tack.

'Gilly, do you know what corps the ATO is in?'

'No, Sergeant.'

'I didn't think so. It's the Royal Logistics Corps.'

He still looked blank.

'It's the RLCs, isn't it, Gilly!'

His face lit up. 'Oh, really? Oh, thanks very much, Sarge. When can I go?'

Being scared of combat wasn't Gilly's fault, because warfare is not for everybody. I wasn't pissed off with him for not liking war. I was pissed off with him for taking the Queen's shilling while thinking he'd never have to see it.

The heat and the boredom had a predictable effect on Louey and his arch foe.

With little else to worry about, Louey had too much time on his hands to remember how John Wedlock had punched him in the cookhouse. He had been brooding over it for weeks. He'd given his fair share back of course, but it was the initial blow to his dignity that really infuriated the normally gentle giant. Whenever anyone asked him about it, Louey would just reply: 'He was wrong to go for me like that. Wrong.'

Hearing that Wedlock had been bad mouthing him over lunch one day finally pushed Louey over the edge.

'That's it,' he quietly announced, as he got up and walked over to the cookhouse.

Wedlock was still at his table with his back to the door,

so he didn't see Louey walk in. That was unfortunate for Wedlock, because Louey calmly strolled up to the hot plates, picked up an industrial size frying pan almost empty of paella, and charged Wedlock straight through a corridor of khaki bodies sitting down eating their scoff.

Wedlock barely had time to stand up before Louey wrapped the frying pan right around the back of his head with a dull metallic thud. Everyone knew what to do now. The cookhouse immediately erupted into two cheering mobs each backing their own prize fighter – Recce screaming for Wedlock, Snipers screaming for Louey. The neutrals just screamed.

Wedlock went down like a sack of spuds from the almighty blow. Louey was straight on top of him, and gave him two massive haymakers in the face.

'That's for last time, Wedlock, you Fijian piece of shit.'

Once the Fijian had literally realized what had hit him, he began to fight back. The frying pan blow was enough to kill most men, let alone the horrendous punches. But Wedlock seemed undamaged. In a righteous rage now, he managed to turn Louey over as the two interlocked in a very uncomfortable looking bear hug. For a few seconds, Wedlock was again on top, and hit Louey hard in the face, before they were rolling over again. After several more blows from each, the fight drew to a standstill with both men pinning all of the other's limbs down on the floor in two of the world's most unorthodox wrestling positions.

Afterwards there were the usual black eyes on the baker's dozen that were brave enough to separate them. It was another trip to Dale for Louey and Wedlock and a major bollocking, along with a hefty fine this time too. As far as Louey was concerned, it was worth every penny. Honour was even.

As it was so quiet, the battle group also introduced three-day mini-breaks for us in Kuwait. They were known as Operational Stand Down (OSD) packages. It was a good idea, because it allowed us to get a much needed change of scene. By the end of July, we'd done more than six weeks of peace in Iraq's brave new world – and we were crawling up Cimic's walls.

Rather than going en masse, each platoon from Y Company would send a fire team of four blokes on each trip, so there would never be a manpower shortage for any specialism. My turn came on 29 July, and I went with Fitz, Des and Oost.

It was a four-hour drive to Kuwait, and we travelled down in a convoy of Snatch Land Rovers. It was a tense drive, as Route 6 still had a high roadside bomb threat. Again, old habits died hard for the more fanatical of Moqtada al-Sadr's followers.

As we passed through the veritable dump of a city that is Basra, to our eyes it was a thriving modern metropolis. We had got too used to shitty, sleepy Al Amarah. However, it was absolutely nothing compared to the extraordinary experience of crossing the border.

Travelling from Iraq to Kuwait was like crossing a 200-year time warp. The difference between the two countries was phenomenal. One second you're on a crappy single-lane potholed road out of the early nineteenth century, then suddenly it turns into a six-carriageway motorway from the twenty-first century, with knobs on.

In a flash, all the mud huts and filth had gone. Everything in Kuwait was brand new and clean. Every house was tiled and looked to be made from marble, and its people were happy and well dressed. It was an acute reminder of what happens when one country spends its oil money for

233

twenty-five years on infrastructure, and the other blows it on war. Kuwait is what Iraq should have looked like. We were impressed; Saddam must have tried seriously hard to fuck his country quite to the state that he did.

We stopped just after the border at a British military post to change into the civvies that we'd brought with us and hand over our weapons and ammunition. It's always a good feeling when you can pull on a pair of jeans after months on end in combat fatigues. Then it was down to the US Army's Camp Doha, in the desert just to the north of Kuwait City. Endless rows of small prefab blocks that doubled up as holiday chalets, each filled with four bunk beds and nicely air conditioned. It wasn't just Brits there, the whole of the 150,000-strong US military from all over Iraq took it in turns to do their operational stand downs at the camp too.

If you're ever in doubt of the size of the US footprint in Iraq, go to Camp Doha. The place blew our minds. It had everything: great big cinemas, enormous gyms, Burger King, Pizza Hut, coffee shops, indoor shopping malls, soccer pitches, the works. It made our own Shaibitha look like a little corner shop. Just going on a wander and a gawp was a great unwind in itself. To us, mundane snippets of normal life that you wouldn't blink at in the UK were utterly fascinating. There were even some decent looking birds around the place, either American servicewomen or civilian contractors. We tried hard not to gawp at them too. The only thing the place lacked was booze. But it was so stupidly hot, you didn't really fancy waking up with a hangover anyway.

Inside the giant Naafi the size of a department store (Yanks call it the PX) was everything you could ever possibly want for service in Iraq. Videos, TVs, stereos, duvets, towels, clothes, rucksacks, boots, tents, laptops, mouse pads, video cameras, PlayStations, Xboxes, gun holsters – the lot. American soldiers did whole year-long tours in Iraq rather than just the six or seven months we had to do, the poor sods. We looked on in pity as they filled up their trolleys to the brim for the long haul.

Des broke the muffled calm of the place with a shout I heard from the other end of the shop.

'Hey, Oost, man, over here! You've got to check out the fucking hardware they've got!'

He'd found the knife section. He was in heaven. It had every blade and serrated edge he'd ever dreamed of. Even some that he hadn't. The South Africans are a lot like the Americans with their shared fascination with guns and killing tools, just a little bit more bloodthirsty.

We also had a good old laugh at their rows and rows of T-shirts. Nobody does T-shirt slogans quite like the US military, and none of them were ironic. 'Who's yer Bag-daddy' was a common one. On another, there was a cartoon picture of a mean looking GI holding out a tin can with the words '100% genuine Whoop Ass' written on it. In a speech bubble coming out of the cartoon GI's mouth was the phrase, 'Don't make me open it.'

Des and Oost bought matching sniper T-shirts, which they cherished from that day onwards. A dirty great big rifle barrel poked out from the design on the front. On the back was printed the slogan, 'Never run from a sniper. You will only die tired.'

That night, we stuffed our faces with burgers. The next morning I woke up feeling like shit; just totally exhausted, and I knew I was coming down with something. Typical. I get ill just when I go on a bit of a holiday.

I spent most of that day in bed. On the next, I felt a bit better so I joined the boys on a sightseeing trip into Kuwait City. It's not an amazing place, with the only real landmark being its twin giant conical water towers. We took a few pictures and hung out on the city's long sandy beaches, because I was still feeling ropey.

After another night of face-stuffing for the boys, while I looked on jealously, it was back up to Al Amarah. Before we set off, there was the obligatory final trip to the jumbo PX where the guys stocked up on as many consumables as they could carry. That meant dozens of bags of salted beef jerky to crates of Coke and platoon-size pouches of American chewing tobacco. We barely all fitted in around the stash. Des and Oost munched throughout the whole journey up, and by the end they were feeling as sick as parrots.

There was a familiar face waiting for us back in Cimic.

After pestering every military doctor in the UK to declare him fit for duty, Daz had finally succeeded. He got himself on the very next plane back out. We greeted him with a lot of warm handshakes, and no small amount of piss taking. Just what he had been expecting.

'Sorry you've missed all the fun, mate. We were a little bit busy while you were lying on your fat arse in some cosy hospital bed.'

'I was gutted, fucking gutted, Danny. I was getting all the sit reps in the hospital. Seething I was, you should have seen me. I just hope you slotted the fucker who got me.'

'Don't worry, mate. I think there's a fairly high chance of that, at one stage or another.'

Daz was technically the 2i/c of the platoon again, but he and Chris ended up doing the job together after his return. There was a lot Daz had to catch up on, and he was the first to give way to Chris's enormous experience.

Despite everything the platoon had been through since April, it was funny to think that Daz had still not fired his weapon in anger once. He'd never even got the chance – he was blown up in the very first attack on us. The last thing he remembered before the morphine kicked in was getting his ammo stripped off him.

Not that any of us had any idea at that moment, but he was about to get his chance.

Daz had got back just in the nick of time. So had we. Within a few days, Y Company was going to need every man it could get. One hundred and six British soldiers' lives would depend on exactly how hard we were prepared to fight.

20

Two days after we got back from Kuwait, I still felt shit from whatever it was I'd got. Corky the company medic sent me very reluctantly back to Slipper City for a proper medical. I hated going back there, even if I was ill.

I checked myself in at the Regimental Aid Post, a single-storey concrete building. The female nurse there told me I was exhausted.

'But I've just come back from my OSD, I can't be. We haven't done anything for bloody weeks.'

'Doesn't matter. You've probably had this coming on for a while. You've got a viral exhaustion infection. Good old fashioned rest is the only way you're going to sort this one out, Sergeant. There are a few ward tents next door that are totally empty at the moment. Why don't you take yourself off there and get some proper sleep?'

She gave me some pills.

'Take as much time as you need. I don't want to see you again until you're feeling a lot better.'

There was a knock on the door, and an orderly popped his head round it.

'Ambulance coming in from Cimic House with a head injury, ma'am. Half an hour.'

I sat up. 'Cimic?'

'Yeah. There's been some sort of accident. That's all we know at the moment.'

Cimic, shit. Was it someone from Snipers? The nurse read my mind.

'No, Sergeant, there's no point in you waiting around for that. There's nothing you can do for anyone in the state you're in anyway. Go on, off you go.'

She was right. I stumbled over to the tents, popped her pills and slept for two solid days. I woke up feeling right as rain on the morning of 6 August, the day of my thirty-sixth birthday. I also woke up in a world that had changed considerably since I last saw it.

Moqtada al-Sadr had fed us the mother of all shit sandwiches.

After a couple of months at playing the politician, he'd discovered that democracy wasn't really his bag after all. He finally threw all his toys out of the pram during a row about how many delegates he was allowed to bring to a national conference to decide how Iraq would elect a new government. He pulled out of the whole process, helpfully branding it 'a sick joke on the Iraqi people'.

Flexing his muscles a little more, Moqtada then issued a series of violent threats at what he and his people might do if he didn't get his way. The rabble rousing was a blatant challenge to the new and unstable government's authority. It was also a clear breach of the peace agreement he had signed, and the Americans weren't standing for it.

On 3 August, the Yanks had tried to nip any trouble in the bud before the streets exploded again. They wanted to avoid the mistakes they had made in April. A company of US Marines and truckloads of Iraqi police were dispatched to al-Sadr's home in Najaf to arrest him. It was the worst thing they could have done.

Moqtada had guessed the Americans were coming. On arrival, the Marines were greeted by heavy gunfire, mortar shelling and a barrage of RPGs, courtesy of hundreds of Mehdi Army fighters who were already defending the house.

Quickly, the clashes spread to the old city of Najaf. There, al-Sadr's fighters had already taken up well-fortified positions around the great Imam Ali mosque.

Round Two was well and truly on. This time, however, it began with one very important difference.

In his passionate plea for jihad to all Iraqi Shia the next day, Moqtada put it about that the Americans had invaded Najaf to destroy the Imam Ali mosque, as a punishment for him not coming quietly. This wasn't true, but it was easily the most inflammatory thing Moqtada could possibly say.

The sprawling, golden-façaded Imam Ali mosque is the most holy site of all for the Shia. Not only is it their Vatican, it's also the tomb of the Prophet Mohammed's son-in-law Ali, the man who led the factional split from Sunni Muslims to create the Shia faith. When Ali was murdered at prayer in 661 AD, he became the Shia's most important martyr and from then onwards almost as highly revered as Mohammed himself. There was no greater insult to the Shia than to destroy this sacred spot at which hundreds of thousands of pilgrims paid homage every year.

In short, a threat to the Imam Ali mosque was seen by them as a threat to Shia Islam's very survival.

Thanks to their itchy trigger fingers, the US military's reputation for heavy-handedness had been well established in Iraq by August 2004. Moqtada's legions of followers believed every word he told them. They soon whipped themselves up into an extraordinary state of fanatical religious fervour.

Redders was also back at Abu Naji having to do a stint in the battle group Ops Room. He had come to the Regimental Aid Post to give me an update on what was going on.

'Put it this way, Danny, threatening the Imam Ali mosque

is like waving a giant blood-red flag with bells on it in front of a seriously histrionic bull with a persecution complex. It's Moqtada's nuclear button, and he's fucking well pressed it.'

'I see.' Clearly it wasn't going to be much of a birthday.

From the peace and quiet of just two days ago, reports were now flooding into the Ops Room of serious trouble all over the country. Coalition forces had come under heavy attack again in the poor Shia suburbs of Baghdad and across all the major southern cities: Nasiriyah, Kut, Kufa and Diwaniya. Basra too was once more in flames. The Mehdi Army there had tried to take control of strategic buildings and were fighting open gun battles with British troops in the streets.

Now it would be nice to say that the people of Al Amarah rose above all the tosh being spoken by Moqtada, and got on quietly with their everyday lives. But if they'd done that, they wouldn't have been the people of Al Amarah. The city was as bad as anywhere. From what it looked like in Abu Naji, possibly worse.

Within hours of the Moqtada pronouncement, the city's mosques began broadcasting a furious call to arms. Thousands were out on the streets in angry protests, and the OMS were in the middle of it all, frantically rabble rousing and sinisterly mobilizing at equal pace. The shooting started almost immediately.

Redders also told me about the head casualty that had come in from Cimic. It wasn't a sniper. It was Ray, the cheeky but lovable private from Mortar Platoon. Ray the Mortar Magnet. He was dead.

'Ray? Jesus, poor guy. How the fuck did that happen?'

'It's unbelievable, Danny. As soon as the trouble started, the Iraqi Army who were manning the front gate fucked

241

straight off. We had to put Ray and a couple of other lads on it instead. It was kicking off pretty badly in town. The OC's rover group in a couple of Snatches came screaming back in and Ray raised the metal barrier on the chicanes to let them in.

'You know the metal chain you use to pull the bloody thing up and down with? The cheese cutter pole on top of one of the Snatches caught it as it went past. That yanked the barrier straight back down right on Ray's head. It must have pretty much killed him on the spot. Don't think he knew anything about it. Which is something, I suppose.'

What a pathetic waste. After all we'd been through, Ray was killed in a stupid little accident like that. It wasn't anybody's fault, but it was the first fatality the battle group had suffered and it was a bitter blow.

Soldiers understand losses in combat, because that's what happens in war. We're all big boys and we know the risks. To lose someone so needlessly like that though was gutting. Ray especially, who'd shaken off everything the OMS had thrown at him. He was their casualty all right, albeit in a more oblique way. Of that we were all sure.

'There's more, Dan,' Redders continued. 'The OMS even managed to cut short a little memorial service organized for Ray yesterday. Just as the padre was saying his bit, the first round of a mortar barrage landed on the cookhouse roof. Everyone had to scarper for cover.'

'Fucking wankers.'

'That's another thing – the mortaring is back something special as well. It's up there with what we were getting at the start of May. Didn't take them long to find all the tubes they're supposed to have got rid of, did it?'

From that moment onwards, I bust a gut to get myself back to Cimic. A new movement ban on Snatches was coming into effect at dusk that evening. After that, fuck knows when the next Warrior column would move.

The situation was deteriorating by the hour. The CO's desperate negotiations with city leaders to try to halt the violence had failed. Instead, the Mehdi Army stormed all of Al Amarah's police stations and assumed full control over the town council. In effect, the town was theirs again.

Cimic was the uprising's next target, and it was taking a pounding. As the most obvious as well as accessible symbol of the coalition's presence in Maysan, the compound swiftly became the focus of the entire province's resistance. For the same reason, it was imperative the battle group as the lawful Iraqi government's agent defended it.

Just as the sun began to dip below the horizon, the two Snatches I had persuaded Featherstone to send down finally turned up at the front gate. I had the passenger door open before the lead vehicle even stopped moving.

'Don't even stop the engine, Sam, fucking go now.'

As we sped out of Abu Naji's front gate, there was a series of mechanical clicks and clunks as everyone in the vehicle made their weapons ready.

We took a back route in up the city's eastern flank as the Red route would be a certain death trap. As we cut into the old town, there were OMS gunmen milling around on pretty much every corner.

'Just put your foot right down, Sammy. Don't stop for anything, got it?'

'Got it, Danny.' He didn't.

I depressed the button on my chest rig to speak into my PRR. 'Everyone else, keep your eyes peeled. With a bit of luck we'll get through without a fight. The first person you see raise their weapon at us though, give 'em blue fucking murder.'

The two Land Rovers' V8 engines roared as we shot past most of the groups of hoods before they even got a chance to see what we were.

Only one problem. It was obvious where we were going. One of the OMS had radioed ahead. We were tearing up Tigris Street only 500 metres away from Cimic when they sprang the ambush. If you can call it that. Slaughter is a better word.

It was the most suicidal thing I have ever seen. Less than 100 metres in front of us, three youngish looking lads in black ran right out into the middle of the road. With their AKs at their waists Rambo style, they opened up on us.

'Top cover!' I screamed up at Louey and Des, as I opened the passenger door and jammed my SA80 down the crack between the door and the window.

That's when I heard the shouts of the men in black. Over and over, 'Allah Akbar! Allah Akbar!'

Louey and Des were already on to them. *Fucking good blokes.* A second later both their Minimis were chattering with fury. Metal on metal, as dozens of 5.56mm shell casings rained down on the roof above my head. With my left foot jamming the door open, I flicked my SA80 onto automatic and sprayed a full mag at them too.

'Hold on,' hollered Sam.

The Snatch's tyres screeched as he swerved it from one side of the road to the other to make us a harder target. Fantastic skills, Sam.

A couple of rounds piled into the Snatch's engine block, sparks flying as they smacked through the bonnet's metal. Another tore through the glass, just missing Sam's head.

The nutters weren't going to beat the Minimis though. By the time we'd reached their position, two had been blasted to the left side of the road. The third fell into a kneel, clutching his badly bleeding gut. Sam swerved to miss him, but the second wagon had no chance. Both its offside wheels went straight over the fighter, finishing him off for sure.

Sam craned round for a second to stare at the carnage.

'Fucking lunatics! What were they on?'

It was madness. If our bullets hadn't cut the men up, we would have knocked them down like bowling pins with four tonnes of Snatch. They'd known that before they even went into the road.

The contact was hard proof that this fight really was going to be different.

It wasn't just about the OMS's ego any more. This time, there was real religious belief behind what these fighters were doing. Their fanaticism took away any fear of death. Death was good, if Allah wished it. Everything was Allah's call to them; it was all out of their own control. Fighting people who don't care about dying is harder because they don't do what you expect them to do. Or what you'd do. Like keeping your fucking head down if two Minimis are going to blow it off.

Luckily, the road kill behind us were only new recruits. Nobody had bothered to teach them how to aim.

Cimic was no longer the holiday camp that I'd left. Instead, it was a hive of activity with blokes running left, right and centre getting ready for another long night. The place was on a major war footing.

The sangars were double-manned, with many of the sentries' eyeballs already red with tiredness. On the righthand side of the driveway as we drove up was a freshly bombed-out Snatch, peppered from top to bottom with holes. A mortar had landed a few feet away, totalling it where it stood. A young lad from Recce was darting about all over the paving stones furiously trying to sweep up dozens of shards of shrapnel into an untidy pile to stop vehicle punctures. The boys had obviously had a busy time of it.

As I jogged into the house, a constant stream of instructions crackled out over the PRR from the Ops Room to various sections of the defensive cordon. On the main stairway, I was almost knocked over by a pair of blokes carrying a fucking great chest of 7.62 link for a Gimpy somewhere.

Behind them was Dale.

'Ah, Danny boy!' He gave my hand an even harder bone crunch than usual.

'Thank fuck you and your boys are back. Thought you might have decided to sit this one out.'

Dale had his helmet on and he wore his body armour over a T-shirt. He had at least two days' stubble growth, as had many of the blokes in Cimic. The house had also swiftly returned to the Black Hole of Calcutta with everyone having to live back under hard cover again. A couple more of the single-storey Portakabins had bought it from the return of the mortar barrages.

'Me? Fuck off mate. Not for all the tea in China.'

'Good. 'Cos I've had to kick everyone out of the faarkin' pool and send them to work again, haven't I. We need you on the roof big style, mate. Grab some water and I'll give you the low down.'

Dale didn't have much good news. It wasn't just the reason for it that made the fight different this time. It was the numbers too.

'The main problem is that every single fucker out there is uniting against us now. It's all about Najaf, isn't it. It's sent them potty. The OMS is a given, we knew they'd be in a bate. But now it looks like we've got the tribal bosses and estate militias lining up alongside them as well.'

'Shit.'

'Yeah, it is shit. They're not even scrapping with each other any more. They're all fucking Sadrists now. And they want us out of Maysan altogether. The Int boys are getting more reports than they can even process at the moment. People are coming in from all over the province to have a go apparently. There's even a few hundred of those fuck-heads from Majar al Kabir who done the Red Caps last year on their way up as well.'

Majar al Kabir. The land of the savages. We hadn't even gone near them on our tour, but that clearly didn't mean they were going to miss a chance at slotting some more Brits if they could.

But Dale had more.

'And if all of that ain't bad enough, al-Sadr has put a price tag on our heads, hasn't he. It's being put about that anyone who kills a coalition soldier gets 200 US dollars in cash from the local OMS. Cheeky sod – I reckon I'm worth at least a grand.'

It was a good incentive. The average labourer got little more than $100 a month. So the greedy now had a reason to line up alongside the believers too. The Maysanis sensed blood, and everyone wanted a bit of it.

Dale scarpered back to the Ops Room while I thought about what he'd told me. Yes, there was no getting away from it, it was a fucking mess. And we weren't holding the same amount of chips that we had during the spring uprising.

We couldn't just do another Operation Waterloo and clear all the bastards out with our firepower. For one thing, we no longer had the air assets guaranteed. With much of Iraq in flames, the American Spectre gunships were busy elsewhere protecting their own troops.

There was also the dangerously high level of feeling among the average Al Amarahan to take into account. To a man they were all Shia, and therefore far more sympathetic to al-Sadr's cause this time. Would another full-scale armoured incursion into their city set every single male inhabitant against us? It was certainly possible. There must be about 100,000 of them – we'd be outnumbered 100–1.

Of course, privately I was quite excited to be in the thick of the action again. I'd missed it badly, we all had. To feel the adrenalin rush of danger again was a liberation because being mortared, grenaded and shot at turned us all on.

Yet this time the stakes were a whole load higher. It was clear from very early on that this was going to be considerably worse than anything we'd ever seen before. Most importantly of all, we had had people killed now too, and that changed the tone of everything.

The situation boiled down to one simple question. Were we really going to be able to handle the immense scale of the onslaught that was now coming our way? For the first time, I had to admit it. I didn't know.

Without even dumping my stuff, I went straight to the roof to catch up with the boys. I could already hear them returning the odd round to some sporadic incoming fire. As always, the boys were my priority. Until I knew their state the bigger picture could wait.

'Some peacekeeping tour, eh, Dan?' said Smudge with a big grin across his mug.

Excellent. The saying was our catchphrase for the tour. After a few months of redundancy, it had become very relevant again. It also told me immediately that the boys' spirits were as high as they'd ever been. That cheered me up considerably.

'Indeed it is, Smudger. I put in a word with the OMS because I knew you were getting a bit bored.'

'Good on you, Dan, thanks for that.'

'Anyone got any kills in yet?'

They had, as well as amassing a few tales of heroics too. Again, Ads had the best one. He'd charged a building full of gunmen with just a sniper rifle in his hands and only forty rounds of green spot ammunition.

Ads had been out on a foot patrol with Major Featherstone when they'd been ambushed at a Route 6 roundabout on the north bank dubbed Red 14. It had started with a blast bomb thrown just ten metres in front of Ads, who was the OC's point man and was armed with just his long. As it went off, a load of automatic fire came in on them.

'Gunmen, the two-storey building 150 metres away,' said Ads, spotting them first.

While still out in the open with Featherstone, he knelt

down on one knee, dropped a gunman on the roof of the building with the single-shot rifle, and threw a smoke grenade in front of him to obscure the gunmen's view. Both men carried on firing, the OC with an SA80, until the smoke had done its job. Over his PRR, Featherstone then ordered an immediate assault on the building and set off for it at full pelt.

Charging by Ads, he hollered: 'Follow me, Somers.'

Ads took a quick look behind him. The rest of the patrol were now scrambling for cover where they stood. It confirmed his suspicions. Featherstone's PRR wasn't working and nobody had heard the order apart from him. Realizing the OC would be desperately vulnerable alone, he ran after him anyway.

The pair reached cover just beside the enemy held house, and finally had a chance to confer.

'Good work, Ads. Right, everyone follow me . . . hang on, where the fuck's everyone else?'

'I think your PRR's fucked, sir. There's only me. Maybe not such a great idea to storm the house with just the two of us.'

Somewhat shocked, Featherstone agreed wholeheartedly and they pegged it back to the safety of the rest of the patrol. It was typical bloody Ads, and I thought it was hilarious.

'Why did you do an assault with only your bleeding long and forty rounds, you crazy fool?'

Ads just shrugged his shoulders. 'It was all I had on me, Danny.'

Once I'd got the full sit rep, I instituted a few more home improvements. Nobody had any idea how long the new crisis might last, so the CO ordered us to be ready to sit it out for as long as we needed to. If they wanted a siege, fine. We'd make Cimic impregnable.

Darkness had fallen, which gave us a good chance to add a roof to Rooftop Sangar to give it some shelter from flying mortar and RPG shrapnel. On top of the few planks of wood and corrugated iron, we slapped on two layers of sandbags and some camo netting. It wasn't going to withstand a direct hit from an 82mm mortar shell, but it would withstand pretty much anything else.

We also built a smaller sangar on the roof of the cookhouse, which was situated about 50 metres north of the main house right on the compound's border with the Tigris. From there, you got a better view over the dam on the west and a different angle on to the old town's rooftops to the east. From then onwards, I put a sniping pair in there at all times, giving us three different safe points of fire now from the sangars on Cimic's rooftops.

Then I made sure all the L96s were properly zeroed. Our lives and those of other soldiers would depend on the accuracy of our rifles so I wanted them all spot on. Normally, you go down the range to zero your weapons. We had to improvise.

That meant the corner house, yet again. On the laser ranger, the house measured exactly 100 metres away from the roof; perfect for what we needed. Its inhabitants had already taken more than their fair share of OMS mortar rounds meant for us. Now they were going to get a hefty amount of green spot as well. It was just tough shit. I made a mental note to go round and apologize later.

'OK, lads, the target is that circular electrical box on the outside of the house's main western wall. Can you see it? It's white and the size of a doorbell.'

Under the cover of the next mortar attack, each sniper cracked on.

To zero a sniper rifle, you fire between three and five

rounds from the same firing position at the same target, and take the volley's average position as the mean to which your sights are set. If they're off a little, you adjust them accordingly. Then you break the fire position, get up, and get back down into another firing position and let off another volley, repeating the process. To get the sights spot on, it normally takes three or four volleys. The idea is also to test that you are shooting properly from whatever position you need to be in.

It took a good hour. By the end of it, we had put around 400 rounds of 7.62mm into or around the white box. It would have done nothing for the family's electricity supply. Or their nerves.

We were ready just in time.

By the end of my first full day back, the rioting on the streets near Cimic thinned out as the gunfire on the compound began to hot up. Nobody wanted to get hit in the cross-fire.

For the first few days, the attacks weren't very well organized. They came at us either as individuals or small groups of five to ten. Fighters would try to creep up on Cimic as close as they thought they could. They'd use dead ground behind the dam, on the north bank or inside RPG alley.

'Enemy movement spotted, wait out,' came the warning over the PRR.

Before any sniper had a chance to get a fix on them, they'd jump out and riddle the place with full AK mags, or let rip with a wildly inaccurate RPG.

'Contact! Get your fucking heads down!' one of us would shout if the fire was at the roof. Then, as soon as they changed mags, we'd be back up again and putting down as many rounds as we could back at where the muzzle flashes were.

Pretty quickly, the attackers would have expended all their ammo and they'd have to bugger off again – if they were still alive.

The ground attacks would be peppered by almost constant single-round sniping from further away. For that, they used the rooftops of the old town, the hospital, the bus shelter or the Aj Dayya estate. It posed more of a threat because it was more accurate.

At that stage, still the only thing that really bothered us was the mortar fire. Up to ten separate barrages a day were being launched at us – one of the highest rates we'd experienced.

A mortar round had to be very accurate to kill anyone on the roof, thanks to our reinforcements. But the sheer weight of that sort of incoming was no small pain in the arse. It made every movement out of cover in Cimic very hard work, and people only ever got about by either sprinting like gazelles or crawling everywhere on their bellies. We became a company of high-speed invertebrates.

Largely thanks to its two water boundaries, Cimic came into its own as a natural defensive stronghold. They weren't ever going to breach our walls fighting like that either, and the volume of incoming wasn't unbearable yet. Also, the stronger we appeared, the sooner they'd go away, or so we thought.

'They can't do us any proper damage if they can't get close to us, boys,' I reminded them. 'Slot as many of these fuckers as you can. They might get the message it's not worth coming back.'

Every now and then, a gaggle of women in black dresses and veils shuffled out on to the dead ground waving white flags. The sight was a good morale boost and was always broadcast all round on the PRR. They were the body parties.

Some Mehdi Army were more obliging than others. There were a surprisingly large amount of looney tunes similar to the three we killed from the Snatches who seemed intent on martyrdom. They'd just charge us in full view blazing away any old how. It would have been churlish not to have given them what they wanted so the lads dispatched them to their seventy-two vestal virgins without any further ado.

Other fighters were a lot more devious and harder to kill.

On the north bank, they soon struck on a particularly cynical ploy of using the refugees' mud huts and slum housing as cover points to attack us. Old women and kids would be ordered to stand at their windows or doorways at gunpoint. Hiding behind civilians has been a coward's trick I've seen the world over from Belfast to Bosnia. How they justified that against the allegedly moral aim of their jihad was beyond me.

The scumbags hadn't counted on Fitzy though. After a day or so of us seeing this, he came up with an idea.

'I can do one of those sods, Danny. If you flush them out, I'll keep my eye on the door.'

'You sure, mate? Wasting some old Doris's kid by mistake isn't going to help our cause much, you know.'

'Positive.'

I took his word for it. There was one mud hut on the north bank that the fighters were particularly fond of, about 600 metres to our north-west. We waited for the next 'holy warrior' to go inside it and push out the human shields.

Ten minutes later, one turned up. He was a well-built bloke in his forties with a bushy beard. Most likely a long-standing OMS stalwart. Once he was inside, Fitzy and I lined up our longs on the building from Rooftop Sangar. I took aim at the open window two feet to the left of the door, where we'd seen the guy's muzzle flash. Fitzy concentrated solely on the door frame.

'Ready, Fitz?'

Thirty seconds of silence, as he studied every single centimetre of the possible target area in turn and mentally banked the lot of it.

Fitz took a last calm deep breath. 'Ready.'

I put a round right into the window's top righthand corner, behind which I could see straight on to the back wall.

There was a commotion inside. It worked. Convinced we were going to waste him in there, the gunman came out the door crouching low behind a twelve-year-old girl. Brandishing his AK in his right hand, he pulled the screaming child's body close to his with his left arm wrapped around her neck. Crablike, he began to slowly shuffle both of them along the building's front wall.

Fitzy let him move three feet before he released his round, immediately pulling the bolt back to drop another in the chamber if he needed it. He didn't.

The bullet ripped into the very middle fleshy part of the OMS man's lower neck, exactly in between both collarbones. It made a big old mess, slitting a major artery and spraying fountain arcs of blood over the back of the girl's head and down her face for a second or two until she threw off his weakening grip. He gradually sank down the wall to the floor, choking violently, and making feeble efforts to stop the blood flow with both hands; it just spurted out between his fingers instead. Thirty seconds later, he was dead.

'Sorry, mate,' came Fitz's brief verdict. 'Fucked with the wrong platoon, didn't you.'

By the fourth day of the siege, stocks in Cimic were getting low and we needed a hefty resupply. Because the violence was still increasing every day, Abu Naji decided they didn't want to make a habit of sending Warrior convoys into the city if they could possibly avoid it. Instead, they loaded an entire company of Warriors up with as much rations and ammo as it could possibly carry to last us for as long as possible.

The convoy got through to us in the early hours of the morning, after the predictable hefty slapping on the way, even though they came via the greatest round-the-houses back route possible. It took us all two full hours to unload everything from them.

'That's your lot, lads,' said C Company's sergeant major as his growling Warriors prepared to set off back to Slipper City. 'Go easy on that lot. I don't fucking fancy doing this journey again just to give you guys second helpings of ice cream.'

At that stage, we weren't particularly bothered at the prospect of not seeing them for a while. We felt very comfortable in Cimic with our veritable new powder keg. Boxes of 5.56mm, 7.62mm ball and green spot, UGLs, L109 hand grenades, 51mm HE mortar rounds and dynamite (Just in case) lined the stockroom's walls from floor to ceiling. We had enough ammo to blow up the Houses of Parliament. Anyway, the solitude was just another exciting challenge for us.

'Eh, it's just like the Alamo here now, innit?' quipped Pikey. 'Fuck 'em all. We'll do a better job without those armoured pansies interfering anyway.'

It was still early days then. A week later, Pikey had shut his big gob. We all had.

22

The resupply also brought us something else: a new OC.

Major Featherstone was exhausted. He hadn't had a break since we arrived in Al Amarah, and Ray's death coupled with the frenzy of the last four days had really knocked the remaining energy he had left out of him. Still under heavy protest, he eventually gave in to the Commanding Officer's insistence that he take some leave. It became obvious even to him that he wasn't going to be any use in command for much longer.

Out went Featherstone on the Warriors, and sadly three of my snipers with him too: Ads, DV and H. Their R&R was also long overdue. All three volunteered to stay, but since we had no idea how long this was going to last I told them to go while they still had the chance.

In came Captain Charlie Curry. Up until then, Captain Curry had been the battle group's Operations Officer based in Abu Naji. Of medium build and height, he was in his mid-thirties with short dark hair, tinged with flecks of grey. He smiled a lot, and was generally thought of as a decent bloke. It was only when he actually got stuck into the job at Cimic that we realized what a fantastic leader he was too.

He proved this on his very first morning. After ordering everyone under cover, he walked around the whole compound personally picking up every single blind mortar round we had at that time and throwing them all in the river.

Blinds considerably hindered our movement around Cimic

because you couldn't go anywhere near the bloody things. Just because they hadn't gone off when they'd landed didn't mean they were necessarily duds. The slightest movement could explode them, killing anyone within a 20-yard radius. It was a job that normally had to be done by calling out the ATO from Abu Naji. It was very dangerous, and one of the bravest things I've ever seen an officer do. It was also great leadership – as the man would have known – and won him a lot of friends immediately.

Captain Curry was not a man for all the PC bollocks that I felt had hindered us in the past. He made quick decisions with total confidence, and he let us be as aggressive as we wanted. A breath of fresh air, and the man for the moment.

The new boss bought himself more brownie points with us by insisting on joining Dale who was taking out a fighting patrol that very night.

By day, we battened down the hatches at Cimic. Night was a different matter though. We exploited the darkness to push out fighting patrols around the city to take it back to the enemy whenever we could. The best form of defence is always attack and it was important not to let our opponents feel 100 per cent comfortable on Al Amarah's streets.

There was never a need for a sophisticated plan to have a go at them. Mostly, it was just a case of stealthily creeping up on the OMS's favourite mortar base-plate sites, the places we had coded Gold, Silver and Bronze. You'd be assured of a decent contact with mortar teams setting up or their pickets. Never Zinc though, which was the park opposite the OMS building at Yellow 3. The building now doubled as the uprising's battle HQ and had been so heavily fortified we couldn't get anywhere near it.

To our delight, Captain Curry encouraged as much of this as possible.

'The CO wants us to go out and keep the enemy on their feet. You're the best fighters in the battalion, so let's give these fuckwits a bit of payback, shall we?'

That was despite Curry getting into a dirty great contact on his rookie outing with Dale on the north bank. My snipers saved his arse from the rooftop, so he swiftly found out what we could do for him too. From then onwards on their way back in, the fighting patrols would also raid RPG alley and its offshoots to blunt any night-time assaults being prepared at the time.

Bad news in Al Amarah then was never far away though. The day after Captain Curry's arrival, we got another wheelbarrow load of it.

Private Lee O'Callaghan, a young lad from the battalion's B Company, was shot dead by insurgents in Basra. He wasn't the only casualty of the battle either.

Some Royal Artillery lads got lost after a big ambush on their patrol of Snatches. They were in a right shit state and didn't even know where they were. Our guys went out in the Warriors to find them and ran slap bang into an ambush set up just for them.

The company commander had various bits of his body blown off by an RPG, including some fingers and a chunk of his shoulder. The sergeant major got a bullet in the mouth, and a couple of other blokes got badly hosed down.

Lee had been standing up doing top cover out the back of a Warrior's mortar hatch. He took a single round through the heart, dying very quickly.

Lee was only twenty years old, and Sam, Smudge and H had all been through training with him. He'd died in Basra of all places rather than up here, where the fighting had always been a lot more intense. It brought us all down a peg or two, and reminded us that this uprising had become a very serious business. It was only a week old, and already there would be two spare spaces in the dining hall at Tidworth.

Just like with Ray, the overriding emotion after we heard the grim news wasn't one of fear or panic. It was anger. The more the Mehdi Army killed our own, the more they hardened our resolve. If they wanted a fucking fight, we'd give them one.

The head shed were no different. After Lee's death, an order went out to the whole battle group from Colonel Maer's deputy, Major Toby Walch.

'I want you all to be *considerably* more aggressive,' he said. Major Walch was another one for not pissing about. He'd served in some pretty interesting places and was a true soldier's soldier if ever there was one.

Thanks to the new OC, we were only too happy to oblige.

For months a huge cedar tree fifty metres to the right of the front gate had been pissing us off on the roof. It degraded our view down Tigris Street, but Major Featherstone had always refused me permission to pull it down. I decided to ask Charlie Curry.

'The problem is, sir, it obstructs our view of the lefthand edge of the pontoon bridge. That's a common area the enemy use to approach the compound.'

'Yeah, do it Dan. Get the Warriors to ram it over.'

Top man.

'There's some bits at the back gate that I want to get rid of as well, sir.'

'Do the fucking lot of it. Lives are more important than trees.'

For the first time, we also got permission from Abu Naji to fire high-explosive rounds for the 51mm mortar off Cimic's roof. The condition was it had to be used only as a last resort. Plopping off mini-artillery shells into the city would win us no friends whatsoever.

Our landscape gardening proved timely. As week two of the siege began, the ground attacks on the compound began to get more organized and professional. It was clear that the OMS had begun to have the sense that, to sharpen up their effect, they needed to impose some form of order on the mayhem of different militias. Soon there were heavily armed groups of around thirty coming to have a go. They'd stay for longer, and were a lot harder to deal with.

They also had the use of a lot more of the local buildings. Our neighbours around Cimic had upped and left, either of their own accord to keep their kids alive, or at the end of an OMS sandal. All of them, that is, apart from the poor old family in the corner house. Not even the OMS wanted to be in that unlucky pile of bricks.

The quality of the enemy fighter also changed. We'd killed most of the young looney tunes as well as the crap ones, and the survivors had learnt a thing or two. They stayed behind cover a lot more and used diversion tactics to occupy our fire while they'd get closer elsewhere.

Our hardest job was to locate them. Then you had to flush them out too. For every new burst of fire, the sniper and spotter pairs facing the direction it came from would replay the same conversation.

'Can't see a thing.'

'All right then, where are they most likely going to be? Behind that bush? In that dark shadow there. That's it, put a round in there, see what happens.'

Bang. 'Nope.'

'OK, what about that window?' *Bang.*

'No. I've got it, how about that pile of rubble? How about I put a UGL behind it instead?'

'There they are in those ruins! Firing at us now, shit! Get your fucking head down!' And the rounds would rake the top layer of the sandbags inches from our faces.

We upped our game, however, and whenever we could too. We were stuck in a one-way struggle, and there was no backing down now.

One thing that kept them at bay for thirty-six hours or so was the sudden arrival of fast air. After Abu Naji were forced to go down on bended knee, coalition air commanders agreed to free up jets to carry out 'shows of force' for us. You don't get air assets unless there's a lot of trouble, and they initially didn't believe we needed them. Then a couple of pilots came over and had a look.

Fast air was assigned on call for short time windows, a couple of hours per morning or afternoon. They'd be anything from British Tornadoes, to American, Italian or Dutch F16s. You'd never know in advance. They were never going to drop their 500 or 1000lb bombs as we were right in the middle of a built-up area. In any case, we had no direct comms facility to talk to them – a must for all close air support.

To begin with, the jets were delightfully effective. We'd pass on where we wanted them to go up the chain. Then out of nowhere, a terrifying screech. Two very pointy looking things would suddenly tear across the sky at just 500 feet, practically breaking everybody's eardrums. The enemy shat their pants and legged it in total panic. Even at that height, the jets still sounded like they were low enough to take your head off.

We'd always be able to recognize the RAF because they would fly the lowest, sometimes down to just 100 feet. The planes weren't invulnerable to a lucky bullet, so that took proper balls. The boys greeted whoever came with a barrage of whoops and air punches.

'Yeah, fucking right!' we'd all shout. 'You're gonna get some of that!'

Seeing friends as mean looking as a pair of Tornadoes gave us a cracking morale boost. Sadly, after four or five bombless flybys, the enemy soon realized they weren't actually going to get any of that and their powerful effect waned. After a while, they just tucked their heads down, stuck their fingers in their earholes, and carried on once the jets had passed.

So all we could do was to carry on giving it back quicker and faster. It was imperative our drills stayed one step ahead of the bastards.

I decided to kip on the roof at night. It meant I was half a minute closer to helping the guys out up there if they had to stand to. Desperate to do what they could too, a fair few of the lads started doing the same.

We held it together pretty well for the next few days, but the pressure was eating up huge amounts of mental and physical resources. At this pace, sooner or later, we were going to get tired. Nerves had already begun to fray a little, with the odd fractious comment emerging between platoons. And still the OMS screw tightened.

It wasn't just savvy that the enemy was gaining. It was also accuracy. It was hard to ignore that our shaves were getting closer and closer. It began to feel like only a matter of time before the Al Amarah OMS paid out its first 200-dollar bonus.

Dawn came on Day 10 with me on an L96 in Top Sangar and Oost spotting for me down Tigris Street. Fitz and Sam were in Rooftop. An hour or so later, a heavy weight of

AK fire hit the roof's northern wall; the first attack of the new day.

'Firing point definitely on the north bank,' came the shout down from Fitzy.

'Somewhere among the army camp ruins, I think. Can't see it exactly yet.'

That meant they were quite close, and Fitz needed our help.

'Right, come on, Oost, over to the north wall with me, mate.'

We grabbed our SA80s and crawled out of the sangar. Just after we reached the north wall, a high-calibre mortar round plunged straight down through Top Sangar's corrugated iron roof, and exploded in a deafening flash of light and noise. It blew the thing to fuck. The small space where we had just been perching was peppered from top to bottom with smoking pieces of red-hot shrapnel. The sangar did its job well though, as none of the blast went through its sturdy sandbag walls, saving us from any splinters.

Oost and I sat up against the northern wall stunned, and our ears ringing.

'Holy fucking Mary. That was a close one.'

'Too fucking close.'

Since the rest of the roof was still getting heftily shot at, there wasn't much time for existential contemplation. No point in thinking about it anyway, there was nothing we could have done. We rejoined the firefight, and rebuilt the ruined sangar after dark.

By midday the next day, I was in Cookhouse Sangar spotting for Des while Pikey had run down to eat. It was during a short lull in the attacks so we chewed the cud a little. A few mortars had come in, so we popped our helmets on just in case.

That time, I had no warning at all.

Since a high-velocity round travels 300mph faster than the speed of sound, I felt the wallop of the bullet before I heard it. A hard smack on the back of my helmet, followed a fraction of a second later by the crack of the round being fired, and the shot's echo off the surrounding rooftops. We both ducked right down below the sandbag parapet.

'Shit, Des, what the hell was that?'

'Dunno. You OK?'

It felt like I was. 'I think so.'

Des had been facing me, and worked it out quicker than I did. I'd been shot for a second time.

'One round, so must have been aimed right at you. From over your left shoulder about 200 metres away I think, judging by the sound. Are you hit, man?'

Des poked his periscope over the parapet and scanned the horizon. With no second shot following the first, he poked his long over thirty seconds later. In a state of semi-shock, I took off my helmet to feel for the damage. Again no blood, but a mighty fucking sore head all the same.

'No, can't see any movement either. Whoever he was, he's gone.'

We looked at the helmet. The fucker had been very unlucky, it was a great shot. On its right side was a gouge five centimetres long and one deep. The round must have struck just to the right of the helmet's rear, causing it to shave one side rather than go straight through.

If the slug had impacted ten centimetres further to the left, it would have taken off the top part of my skull, with half my brain probably still attached to it.

Des whistled.

'Fuck, man, you lucky bastard. No wait, you're an unlucky

bastard. You know what, Danny, I don't know what the fuck you are any more.'

Des had a point. That was two extraordinary calls in twenty-four hours. I picked up another sandbag and put it behind my head and stayed with Des until Pikey returned. Then I went back up to the roof and showed Chris my helmet.

'You know what, mate? I think someone's telling you to go downstairs for a bit. Go and get yourself a brew or something. We're fine up here for now, mate, I'll call you when it kicks off again.'

For four days in a row now I hadn't left the rooftop for longer than fifteen minutes and only to eat. Maybe Chris was right, perhaps I had started to lose concentration, and that wasn't good.

I went down to the cookhouse to get a cup of tea. Just off from the kitchen was Corky the Medic's room. I could hear him pottering about in there so I popped in to see how he was.

The room had changed a lot too since I'd last seen it during the ceasefire when I'd had to visit Corky about my viral infection. Corky had turned it into a proper dressing station. Everything was laid out there next to the bed: neck braces, bandages, scissors, scalpels, tweezers, IV drips; the lot.

'Nice place you've got here, Corky.'

'Thanks, Sergeant. Hope I never see you in here again. In a nice way, of course.'

'Funny you should say that really.'

'Why?'

'Doesn't matter.'

Stuffed underneath a sideboard was a big cardboard box with some company's logo stamped on it. I didn't recognize it from my previous visit either. Being a nosy parker, I gave it a little shove. It was heavy.

'What's in there then, Corky?'

'Oh, er, you don't worry about that, mate.'

We both made a start for it. I was nearer than him.

'Easy tiger. Bit of contraband booze do we have here? Don't worry, you can share it all with me.'

'No, mate, it's not. Listen, honestly, don't worry about it . . .'

It was too late. I already had a paw inside it and had got a hold of whatever it contained. Out came something folded up and made out of a rubbery nylon material, but unusually dense and thick. As I unfolded the thing, I saw there was a zip on it too.

'Oi, oi! Is this your gimp suit then, Corky? You filthy little bugger.'

Then I realized what it really was, and stopped dead in my tracks. A body bag.

Fuck.

'They delivered a whole load of them during the last resupply,' Corky explained. 'Sorry. I did try to tell you.'

Well, that was a nice touch. Someone somewhere thought we'd obviously be needing a few of these as our early transport home. The discovery did little for my mood, so I left sharpish.

Poor old Corky. He had a tough deal in that room. All his trauma kit was clearly carefully looked after and ready to go. That's because he knew he might be called upon at any moment to do every single thing he could to save our lives. But he also knew if all his efforts failed, he had a second job. To bag, tag and watch over our dead bodies.

*

The battle group knew it had to go into Al Amarah and do something about the uprising's increasing intensity. If not a knockout blow, then something if only for the sake of it. For the Warriors to keep sitting back in Abu Naji while the OMS ran amok looked weak and gave the OMS a propaganda boost. In Cimic, we were also beginning to crave a respite, even if only for twelve hours or so just to take the consistent pressure off for a little bit.

On Day 10 of the siege, the day of my close call in Top Sangar, Operation Hammersmith was launched.

The enemy was now considered too strong for the battle group to be able to retake all the town's police stations and then, crucially, hold them as we'd done in May. Instead, a full-on offensive on the Aj Dayya estate was launched. We knew that's where most of the OMS's most effective manpower was based. If a fair few of its key players were taken out, it would surely help to lance the angry boil.

Under darkness and in the early hours again, the plan was to punch into the city with four Challenger IIs, then encircle Aj Dayya with a ring of steel made up by C Company's fourteen Warriors. Finally, the Royal Welch Fusiliers would carry out a series of search and arrest operations. In a rare triumph of persuasion, we were given Spectre on call for the first three hours.

This time, Sniper Platoon was restricted to overwatch where we could from Cimic. Charlie Curry wisely judged that the basic defence of the compound couldn't spare us if a massive counterattack came its way.

What we missed we were only too glad to.

The column came in and, as everyone from the CO downwards had expected, it got properly creamed.

Along with Captain Curry and the company's other platoon commanders, I spent most of the battle in the Ops

Room trying to keep track of the carnage going on all over the city.

Redders shouted out the vehicle crews' snatched radio messages as he heard them over the net. One of the first set the battle's grim tone.

'Lead Challenger now immobilized. Twelve RPG direct hits.'

Jesus. Until then, we'd thought our main battle tanks were unstoppable. But there was worse.

'Warrior call sign Whisky 28 in such deep shit. In a dead end with enemy all around it. Calling in a danger close strike from Spectre now.'

Danger close means dire straits, and we all knew the chances were they were going to catch a bit of the Spectre's cannonfire themselves. There was a tense silence in the Ops Room for two minutes as all eyes fixed on Redders.

'Whisky 28 OK,' he finally said to a group exhale in relief. 'Extracting now.'

Somehow they had got away with it.

Many others hadn't though. A total of five Warriors were also lost with enormous battle damage throughout the operation, and there were six serious casualties.

The whole thing lasted twenty-three hours, almost double the time planned. All call signs from the battle group including those inside Cimic were contacted by the enemy no less than 103 times that day – a modern record for the British Army.

It was also appallingly hard and hot work. The entire crew and dismounts of another sorry Warrior went down as heatstroke casualties and had to go back to base early, vomiting and slurring their words.

As for the operation's outcome, nobody could say it was anything more than a score draw for each side. The pluses were that a lot of enemy were killed. With the armour drawing them off us, we also got our little respite. It was just miraculous again that in the most intense furnace of combat, no British soldiers had been lost.

On the downside, one or two bad boys were arrested but a lot more weren't home. We also knew we wouldn't be getting Spectre again in a hurry with the conflict in Najaf still going at full tilt.

Worst of all, the thorough pasting the column got had confirmed our fears: we couldn't rely on a resupply any more because the Warriors were no longer guaranteed to get through to us. Effectively, we were on our own.

Then, the day got even worse. A double whammy was waiting for us in Captain Curry's O Group.

'I'm afraid it's the bad news, then the really bad news tonight, guys. A 21-year-old private from the Black Watch was killed earlier today in Basra. Roadside IED, followed up by small arms fire ambush.

'Unfortunately, what's happening in Najaf right now makes the loss of that poor sod pale into insignificance. The US Marines have gone and done us no favours what-soever today.'

In their bid to crush Moqtada with an iron fist, the US Marines had surrounded and sealed off Najaf's Old City, putting the ultra-precious Imam Ali mosque fully under siege. Moqtada and the rebels barricaded themselves inside it. Then a Marine artillery shell damaged two of the mosque's golden minarets and hurled shrapnel into its courtyard.

Meanwhile, all of this was being pumped live into every Al Amarah sitting room courtesy of Al Jazeera TV. Moqtada had seen to that. Tactfully, he added: 'The final battle for humanity has begun.'

We knew we'd feel the backlash the next day, if not later

that night. Our position in Cimic was balanced on a knife edge, thanks yet again to events elsewhere controlled by our 'coalition partners'. Worse, there wasn't a damn thing we could do about any of it.

We were just holding out against the insurgency's current level of force and violence. But if the Yanks went into the mosque, it would effectively mobilize most of the male population of southern Iraq. In Al Amarah, they would descend on Cimic House like killer flies on cow shit.

Sure, we'd kill truckloads of them as they tried to get over the walls. But we couldn't kill thousands; we simply didn't have enough bullets. If the Challengers and Warriors didn't get through then, we would soon be overrun.

Charlie Curry's final bit of O Group news: the whole miserable day had been Moqtada al-Sadr's thirty-first birthday. I only hoped he choked to death on his cake.

23

As it turned out, we got our first vote of no confidence the next morning from our own Iraqi workers inside Cimic. Just watching Al Jazeera overnight proved enough for them. No matter what else was to happen in Najaf, they had decided our time was already up.

I was in the Ops Room discussing our ammo supply with Captain Curry when Daz ran in.

'Danny, sir; you've got to come and have a look at this. It's something else.'

Daz led us out to the balcony that overlooked the back gate, the entrance the locals used. There below us were the interpreters, the two laundry men, the gardener, the cleaners, the water plant operators and its guards. They were going backwards and forwards from the abandoned accommodation blocks to the gate in two lines like ants.

Poised precariously in their arms or over their shoulders were washing machines, spin dryers, air conditioning units, mattresses, shelves, bedside cabinets, TVs. Then they came back for second helpings. They were having away everything and anything that wasn't bolted down. It wasn't just that they were nicking our stuff, but they were doing it in broad daylight and right in front of our very eyes. Rasheed the porn merchant even waved at me with a smile when he saw us looking down.

It meant one very obvious thing. They no longer gave a ha'penny if they got fired because they were convinced there soon wouldn't be anybody left to pay them anyway. Like all good Arabs, they weren't going to let a good business opportunity pass them by. They were taking what they could, then and there, while they still had the chance.

'Cheeky bastards!'

'Like rats abandoning a sinking ship.'

'Fuck them,' said Captain Curry, shaking his head. 'Most of that stuff is so badly fragged it's no use to us anyway. Sooner they're all out of here the better.'

He was right. Nobody had any interest in doing any washing and spin drying right then. Having Iraqis inside the camp was also no longer a great idea either. We couldn't trust any of them. After the morning's plunder, none of them came back. But two had the brass neck to ask for that day's wages.

They'd done us a favour anyway. When the frequency of attacks against us inevitably increased that day with the new developments in Najaf, Curry ordered the disposal of any loose obstacles about the compound. Anything that we might trip over while sprinting from A to B, or that could become secondary shrapnel underneath explosions. Patio chairs, the table tennis table and the gym equipment all went over the wall for locals to scavenge.

The day was filled by fresh calls of 'Allah Akbar' from around the surrounding streets. Sniper fire on us from the old town's rooftops increased to pretty much constant and the rebels turned up with renewed vigour to discharge whatever arms they had at us. From then onwards, we stopped going out at night.

Events in Najaf had perched southern Iraq on the edge of an awfully steep precipice. After smashing up the minarets, the Yanks were for the moment holding back from a full storming of the Imam Ali mosque. Nobody knew for how long though. Neither did it stop them from issuing ever more incendiary threats against Moqtada and the Mehdi Army on an almost daily basis.

For his part, Moqtada had ordered his offices all over the nation to empty their coffers and secure the services of as many combatants as possible. Intelligence came through that young men were now being paid as much as US$50 a day to fight the coalition; a king's ransom.

Added to that, we heard that many of the new recruits to the jihad in Al Amarah were also high as a kite. OMS leaders were feeding them with a lethal combination of amphetamines and opiates that made their brains tell them they were invisible. Then they let them loose on us.

We were now so busy that the platoon's system of shifts on the roof became irrelevant. If everyone wasn't stood-to together at any given time, then the likelihood was they would be soon enough. Instead, I sent a pair or two down for a couple of hours' kip during a lull. When they came back, another lot would go down. If they were unlucky, it would be only five minutes before someone screamed 'Stand-to' again.

The other platoons would be doing the same around the rest of the camp: in the sangars, on the lower balconies or at the two Warriors. With the adrenalin kicking in the moment you woke, an hour or two of sleep a day was all we actually needed. Your body gets used to replenishing itself in the time it has. Nobody really needs eight hours' sleep. It's a bad civilian habit.

· At that stage, the drug-addled loonies we could handle. However, the OMS were also training up dozens more mortar teams to ramp up their endless bombardment on us. That made things far worse. The sheer volume of stuff they began to lob in was just unbelievable. Between 11 and 13 August alone, 400 separate mortar rounds were launched on Cimic House – an average of one every eleven minutes for three full days in a row.

Mortar shells arrived from everywhere, a 360-degree spread around us. The problem was still Cimic's water tower, as you could see it from all over the city. With the crews' work uninterrupted as we were no longer out on the streets, a decent aiming point was all they needed. We even discussed blowing the water tower up, but we couldn't be sure it wouldn't fall on the house.

The only thing that gave us even half a chance was the pop of the shell's launch. That meant we had five or six seconds to hurl ourselves into cover during its flight time. Then *boom*; and fuck, another close one.

That amount of incoming, far more than we'd ever seen in May or June, began to unnerve even our steeliest soldiers.

'I wish these fuckers would give us a break,' even Des conceded. 'Why don't they just go and shag their ugly bitch wives for a while instead?'

In May it had been exciting. Now we all knew the huge increase in volume also hugely increased our chances of getting hit. People being dead made a difference too. It reminded us of our own mortality.

Nerves started to jangle. A strict ban was imposed on doors being slammed. Any big bang was making the more jittery like Redders jump out of their fucking skin.

Yet again though, and through it all, I never once failed to get a single volunteer to go up to Rooftop or Cookhouse Sangars, the most exposed and dangerous places in the whole compound. Quite the opposite, I had to order people out of there to give someone else a turn. This was the calibre of the boys.

It certainly took mental strength to do that. Each person

275

would have been having his own private conversation with himself. I know I did. This is how it went:

'This is shit awful unpleasant. Yes, but hold on, this is what I'm actually here for. I'm going to fucking do this. I've got a uniform on, and I'm going to rise above it.'

You have to harness the fear and just go with it, use it to your advantage. We were snipers, we always get the shit jobs. Fucking deal with it.

It was all the more important for me not to show any fear. As a commander, it's vital you set a good lead. If you do, and you've got your blokes' trust, you can be sure they'll follow you most places. But it wasn't really about me. What really made everyone stick it out was the fact that we were all in it together. Nobody wanted to be the one to let the group down. Keeping your end up for everyone else became much more important than the fear of physical injury. If you had to die, it would be right beside your best mates anyway.

Oost put it well to Des.

'Look at it like this, brother. If you buy it, the chances are I'm going to buy it with you. Then think, you can spot for me in the sky.'

'Fucking awesome, man!'

If we were all still strong mentally, the same could no longer be said for Cimic physically. The heavens shitting down high explosives and shrapnel like rain was taking its toll. The place had begun to collapse.

Dozens of unexploded mortar blinds now littered the camp. The ones on main pathways that seriously hindered movement were all marked up on the Ops Room white board. It was now far too risky for Charlie Curry to do another of his walk rounds.

More Snatches in the vehicle park got fragged beyond

repair. A civilian Land Rover Discovery for the Civil–Military Cooperation (CIMIC) unit's use also took a direct hit right through the roof. That was going to piss off some pencil neck in the MoD.

There was barely a window in the main house that hadn't been blown in or badly cracked. Every day we seeped lower into a squalid cesspit. Among the first things to go were the satellite dishes on the roof, so no more telly, Internet or phone calls home. None of that mattered a jot. But when the water and electricity started to go off for six-hour bursts, things were getting a bit more serious.

No one could wash properly. All but one of the Porta-kabins had been blown up, so the only water supply left apart from the bottled drinking water was a tap on the back wall of the house. When it was working, you could put your head under it.

For peeing and pooing, there were just the two toilets in the house itself for more than 100 blokes. One was an Arab drop hole, the other a sit-down porcelain number. When the water was off they didn't flush, so you'd just have to do your business on top of the bloke's who'd been in before you. Six hours of no water and the shit really stacked up.

We stopped bothering going down from the roof for a piss. Going up and down the ladder was too dangerous. Instead, we filled up empty two-litre plastic water bottles and emptied them out later. More than once, blokes in a rush at night took a bloody great big gulp from a urine-filled bottle mistaking its contents for water. In that heat, all liquids were at the same lukewarm body temperature.

Fresh food supplies were also running out fast. To conserve what was left and cut down on movement again, the cookhouse went down to producing just one cooked meal a day in the evening. Breakfast and lunch were out of ration boxes.

Everyone was also sleeping like tramps now. Very rarely did you ever sleep in the same place on any consecutive night. A few bunk beds had been salvaged from the accommodation blocks, but if none of them was free, you'd go for an armchair or a sofa, or otherwise just curl up where you could on the floor. If you didn't wear a head torch while moving around at night, you'd step on twenty bodies in the corridor.

When the Ops Room staff finished their long shifts, their desks became their beds, and someone else would kip on the floor beneath them. The CIMIC guys' lives had become totally meaningless with the uprising, so they had their offices torn up underneath them to make way for a little more precious living space.

With all that toil, sweat and closeness, the place properly stank.

Then there was the August heat. We didn't think it was possible for it to get any hotter than July, but it did. On bad days, the temperature even hit 60°C. That's fucking potty heat. No matter how long we'd been there, we were never going to acclimatize fully to that. We drank litres more water, but were still losing the same amount of body fluids. Salt deprivation meant more attacks of cramp in sniper fire positions, and that got properly painful.

All in all, by the end of the siege's second week we were in need – desperate need – of any form of relief.

We got it.

Captain Curry had mentioned to me that there might be another sniper pair coming our way from somewhere. When they turned up one day in the middle of a big firefight, it was totally out of the blue. Nobody quite worked out how they'd got there either; not even Captain Curry.

I was over in the Pink Palace when I got a call on the PRR to come up to the Ops Room. Curry wanted to see me.

'Oh, hi Dan, thanks for coming over. I want you to meet these two chaps. They're a sniper pair from the . . .' he paused, as if considering the options, then continued, 'er, the Royal Marines. They've come to help us out here for a little bit.'

The first bloke extended his hand. He was in his late twenties, clean shaven, with mousy blond hair and a West Country accent. His haircut was the normal regulation short back and sides and he wore the usual British military combat fatigues.

'Hi, Marine John Withers.'

Then the second stepped forward.

'Hello, mate, I'm Buzz.' He was a cockney.

Interesting. First name only. And Buzz didn't wear any rank either.

'Dan Mills. Good to meet you.'

Buzz looked nothing like us. He was older and shorter than John, in his thirties and stood at about five foot seven, as well as unshaven, with at least three days' stubble. He looked scruffy, with just a dark T-shirt on and a thin blue flak jacket over it, and a pair of civvy boots that weren't desert coloured. In fact, the only military thing he had on was a very dirty pair of desert combat trousers.

It took me about five seconds to work out he wasn't Royal Marines. Might have been once, but not any more. He also carried a bloody great valise over his shoulder that was almost as tall as him and looked extremely heavy. *What was in that?*

279

Despite Buzz's appearance, both men were very polite and professional.

'Can you give us a bit of a show around? We'd be grateful,' said Buzz.

'Pleasure.' I was happy to have any help we could get.

Chris and I showed them all the positions we were using, and gave them a visual tour of the city from the roof. Buzz asked if it was OK if they worked from Rooftop Sangar.

'Be my guest, mate, shoot from wherever you want.'

'Thanks.'

'Just one thing. John is, but you're not Royal Marines, are you.'

Buzz just smiled. I'd come across a few of his type in my time. Always the same. They don't say, and you don't push them. You don't need to. Everybody knows the game.

Buzz had come down from Baghdad. He was a sergeant with his unit. He was too polite to say it, but it was obvious to us that for him Al Amarah was just some shit hole of a town he'd never heard of in the middle of nowhere. Compared with what he was used to doing, he must have been expecting to be bored off his tits. When the call came in, there'd been no other volunteers to go south with him from the unit. Instead, a regular Royal Marine had been collared for the job of being his Number Two instead.

'The common conception in Baghdad is there's fuck all going on here,' Buzz explained.

'Is it now? Terrific.'

Buzz had been brought in for a specific reason. Our longs had a range of up to 1,000 metres. Any target further away than that, and we were just pissing in the wind. Literally, because the smallest gust would blow the round off trajectory at that distance.

That put a lot of places the enemy loved to use out of

our range. The bus depot on the north bank was 1,200 metres away, and the Yellow 3 junction right by the OMS building was at 1,700 metres. It was infuriating, because we could spot them running around up to no good but were powerless to stop them.

Someone in Abu Naji had good connections with his unit, and had put in a request for one of their sniper pairs because of the additional range of the weapons they use.

We explained the problem to Buzz.

'OK, roger that. We'll see what we can do for you.'

Up at Rooftop, they unpacked their kit. They had two grip bags with them. One was full of ammunition. Out of the second came some whopping great big sights and two pairs of ear defenders. That meant only one thing.

Buzz finally unsheathed his valise. And there it was. A .5-inch calibre Barrett sniper rifle.

Oh fucking yes.

I'd seen a Barrett before, but never fired one. It was known in the trade as the big bad mother of the whole sniper rifle family. Weighing a whopping 14 kilograms (or more than two stone), it measures five feet from the end of its specially designed square-shaped stock to the tip of the thickly grooved muzzle.

It was designed by the Americans primarily for use on the battlefield to take out armoured vehicles; drivers or the engine blocks, it did for both. It was also excellent for destroying enemy inside strong defensive positions such as sangars.

The weapon took rounds the same size as the Soviet-made Dshke heavy machine guns that had cut us up so badly on patrol with the OPTAG sergeants. The regular army uses .5 calibre Browning machine guns too, but only on a heavy tripod or welded to the roll bars of Land Rovers.

The Barrett has an accurate range of at least 2,000 metres, and sometimes further still. Simply, the more gunpowder there is in the bullet, the faster and further it will fly. You can only use them in a static position because it's too bloody heavy to carry around on patrol. The IRA had a Barrett in Northern Ireland, and used to fire it from inside a specially modified car boot. They wreaked havoc with it for a few years on isolated army patrols in bandit country.

Buzz's toy was going to do us a whole load of favours, and we were chuffed to bits just at the very sight of the thing.

First, he put down a couple of zeroing shots into some rubble on the dam to make sure the journey hadn't screwed up his sight settings. That's when we really understood the need for the ear defenders. Hearing it fire was a joy in itself. It made a deafening boom like a miniature artillery piece, and gave off an echo that lasted a good ten seconds. A big puff of dust erupted from the sandbag wall underneath the thing, and the whole wooden sangar quaked on its foundations. From that moment onwards, we dubbed it 'the Beast'.

'Fucking hell, man, that thing's awesome,' whispered Chris.

'Tell me about it. Imagine what one of them slugs would do to an OMS man's guts, eh?'

'What guts. Put a round through his kidneys and he could stick his hand through his body to wipe his arse.'

Neither of us wanted to look unprofessional in front of Buzz and John, but it was damn hard to conceal our excited giggling.

The pair didn't have to wait long for their first long-distance kill.

That afternoon, they spotted what must have been a senior

OMS man standing on a rooftop right at the back of the bus depot. He was coordinating a group of gunmen having a hefty go at us from the north bank and an AK47 was slung across the front of his body.

Sitting next to them, I followed the shoot through the sights of my L96.

The target was at least 1,600 metres away – the equivalent of sixteen football pitches placed end to end. It was right on the limit of my eyesight in the heat mirage, even through my Schmidt and Bender sight. I had to strain to make the guy out.

Buzz fired. The round impacted right on the firing mechanism of his AK. Then a technicolour explosion of blood and flesh. Simultaneously, the man went flying backwards out of his flipflops like he was a puppet on strings, and straight off the back of the other side of the roof. No more senior OMS man.

It was the first of a good handful of kills that afternoon. The insurgency's increasing mayhem provided no shortage of targets. Buzz was loving it.

'Fuck me. I thought it was supposed to be quiet down here. Is it like this all the time, Dan?'

'Yup.'

'Bloody excellent. This is proper war fighting down here, you know?'

'Yes we do, mate.'

'We don't get any of this sort of work in Baghdad. If only the guys knew what they're missing now. They'll be gutted when I tell them about it.'

At midnight after a good twelve-hour session, Buzz and John announced they were going to get their heads down for a bit. They'd been travelling overnight, and, amazingly, the Beast actually seemed to have quietened things down just a fraction in the city. There was one mean new bastard in town and they all knew it. The noise of the Beast alone was enough for the OMS brass to sit back and ask themselves what the hell we'd got our hands on. Then there was the damage it did to their men who'd got on the wrong end of it.

'I'll leave my rifle up here,' said Buzz as he got up. 'So any of your lads can use it if a long-range target pops up. Don't be shy with it, she's a real beauty.'

No danger of that, matey.

'Use this bag of ammunition.'

He chucked over a tightly cross-squared bag fastened by a draw cord. It reminded me of the old bags you used to keep your plimsolls in at school. We respectfully waited until they'd got at least as far as the stairs down into the house. Then, as soon as they were out of earshot, we were like little kids in a sweet shop.

'Oi, Danny, pass the Beast over here,' whispered Smudge immediately. He was salivating to have his photo taken while firing it. 'They did say don't be shy.'

'Fuck off, Smudger. I'm the boss here, and anyway – you're not qualified to use it.'

– A cheap trick, but true. And the only time in my whole career that I've ever relished quoting poxy army red tape. Since Chris was also qualified to use such a marvellous weapon as the Beast, I justified us a few practice shots just in case we did need to have a go at any long-range targets.

And marvellous she truly was.

In every sense, the Beast gave off one hell of a kick. If you didn't grip it good and hard, it could recoil off your shoulder blade and smack you in the face hard enough to crack your jawbone. Also, you'd be deaf for ten minutes without the ear defenders. Chris and I put a couple of rounds into the giant metal leg supports of Yugoslav Bridge. They made a terrific row just rocketing around off its different struts.

While Smudge posed for his snaps, I had a poke around Buzz's plimsoll bag. There were three different types of round in there: the normal 'full metal jacket' brass ball rounds (like our green spot but a shit load bigger), some with tips painted yellow and red, and a third lot with tips painted grey.

'Right, give us the Beast back over here. I want to know what these yellow and red ones do.'

I popped one into the chamber, pulled the cocking bolt back, and let it fly at the bridge again. On impact, it gave off a big bright yellow ball of light. Excellent. They were flash-tips, to illuminate the target so you could see where your rounds were hitting at very long distance.

Oost and Des were awe-struck, and watched every move-ment I made like two obedient little puppy dogs.

'Try a grey one, Danny,' suggested Des.

'Yeah, let's see what the grey ones do.'

I popped a grey one off. *Boom*. It impacted on the bridge with a bloody great explosion.

Des was beside himself. 'Wow, man! What the fuck was that bad boy?'

I had a good idea. I took aim at a car that someone had abandoned on top of the bridge. It had been bothering us there anyway. OMS fighters could use it as cover to shoot at us. At least that was my excuse.

Boom!

The round piled straight through the engine casing and exploded somewhere in the middle of the block, causing a small fire to ignite. Yes. They were armour-piercing.

'Awesome, man, awesome!' They were Des's new favourites.

An armour-piercing round fired from a Barrett would punch through steel with some ease. Its greatly strengthened casing and specially shaped nose do the initial damage, before the bursting charge encased within its body finishes the job.

Chris and I popped a good dozen more grey rounds through the abandoned car until we found its petrol tank. Then it properly exploded and burnt down into just a shell we could easily see through. No more hiding behind that.

Buzz was back up at dawn.

'By the sound of things, you had a decent turn on the rifle last night, eh? I forgot to tell you, don't use the grey-tipped rounds. They're armour-piercing and they're really expensive.'

Oops.

'Ah, right. Sorry, Buzz, might be a little late for that . . .'

Buzz and John fitted in very well on the roof. By and large, they worked to their own remit and picked out their own opportunity targets. They didn't need me to spoonfeed them anything. That was their discipline and expertise, and it was fine by me.

Buzz didn't tell us much about what he did elsewhere. Out of respect we didn't ask. It was enough for us just to know they were there with the Beast. They certainly made life a bit more difficult for the enemy's hordes. After a few days of death-by-Beast, the OMS coordinators learnt to get their heads down and were forced to go about their warfare in subtler ways.

But the one thing Buzz and John couldn't do much about was the mortars. Incoming shells were still our most perilous threat, and they hadn't let up one bit. No matter how deadly the Beast's rounds were, they still couldn't go through two sides of a thick concrete building, and that's where the mortar crews knew to set up their base plates.

Around the middle of week three, we seriously started to feel the pinch of their endless projectiles. Power was totally knocked out. One mortar round destroyed the big outdoor generator with a direct hit, and a second sliced straight through the underground connection to the local electricity grid. All we had left was the Ops Room's emergency petrol generator that was just strong enough to power its essential radio equipment.

The tap water supply then dried up altogether, either from mortar damage or because the OMS turned it off; we never discovered which. Blokes started to use the bottled water for shaving as it's part of army standing orders. Then it was realized we were in danger of running low on that too, so all shaving was knocked on the head. We all started to look like Buzz.

A lot of the bottled water supply was being lost to shrapnel damage, as the crates were always stacked along one side of Cimic. To preserve the rest, it was all brought inside the house to be stored away safely under stairs or in any secure cubby hole we could find. In that heat, it was just as important to us as bullets; and it would soon become more valuable to us than liquid gold.

Chef's luck finally ran out too.

24

It happened one evening when Recce Platoon were at full-on scoff mode in the cookhouse. Full credit to Chef, despite the appalling levels of incoming he'd still got a hot meal out for 100 blokes once a day, every day, working under just his green field tent with no other cover. When mortar barrages started, he'd have to peg it back into the cookhouse and wait it out there. If that meant his food got burnt, he'd have to chuck it all out and start all over again.

Recce were ravenous after a tense day in the sangars.

'Any more chips, Chef?' someone asked.

'Yeah, just put some on. Give us a sec, I'll just go and get them.'

A minute after he left, a new mortar barrage struck up. Twelve shells later, he still wasn't back.

'Where are those bleeding chips then, Chef?' the greedy bastard shouted.

They heard his screams then. He'd been hit by the barrage's first round. It had come straight through the roof of the tent as he was leaving it with a big baking tray of chips in his hand. A nasty lump of shrapnel had torn straight through his leg just below the knee. It was hanging off him by little more than just the skin.

Chef lost a hell of a lot of blood, but Corky managed to save his leg.

After that, we were all down to eating just hard rations from the emergency supplies. Chef's emergency kitchen had been blown to fuck now too. That meant nothing but boil in the bag meals. They tasted a lot better when thrown into our 'all-in' stews brewed up on a camping stove in a corridor, with a good dollop of Tabasco sauce.

To conserve it, all our ammunition was also pooled. Our stocks were depleting, and fast. Until then, each multiple commander had supervised his own stocks. Instead, all the ammo was called in and stored in a windowless room off the Ops Room. That way, we knew it was safe from incoming. Dale could keep an eye on how fast it was going down, and everyone knew where it was if they needed it in a hurry.

Sleep deprivation was now also becoming a somewhat serious problem. During lulls in fighting, soldiers from all the Y Company platoons were starting to fall asleep at their posts, no matter how hard they tried to fight against it.

In a bid to ease the pressure on the company and give the lads a chance of some rest, Captain Curry ordered the CIMIC guys into the sangars as well. That meant Major Ken Tait's lot. There were less than twenty of them, a lot were warrant officers and captains, and almost all were TA. Their job was to administer the reconstruction of Maysan, and most had spent the whole tour at their desks. They came from a huge hotchpotch of regiments: Highlanders, sappers, loggies, and Adjutant General's Corps largely. Back home, they were clerks, bank managers and solicitors. One was even a millionaire record producer. From that moment onwards, however, they were poor bloody infantry, like it or not. Here's a weapon, now go and fucking use it.

Captain Curry assigned them two-hour stints in the middle of the night when the attacks normally died down a little.

On their first night out, Pikey got a bit cruel.

'Hey hey! Look, here comes fucking Dad's Army.'

Admittedly, it was funny to watch them, looking all white

289

and pasty faced to us, venture desperately nervously out to their assigned positions for the first time. Most hadn't fired a round in anger their whole civilized lives, let alone on that tour.

But credit where credit's due, most fought when they had to with just the same tenacity as the rest of us. The millionaire record producer, who showed particular balls, even said he was pleased he could finally stand up and be counted having watched us do all the defending so far. And at the head of the lot of them and always spurring them on with steely Glaswegian growls was Ken Tait. Without fail, a Benson and Hedges permanently smouldered on his lower lip as he prowled the walls. Inside, he'd been a coiled spring. Outside, he was in his element.

It was ironic, but just about the only thing the OMS's umpteen mortar rounds still hadn't destroyed was the Iraqi flag on Cimic's roof. It still fluttered proudly on its pole – shredded a little maybe, and the white part was now grey with soot, but still very much there. We didn't give a shit about it at first. Then it became a talking point, and after a new barrage someone would always have a peak out of a sangar to see if they'd finally nailed it or not.

'Flag's still there.'

'Still? After that lot?'

'Yeah.'

'Blimey.'

The day after the first Dad's Army show, we were treated to something really special.

As well as the Beast, Buzz had another pretty smart string to his bow. The time had come to use it.

That morning, we took two more direct hits from mortar rounds on the roof, leaving two more crumbled concrete craters covered in nasty scorch marks. Everyone had managed to get their heads down in the sangars before the hot shrapnel shards had zipped off in every direction. But it had been uncomfortably close. One of the flying embers had smacked into the barrel of one of the boys' longs, putting it – and almost him – permanently out of action. Both rounds had come from Zinc, the big park opposite the OMS building.

It was their best mortar base plate spot by far. Annoyingly, they were getting more and more rounds on target from there every day. It was also a piece of piss for them to use. They'd come straight out of the OMS building and set up in permanent pits already dug in the grass.

The Beast couldn't touch them because a big white ware-house three-quarters of the way down Tigris Street on the riverbank obscured our entire view of the park.

I let out an idle thought.

'Fuck, it would be nice to go down there and take those bastards on with a big stick.'

That plunged Buzz into thought.

'How far is it from the park to the nearest buildings, Danny?'

'Depends where in the park. A good hundred metres or so. Maybe three hundred at the furthest point.'

'That should be far enough.'

'Why?'

'To avoid collateral damage.'

Buzz looked up from the Beast's sight and turned to face me.

'I can bring some air down on that fucking place, you know.'

As with all soldiers of his ilk, Buzz had the knowhow to call in close air support. He had also brought down from

Baghdad the radio and frequencies he would need to do that.

It didn't take long to persuade Abu Naji to authorize the bombing. Zinc was bang in the middle of a crowded city that was home to a third of a million people. On any normal tour, an air strike on a place like that would have been totally unthinkable. This wasn't any normal tour. Our time was also running out.

Since it was unlikely that there would be kids picnicking in there with their mums while the Mehdi Army was hurling mortars out of it, Zinc was declared a legitimate air target.

The fast air request for that night went in to coalition air command. At sunset, the message came back that we'd have six jets on call; three pairs of two. They'd last us the whole night. Now all we needed was for the OMS crew to turn up.

We got smacked by base plates in a lot of places in town that night, but none of them was in Zinc. Surely the OMS hadn't picked the one night we had something big to hurt them with to have their annual summer barbecue? That would be just our luck. In all my born days I never thought I'd ever pray to get mortared. That night I did.

My prayers were answered. Just after 1 a.m., a barrage rocketed up at us from right in the middle of Zinc. It was heavy stuff too: another 82mm tube.

We were on.

The Ops Room told Abu Naji and Buzz switched on his radio gear. Half an hour later, his radio came to life. The voice had an English accent.

'Hello, Buzz? Buzz, are you reading me?'

'Is that you up there, Jimbo?'

'Yes, mate, it is.'

Buzz and this bloke Jimbo obviously knew each other so well they didn't even bother using their official call signs. First name terms. Simple. Jimbo was the air controller in an RAF Nimrod MR2 spy plane. That meant he was probably from the same unit too. The Nimrod was somewhere in the night sky up there above us, cruising at an altitude of around 25,000 feet.

'Oh, you took your fucking time getting here. There's a war on down here, you know, Jimbo.'

'Sorry, mate, we came up from the Gulf. What can we do for you then?'

At that very moment, another crump erupted out of Zinc. The team had begun their second barrage.

'Did you catch that one, Jimbo? Directly south from our position, about one point seven klicks.'

'Yeah, copy that. We're on to it. Six mobile heat sources moving around a static one. That will be the mortar tube. I can see you too now, Buzz, if that's you in that highest sangar. Ugly as ever, I see.'

Amazing. We couldn't even hear the bloody Nimrod. The wonders of modern technology.

'Wait out for a few minutes, Buzz. I'm tasking the fast air now. By the way, they're putting another round down the barrel now.'

'OK, thanks.'

Three seconds later, we heard the crump.

Buzz had done his bit. From then onwards it was over to Jimbo to bring the jets on to the base plate in Zinc.

Now this was a major event for us at Cimic. During major engagements, the Ops Room makes a point of keeping everyone informed of what's going on over the PRRs. As far as we were all concerned, an air strike qualified as a major engagement. Word of it had already spread like wildfire

293

around the compound long before anything was ever mentioned over the PRRs.

It was close to 2 a.m., but the whole of the house was wide awake. There were blokes craning out of every window on its southern side trying to catch a glimpse of something. The entirety of Sniper Platoon had crammed into the two roof sangars. Mortar barrage or not, there were people hanging off the fucking chandeliers to see this.

It wasn't just Y Company either. We later found out that anyone in Abu Naji who could get to a VHF had done so once they heard there was an air strike on. The general call sign when a message goes out to all ranks is recognized across the British Army as Charlie Charlie One.

'Charlie Charlie One, be advised. Fast air coming is two F16s,' said Redders from the Ops Room across our PRRs.

'F16s? Oh yes!' yelped Rob Green. 'Come on son, bring it on.'

In Top Sangar below us were Rob and Smudge. Rob had unfortunately lost his cool totally by then. So had Smudge.

Rob was a full screw in the platoon. A course had kept him behind in England and he'd only joined the tour in July. He was normally a quiet and consummate professional. That night he was a snot-gobbling adolescent just like the rest of us. He had decided to video the whole thing from start to finish on his digital camera.

For Smudge's benefit, Rob also insisted on launching into a speech on everything he knew about the aircraft the moment it was identified. It wasn't much.

'F16 Fighting Falcon, Smudge. That's the fastest jet in the world. They fly off carriers in the Gulf. They can see everything. They've got the heat-seeking fucking shit and all.'

'Fucking awesome,' replied Smudge in wonder.

'Charlie Charlie One. Target acquired.'

'Hah! Did you hear that Smudge? Target acquired!'

'Oh, come on, please do it. Pleeeease.'

Every new burst of information sent the two of them into an ever more frenzied ecstasy. We still couldn't hear any sound of the jets at all though.

Crump. Barrage number three from Zinc had started. It was a good one too. Rounds started to come in quite tightly around the house. We didn't give a fuck. We'd all have taken a direct hit on our sangar as long as we were allowed to live long enough to see the bomb drop.

'Danny, Ops Room. Are there any vehicles near the target?'

I had a look through the Beast's sight. Tigris Street was totally empty. So was Yellow 3, as well as the bridge that led from it over to Red 11. Before the CO in Abu Naji could give specific clearance for an F16 to engage, he had to be as sure as he could that they weren't going to fry any civilians.

'Ops Room, Danny. That is a negative. No traffic in the area at all . . .'

Crump.

'. . . also tell Abu Napa the target is still very much live. Tell them they are clear to engage right now.'

Abu Naji didn't need to ask twice. They'd learnt by then that our word from the roof was as good as gospel. We'd earned that reputation the hard way over a long hot summer. The CO didn't make us wait very long. The next message from Redders came just ten seconds later.

'Charlie Charlie One. Weapons cleared for release.'

The CO had given the green light. The F16 pilot went to work.

'Charlie Charlie One. He has eyes on the target. Commencing bombing run now.'

Buzz leaned out of the sangar to speak to Rob and Smudge.

'Eh, boys, watch this. You're gonna like this, I promise you.'

To my right, Chris couldn't hold his excitement in any longer.

'Yes! Drop it baby, drop it!'

Jesus. Even Chris had started gibbering like an idiot. It was impossible not to. As the supposed mature commander I was trying as hard as I could to keep a straight face. In fact, every sinew in my body was urging that bomb to fall right on top of those sweaty bastards.

Then, what we'd all been waiting to hear.

'Charlie Charlie One. Weapons released. Time to impact, figures Three Zero. This is it lads.'

The bomb was in the air and there were thirty seconds to impact. Gleaming.

Very soon after that, we began to hear the jet. A quiet rumble at first, then the noise grew rapidly. After releasing the 500lb device, the pilot had locked the F16 into a steep dive after it. He was guiding the bomb down on to its target from the laser in his nose cone.

'Here it comes,' I shouted. Bollocks to maturity.

The closer the F16 came to earth, the louder the jet engines screeched. We craned our necks out of the sangar frantically to catch a glimpse of it, but it was impossible to make anything out in the black of the night sky.

Soon, it sounded like it was coming straight for us. Surely it couldn't get any lower? Just as the furious scream passed right by, a huge white flash engulfed the whole of the horizon for an instant, followed by a giant ball of flame at

Zinc that licked up 50 metres. A fraction of a second later, *BOOM!*

Cimic erupted. Cheers and maniacal laughter burst out from all over the compound.

'Yes! Yes! Yes!' shouted Smudge, jumping up and down on the spot.

'Fucking 'ave it,' jeered Rob.

It was a great feeling. For countless days on end, the OMS mortar teams had been blowing us to pieces. They'd badly wounded our cook, they'd nearly killed Oost and me in the sangar, as well as at least a dozen other blokes, and they'd smashed our home to bits. Now they knew what it felt like to get pasted.

The blast must have taken out a few power lines too, because all the lights went out over three square blocks of houses around Zinc. That included the OMS building. Good. Now those fuckers couldn't boil a kettle either.

A few minutes later, the Nimrod, still circling somewhere above us, passed the battle damage assessment down to Buzz. The 500lb bomb had been landed exactly nine metres west of the mortar base plate to limit any damage to the flats to the east. All six members of the mortar crew were vaporized instantly.

A dirty great crater now sat in the park, and the air controller said around forty people were in it pawing over what was left.

'That OK for you, Buzz?'

'Spot on, my man. Pints on me next time I see you, Jimbo.'

'Glad to oblige. Guess what, the F16s wanted to come by and put another one down there on the forty mourners. I had to tell them we couldn't ID them all as hostiles.'

'Don't you just love the Yanks. Shame they didn't.'

'Yes it is. That's us going off task now, Buzz. Cheerio.'

'See you around, old mucker. Out.'

The air strike wasn't going to change a great deal. We all knew the OMS would have another mortar crew in the park by tomorrow night. Even if it was just for a few hours though, we were just a little bit safer. It also meant we could draw up a new column for the Ops Room stats board. It read: 'Air Strike = 1'.

Most importantly, the OMS now had six of their best fertilizing the roses. Fantastic compost.

For the rest of the night, the mortar teams left us alone. The whole town had heard the air strike and knew we had jets up there now. None of them wanted to be the F16s' next prey. But by mid-morning the crews were back to business as usual.

Unfortunately, that morning we also had to say goodbye to Buzz and John. Their time with us had come to an end. Buzz said he was sad to go, and this time we genuinely believed him.

'Baghdad want to know when I'm coming back. They want me up there as soon as possible because of the workload. I've already delayed it twenty-four hours. I asked for another twenty-four, but they'll get proper shitty with me if I don't leave today.'

They were running low on .5 inch ammunition anyway. All the ball and flash tipped rounds had been used up, leaving just the armour-piercing rounds left. You should see the mess that made of people.

They shipped out of Cimic before dawn the next morning, just as discreetly as they had come.

No more Buzz meant no more Beast and no more air strikes. We were on our own again.

25

That was a shame, because we could have done with Buzz and his entire bag of tricks with the news we got the next morning.

The Intelligence Cell at Abu Naji had passed on an alarming new warning. Working next door to the battle group Ops Room, the Int Cell collated all the snippets of information and gossip they could pick up about the enemy's movements. It was all graded in terms of its reliability; some things were very accurate, other stuff total fantasy. The new warning had the highest reliability grading possible. It came from a tip-off from a senior insurgency source.

Abu Hatim, the brother of the disgraced ex-governor and the self-styled Lord of the Marshes, was back in town. Over the years, he had built up a sizeable and well-armed following at the head of the terrorist resistance against Saddam in Maysan. Amid the chaos of the uprising, he had sensed this was his chance for power. Abu Hatim had struck an alliance with the OMS to join forces and drive us out of Maysan for good. Under the deal, the Lord of the Marshes would then rule it as an extremist Islamic province under Moqtada al-Sadr's supreme authority.

The tip-off also had it that Abu Hatim and the OMS were to launch a major new offensive against us that afternoon. For the first time, all the armed militias in the province would be fighting under a single coordinated military leadership. That spelt big trouble.

The moment the warning came in, all of Sniper Platoon

were dispatched to the roof to keep a lookout for the first sign of any attack. There was nothing for hours.

Then, once the midday heat had died down, a large crowd began to gather outside the Pink Palace. They carried placards and chanted slogans about Moqtada and Najaf. A man in his fifties bleated fury into a loudspeaker, whipping up the mob's passions further. None of them was armed, so they could stand there all day for all we cared.

Then we spotted something of more concern. Using the crowds to distract some of our attention, half a dozen gunmen were creeping up on us through the shadows of Tigris Street.

I went straight for my PRR speak button.

'Stand-to! Stand-to!'

First it was just that handful; then we spotted another small group approaching elsewhere from the west, and then another in the east too. Others had slipped among the rubble of the north bank. Soon, we'd identified at least twelve different concealed enemy positions. Without firing a shot, the fighters had fanned out in a large circle around us. There were easily over 100 of them in total.

Shit. The intelligence was obviously spot on. Three minutes later, every Cimic defender was in his battle position. Another message over the PRR from a sentry.

'Ops Room, Front Sangar. RPG men ducking in and out of the alleys in front of us. Must be a dozen of them in there.'

That prompted a suggestion from Des. His South African blood was properly up now.

'Want me to get out there with my blade, Danny? I don't mind knifing a few of them.'

Before I could reply, an RPG warhead soared up at us from the north bank and shot straight over all our heads.

It was the signal for the lot of them to open fire.

Immediately, we were giving it back at them just as good. Half a dozen Gimpys roared out from all round the compound, interspersed by the constant chatter of Minimi bursts and the single aimed shots of two dozen SA80s.

We were putting down a good weight of lead, and managed to slot the odd one or two; but on the whole, the gunmen were all being very careful to stay back at least 500 metres from us. That way, neither side was really close enough to do each other any real damage.

After the attack's initial fifteen minutes, the 360-degree fire tailed off to be replaced by shorter exchanges between individual positions. That went on for another half an hour or so. Then the enemy ceased firing altogether, and we followed suit. In small groups again, they began to withdraw.

Chris was livid.

'What the fuck are they doing? Come on, you fucks! We're fucking ready for you, don't run away.'

It hadn't been much of an all-out attack. The biggest force we'd seen so far had clearly massed for what had threatened to be a proper assault. Bizarrely, it had finished before it had even really begun. The question was why? For once, the enemy had amassed a seriously potent and coordinated force, but they didn't seem to have any intention of using it. Could they really have lost their bottle that easily?

Pikey thought he had the answer.

'Hah! It's obvious. This Abu Shat-im-self is obviously a fucking pussy.'

It wasn't the Abu Hatim we'd heard all about, and it certainly wasn't the OMS we knew either. By the time the engagement had been over for an hour though, nobody bothered to give it any more thought. As far as we were concerned, they were all fucking mad anyway. There was never any point in trying to get inside a Maysani's psyche. You'd soon end up in a loony bin yourself.

As we gloated over our mini-victory, back in Basra there were graver moves afoot. There was no mood of celebration in Brigade HQ. The senior brass had heard enough. The situation in Najaf was still no better, and southern Iraq remained on the brink. No matter how ineffective their assault on us had been, the brigade staff didn't like the sound of the new intelligence about Abu Hatim and the OMS one little bit.

On top of that, we'd also lost another soldier in action. A lance jack serving with the Cheshire Regiment had been shot dead during a gun battle with the Mehdi Army in Basra. The brigade's fourth death since the start of the month.

Enough was enough. It took us all by surprise, but the reality was it had been in the pipeline for ages. An order came through for us to prepare to withdraw from Cimic House. We had to be ready to move by 1600 the next day.

Strategically, it was a difficult call. It was hard to deny that the cost of holding Cimic was beginning to outweigh its purpose. The place had been smashed up so badly that there was nothing really left to defend. Being there for the sake of it made less and less sense, and a massacre was indeed far from out of the question.

On the other side, a withdrawal might save a bit of blood in the short term, but we'd have to come back into Al Amarah sooner or later. We were never going to abandon the city for good. Everyone who'd actually been to Al Amarah knew that fighting our way back in would prove a full-on nightmare.

Personally, the idea of a withdrawal really pissed me off.

Letting the OMS win really stuck in my gut. Orders are orders though, so I just got on with it and told the boys to start packing.

'Remember, lads, we're all leaving on foot. Whatever you can't carry gets left behind.'

For the rest of the day, Cimic resembled a madhouse. It was like a scene out of a World War Two movie.

Everything of any military value that we couldn't carry had to be destroyed. That meant huge piles of papers had to be burnt. A pit was dug in the garden for a bonfire, and on it went company admin documents, spare maps, and endless bundles of CPA and CIMIC paperwork.

Blokes were dumping all sorts of kit in great piles around the house. A ton of stuff had been accumulated over the tour. Now that nobody had the luxury of freighting it home, it all had to go. TVs, fridges, PlayStations, souvenirs, toiletries, Arab rugs, extra webbing, duvets – even Ads's mammoth porn stash; it all got binned.

The place was also rigged for detonation. Nothing was to be left in the hands of the enemy. Assault engineers put strips of plastic explosives inside the boats, over their outboard engines and in the few remaining vehicles that still worked. The rooms in Cimic where we would have to dump heavy equipment such as big radios also got wired up, along with the equipment for good measure. It was all ready to go, and just needed a few live detonators to be slipped in at the last minute. The second we left it, the camp would be blown to smithereens.

As they dismantled everything on the roof, the boys aired their feelings about the withdrawal. I was proud to find them just as angry as I was. They were being offered a ticket out of that pit of squalor and degradation. But none of them wanted it.

A Chinese parliament gathered. Pikey took his usual considered approach.

'Fucking twats, cunts, wankers and bastards. We get battered to fuck, mortared to death, shot to buggery, and all those hoops in brigade have to say is, pull out?'

'Bollocks to them,' said Daz in agreement.

'Never mind all that,' chimed in Oost. 'We're going to be bored stiff in Abu Napa. All I'll get is the RSM going on about getting my hair cut again.'

Des backed his countryman up.

'Too fucking right, man. Where's the fun to be had back there, hey?'

But Chris had the best point of all.

'What about Ray? If we pull out now, what did he die for then?'

The whole platoon yessed in agreement to that.

Being the gentle giant that he was (when John Wedlock wasn't about), Louey almost always kept his opinions to himself. At that moment though even he felt motivated to speak up, and directly to me.

'Full respect, Sergeant, but I think it is wrong to leave. You know, man, Cimic is our home.'

Right. I had to tell Captain Curry about the strength of the boys' feeling in the O Group. I felt it was important he knew. All the multiple 2i/cs and the CIMIC boss were brought in especially for it that night too. It was an important occasion. As it happened, Captain Curry asked for our thoughts first before I even got a chance.

'Right, chaps. The CO has been on. He's very uncomfortable at having to send the battle group back into the city if we pull out of it. Some are saying we could do it when Najaf is all over. But you and I and he all know the OMS won't let that happen peacefully in a million years.

304

'He's spoken to the brigadier and persuaded him that the final decision should rest with the men on the ground. Only we know what we're capable of. So whether we leave or not tomorrow is now up to me. That's why I've got you all in. I want to know what you think.'

We discussed the merits of both arguments for almost an hour. To my delight, other platoon commanders reported back the same thing. Nobody wanted to leave.

One of the junior officers made the best speech.

'Look, sir, we've had a fair few nasty injuries and even more close shaves, admittedly. But we haven't actually had a single fatality to hostile fire yet. We're fighting brilliantly and we've still got a bit of ammo left.'

'That's true, sir,' confirmed Dale.

The officer concluded. 'The point is, sir, we don't need to pull out yet. I say let's see if we can finish the job.'

There were furious nods and 'hear hears' all round. Captain Curry waited ten seconds for any last comments, then gave his reply.

'Fine. I agree wholeheartedly. In fact, I was secretly hoping you might all say that. If you want my opinion, I don't see why we have to hand over this place to the modern day equivalent of the Nazis. We'll withdraw when we're ordered to, or if we really have to. Until then, we're going to sit it out.'

The decision got a spontaneous round of applause and a room full of proud smiles. We walked out of the hot and sweaty briefing room into the cooler night air and back to our respective platoons with our chests puffed out and a renewed sense of determination in our stride. We were professional British Army soldiers doing what we were paid to do. It was in our blood to stand our ground.

The boys were pleased too when I told them the news.

Despite our exhaustion, it gave us a fresh new burst of confidence.

That night proved to be the quietest of the whole siege so far. It reaffirmed everything we had begun to suspect about the new rebel alliance. First there was their piss poor attempt at a compound assault. Now, they could barely be bothered to lob in more than one or two mortar rounds at us.

Yet again the Int boys had heavily overexaggerated the threat they really posed. Maybe they had all turned chicken at the sight of the air strike on Zinc. Whatever the cause, it was clear to us that the numpties were already beaten. Pikey was right: Abu Hatim was a pussy after all.

With not much fighting to be done and the tension swiftly receding, conversation on the roof that night for the first time turned to home. We were a good two-thirds of the way through the tour, so we allowed ourselves a start at that traditional end-of-tour conversational gem: what our dream first meal at home would be. It's a conversation that never normally lasts less than a month.

Quiet precedes most storms. Even hurricanes.

26

It turned out the previous assault had been no more than an elaborate dress rehearsal to gauge our firepower.

The next morning, the mortaring returned with a vengeance. It didn't stop Pikey from banging on tirelessly about jellied eel served with deep-fried Mars bars. We'd opened a can of worms with the first meal chat there.

The incoming got heavier as the day went on. By the afternoon, Pikey had shut up. By darkness, we were on the end of one of the heaviest daily poundings we'd had the whole tour. It was relentless. After the calm of only the night before, and our absolute certainty the worst had passed, the renewed heavy incoming confused the hell out of us. If these fuckers knew they were beaten, what was the point in mortaring us so hard?

The onslaught continued overnight and throughout the next day too, with just the same intensity. Yet more of the camp was being blown to bits. Repeated blasts left sand and shrapnel everywhere, and the sniper screen fencing had begun to collapse. Nobody could clear it up. All we could do was hunker down in the sangars and pray against direct hits.

Our confusion at what it all meant was nothing compared to what we felt the morning after that.

I got up at dawn after finally coming down from the roof at 2 a.m., when the mortaring had still been incessant. The first thing I noticed before I'd even opened my eyes was the extraordinary quiet. I think it was peace that woke me up.

By the time I was on the roof fifteen minutes later, the sun was steadily rising over a ghost town. There was very little traffic on the streets, very few people going to work on the pavements. By 8 a.m., all of the souks were still closed. That was very odd, because it was a Monday. We'd never seen the city like that. It felt like a dream.

'It's fucking weird,' said Chris, who'd gone up to the roof when I went to bed.

'How long's it been like this?'

'The mortars packed up just before dawn. Then nothing, Danny. Not a bloody thing. It's like they all know something that we don't.'

It didn't take very long for the penny to drop. Silence was the most obvious of all combat indicators. The whole town must be in on this one, whatever the hell it was.

We stood-to, just in case. Dozens of belts of GPMG 7.62 link were hung over the sandbag walls of every sangar. Tins of 5.56 ammo were stacked outside each entrance, alongside crates of water, all ready for the off.

We waited for hours as the August sun just burned us redder.

Oost couldn't stand the tension.

'Where the fuck are these shits, then? They're doing my nut, man.'

When still nothing had stirred by 11 a.m., half the company stood down. It was too hot for the enemy to try anything then, and concentrating on nothing drains people unnecessarily. I went down to the Ops Room and volunteered for a shift on the radios so the 2i/c could get some kip. We'd all stand-to again at 3 p.m., when it was cooler.

The enemy guessed we'd do that. So they attacked at midday on the dot.

It started with snipers on the old town rooftops and a new heavy mortar barrage from two different positions. They were smacking stuff in on us from both Zinc and the north bank at the same time.

'Stand-to! Stand-to!'

A dozen frantic shouts were coming from every sangar in the compound.

All over, blokes were throwing on their body armour and helmets. Fast-moving bodies crammed the corridors and crashed up and down the main staircase.

I legged it up the stairs to the roof three steps at a time. I looked down to guide my feet. Bugger it. I still only had my sandals on. I'd left my boots in the Ops Room. Too late. Just before I reached the roof door, the steady thumping of Top Sangar's Gimpy opened up. I burst out on to the roof to feel the crack and snaps in the air as bullets zipped past splitting the atmosphere around them.

'Fucking get down!'

As my body hit the floor a neat burst of four rounds smacked into the door frame behind me.

Thank God for the roof's all-round three-foot wall. Nobody could raise their heads even a centimetre above it because the air was thick with flying lead. Small chips of stone and concrete shot off its exterior on all sides. Enemy bullets also piled into the sangars' sandbags every few seconds with puffs of dust erupting from each one. Noise was everywhere.

Top Sangar had practically the only eyes on. Des braved the hail of lead to scream out all the information about the enemy he could for everyone's benefit.

'Three buses pulling up at Yellow 3 . . . at least twenty

UKMs dismounting with AKs, RPGs, heavy machine guns ... Separate dismounted attack coming up from Tigris Street, maybe twenty more men ... No, make that the pontoon bridge *and* Tigris Street now, another dozen there ... Another big group going over the bridge to Red 11. Heading up to the hospital and dam ... Targets on the river road too now ... Hang on; now there's activity on the north bank as well. Minibuses pulling up. Get the fucking Gimpy onto them, Oost. Passengers are armed UKMs; taking positions in the rubble ... It's a 270-degree, no fuck it. It's just a fucking 360-degree contact ... Targets approaching from all sides. Repeat, targets approaching *from all sides.*'

They were crawling all around us like ants. Attackers were closing on us from the east, south and west, supported by constant static fire positions over the river to the north. There must have been hundreds of them; far too many to count. At least three times the size of the dress rehearsal mob.

Shit. We had to start getting our heads up, or they'd be all over us in five minutes.

'Get the fucking rounds back down at them!' I shouted over the din. 'Lads, everyone's got to start spotting for targets.'

Dale burst open the roof door and hurled himself down on the floor to join me giving out commands.

'Oi, all of you get your faarkin' heads up! Wait for the incoming to stop. Heads up, rounds back, heads down again.'

Dale grabbed at his PRR.

'Ops Room, Sarn't Major. Get every spare fucker up here now.'

This was it. There was no doubt we were facing a clear and concerted attempt by the enemy to completely overrun us, and with everything they'd got. They seriously meant business. Cimic had always been their prize. Now they were coming to get it. There was no doubt either that they thought they could do it. OMS mortar crews had landed a shitload of incoming right on us in the last sixty hours, let alone the last three weeks. Surely these British infidel dogs have had enough. They're getting mortared to fuck, they've been on their own for ages; they'll be a pushover. They'll run away or surrender. If they don't, we've got enough men to force our way in.

If you want to gain access to Cimic, there's only two sides to do it from: Tigris Street and the dam in the south, or straight over from the alleys in the east. So they hit us from both. Dozens of small teams steadily approached, firing and manoeuvring just like we would. On the roof, we got bullets and mortars, while the front and back gate sangars got never ending RPGs. They were good.

If only Spectre gunships flew in daylight. They'd be in Shangri-La with this lot.

Nor could we expect any help from the battle group either right then. It would take hours to assemble a column big enough to have a go at getting through all those lunatics. We didn't have hours. Got to suppress them and slow them up. It was our only chance.

Showing big balls, Louey was the first to scamper over to the western wall.

'Watch out, watch out,' shouted Des, as the whistle of a descending mortar round grew rapidly louder. It landed just long in the river as Louey poked his SA80 over the wall's edge and began to squeeze off second-long bursts at whatever he saw.

A dozen blokes from Recce Platoon then joined us on the main roof. Another four with Minimis piled up the ladder double quick time to Rooftop Sangar with Des and Oost, and Dale now too. The L96s were abandoned. They couldn't put down enough fire. Showing considerable pluck, the blokes followed Louey's lead and started to get their heads up long enough to spot targets, and share them out.

Once the enemy started to get within range of their own mortars, their crews were ordered to silence their tubes. That allowed our spotting to pick up.

'Gunmen running out of Baghdad Street now.'

'Enemy at 500 yards, the river road.'

'OMS grouping behind nearest tree to the dam crossing.'

They were the cues for anyone who could to concentrate their fire in the target's general direction. Eventually we began to drop a few of the attackers.

A whoop went up from a young Recce lad who wasted an RPG man the second he emerged from behind the Pink Palace to fire.

'Fucking get it! Whooooh!'

His four mates all cheered just as loud and air punched as the adrenalin of the tiny success hit them too.

'Oi, keep the fucking noise down,' Dale shouted. He was trying to listen in to the frenzied radio chatter to bring guns on to the closest enemy positions first. He also knew the importance of everyone keeping in control. Let the rush of blood go to your head, you lose concentration, you get shot.

I darted around the roof shouting out 'covering fire' as I moved; spotting, bringing lads on to targets, and letting rip on my SA80 when I could too.

After the initial twenty minutes of chaos, we began to find a good battle rhythm. The battle engine was ticking over nicely.

Another four gunmen began a sprint across Tigris Street in the direction of the dam. Reloaded now, the Rooftop Minimis were on to them in less than a second and cut the last two down right in the middle of the road. Then they slotted a third, who was stupid enough to go back for his mates.

Next, a black saloon car with an RPG sticking out the back window swerved out of an alley on to Tigris Street right by Front Sangar. Just as the RPG man leant forward to fire at point blank range, the sangar Gimpy filled the car full of holes. The driver swerved sharp left and away hurling the RPG man backwards into his seat. His warhead shot off high into the sky instead.

'Out of rounds,' yelled Pikey on the GPMG in Top Sangar. A second later someone sprinted over from the roof door with half a dozen fresh belts.

Rob Green's call of 'Minimi ammo' was met by another young lad dashing a few metres forward from the stair block to skid a full tin of 5.56 along the floor at him. The moment it left his right hand he nimbly changed direction for Rooftop to deliver a second tin in his left hand for the gunners up there.

As the tin arrived against Rob's thigh, the two blokes either side of him leant round to tear it open with greed.

'If you need oil, it's over here', shouted someone else.

Soon Dale's fears turned from not enough outgoing fire to too much.

'Disciplined fire, boys. Disciplined fire.'

It was still his job to keep one eye on the ever depleting ammo pile. We were using it up fast. But there was a more pressing problem than that.

'Enemy at 200 to the south west,' screamed Des with renewed urgency.

I ducked down beside Louey on the western wall and poked my head up over its lip. Dozens of them were over the dam on our side of the Tigris now. They were gathering behind the huge piles of hardcore from the waste ground's building site. It gave good cover, and an even better position to shoot at us. RPGs on target from there would do us some proper damage.

Smudge, Longy and Pikey all popped off grenade after grenade from the UGLs on their SA80s into the building site, but to no avail. The grenades had too small a bang to have any real effect.

Bloody hell. We were dropping them, but no way near enough to put the rest of them off. No matter how accurate our shooting was. The sheer volume and blinding fanaticism of the attackers made that irrelevant. They were getting nearer and nearer. We were at full stretch, everyone was battling their bollocks off, and we *still* weren't halting the advance.

'Look, Sergeant, man, see them guys behind the iron poles? They're even wearing body armour and helmets.'

Jesus. Louey wasn't wrong. Probably all nicked off the Iraqi police. *These guys aren't fucking around.* Their number was also growing all the time.

I had an idea. Time for the 51.

'Right. I'm going to get some HE on these bastards.'

We'd been ordered only to fire high-explosive rounds off the roof from the 51mm mortar as a last resort. This was a last resort. Soon, they'd be at the walls. The whole city was blown to pieces anyway, it wasn't as if there was anyone who'd care any more.

'Ops Room, Danny. Permission to fire the 51.'

'Danny, Ops. Yes. Go.'

I chose a spot behind Top Sangar to give myself a little

bit of cover from the direct fire from the dam and Tigris Street. On my knees, I rammed the mortar's base plate deep into a couple of sand bags so they would absorb its kick.

'Want a hand, Danny? I'll feed you the rounds.'

It was Corky the medic. This was no time for him to be waiting around for business in his dressing station, and he knew it. It was all hands to the pump. He squatted down beside me and ripped the lid off a brown tin of ten dark green HE mortar rounds cushioned in plastic casings.

As he carefully passed me the first, he pulled the pin out of its tail fin, making it live.

I slid it down the tube. Holding the barrel by its leather grip with my left arm, I pointed it towards the dam and studied the ranging spirit level in an attempt to angle it for a correct trajectory on to the target. It was educated guess-work at best as I'd never fired HE from a mortar before. Hell of a time to learn. When it felt about right, I grabbed hold of the firing mechanism, a piece of rope at the mortar's base.

'Firing 51.'

'Firing 51,' came the refrain from Rooftop Sangar so everyone knew the next big bang wasn't incoming, and then I gave the lanyard a firm yank. *Boom.* It was just like firing an enormous shotgun. It was a good job I kept a firm hold on the tube too or the huge kick of it would have bounced the thing right back up into Corky's face.

'One hundred metres too long and 50 too far to the right,' called out Chris, spotting for me in the sangar in front of me. The round had landed in the middle of the river just behind the pontoon bridge. Getting the bastard on target was clearly going to be an art form.

I popped the second round down the barrel, turned it a little to the left and straightened the barrel a fraction.

'Short by about 50 metres, Danny.'

Bugger. Maybe third time lucky. The third's explosion was a lot louder.

'That's good, mate, that's good! That's target on!'

It had impacted on a harder surface, meaning its shrapnel wouldn't just absorb into the ground and it could do more damage. The mortar would have to land within 15 metres of the enemy to be fatal.

My third touched down just on the lip of our end of the dam, where enemy fighters were massing. So I popped three more over on exactly the same heading. Big cheers erupted from the two roof sangars.

The shells dispersed or killed one big group. Their positions would be filled soon enough by reinforcements though; there seemed to be no end to the enemy's available manpower. The 51's tube was red hot now, so I doused it down with almost two full two-litre bottles of water. I took a swig from the second for myself. I was gasping with thirst in the intense heat of the glaring sun. We all were. No time to worry about sunburn now.

'Right, give us some more, Corky.'

Then, the unmistakeable deep crump of an 82mm OMS mortar tube. The enemy were replying.

'Mortar incoming from the east!'

Everyone ducked down and hugged their helmets tight. The round whined just over the roof and dropped on the compound driveway no more than 50 metres away. Jesus Christ. The enemy were insane. Unless their rounds were incredibly accurate, they were just as likely to kill their own men as us. They didn't give a shit.

It was an unbelievably close shave. Every one of the twenty-odd soldiers on the roof behind the three-foot walls had their backs fully exposed to a blast anywhere on the roof. Dale wasn't impressed.

'Right, you lot,' he bellowed. 'The second you hear incoming, you're straight in the fucking sangars.'

Pointing at the series of scorch marks left on the roof from earlier barrages: 'You can see where they land. They do that again, that's it. You're fucking dead.'

27

But there was a new drama elsewhere. An urgent report crackled over the PRR.

'Ops Room, Back Sangar. We've got a rocket down here. It's fucking facing right at us.'

A clutch of enemy used the latest mortar barrage to break cover and run out into the river road 50 metres east of Back Sangar. There, they dumped a homemade firing frame loaded with a 107mm Chinese rocket – a projectile big enough to do away entirely with Back Sangar and the five men in it. It was all set and ready to launch on a ticking timer. It would go off in seconds; no longer.

Captain Curry didn't waste any time.

'Back Gate Warrior, Ops Room. Get out there quick and give it some pedal.'

The moment the OC's order was given, the Warrior's engine revved up and its clumsy tracks began to grind over the driveway's paving stones. Two sentries ran to the back gate to pull it open.

As soon as the 30-tonne beast's gunner had a direct line of sight through the opening gap, he stamped on the foot pedal and opened up the chain gun with an enormous thirty-second burst. The hailstorm of pinpoint accurate rounds demolished the threat completely; the frame first in a shower of sparks, then the rocket eventually went up where it had fallen on the road with a boom and a large puff of grey smoke. Just as quickly as it opened, the back gate slammed shut again.

Then a yell from Smudge inside Rooftop.

'Shit! Target on the civilian gate!'

He'd been duelling with enemy snipers on the rooftops above RPG alley, when movement caught his eye below. A gunman had sneaked across the road and behind the compound wall in the blind spot between the two gate sangars while the rocket drama had been going on. He was followed by a second. The first man climbed up on top of the iron gate used as an entrance to Cimic by civilians.

Sixty metres from Back Sangar and just five feet tall, it's the weakest point in the compound's perimeter because it has no sniper screen. The man had already got one leg over the gate when Smudge spotted him. Jumping up on the sandbag wall to get a better aim, Smudge raised his Minimi to his shoulder and began blasting away with well-aimed three-second-long bursts until he ran out of ammo. He killed the first man, and hit the second trying the same thing in the arm.

It gave the soldiers on the ground enough time to turn their fire on the threat. Five seconds later, half a dozen Minimis and SA80s plus a Gimpy were hurling everything they had at the gate, riddling it from top to bottom. More troops sprinted round to it and engaged the enemy from over its top, driving that attack back.

Unfortunately the rocket and the civilian gate had been just a sideshow.

'Enemy to the west at 100.'

Des's urgent shout refocused all our attentions in a second.

'They're moving up and down like jack rabbits.'

One hundred metres away was too close by half. The wasteland after the dam and its dozens of piles of earth presented the perfect ground to approach on. The enemy were using it like seasoned infantrymen. At least fifty SA80s, Minimis and Gimpys were hosing down anything that moved on it now with furious vigour. But they were too quick for us to nail any more than a handful.

Fuck, could we do with a dirty great F16 right now. Screw Danger Close, just slap a 1,000 pounder right on them.

I grabbed at the 51 again.

'Corky, give us some more HE.'

'We've done the whole tin already, Dan.'

'Well, crack open another, then. Quick.'

I raised the 51's barrel still higher towards me, and slid a round down the tube. The things would be practically going straight up and down now. If I wasn't careful I'd mortar us.

After we threw a few out, Fitz in Top Sangar in front of me spotted an opportunity. A long, deep pile of jagged shale stretching 30 to 40 metres sat right in front of the advancing fighters' path.

'Danny, if you can get a few rounds in the shale, it'll give you a million secondary projectiles.'

'Roger that, Fitz. Where is it?'

'Starts about 20 metres short and 30 metres to the right of your last.'

'Got it.'

Boom.

'Still 10 metres too long, Dan.'

Boom.

'That's 20 too short now.'

Bugger it.

Boom.

'Good length now. But 15 metres too far left now.'

Fucking bloody thing. I was ready to hurl it off the roof if the next one didn't work.

Boom.

Fitz didn't need to say a thing. Red hot shrapnel and shards of shale tore through the enemy's ranks like meat through a grinder. Because of their proximity, I could hear each and every one of their screams.

Good. Now you wankers know what it feels like to get mortared up the arse. Des started to cackle in his maniacal high-pitched laughter. Another very positive sign.

'Keep 'em coming, Corky.'

I held the mortar tube in precisely the same position. Another full tin on exactly that trajectory should do the trick. The next load of shells sent the Mehdi Army fighters running around the wasteland like headless chickens. As they were forced to expose themselves, the boys cut them down.

One bloke clutching a badly bleeding right arm made it 75 metres to a waiting car on Tigris Street. Sadly for him, the back door he tried to pull open was still locked from the inside, so to buy time he gave us another burst with the AK still in his right hand. Silly. He was riddled with a dozen rounds on the spot. As the driver got out to help, he popped away at us with a little pistol. So the boys killed him too.

The rate of small arms incoming we were receiving began to drop considerably. Means nothing though. Dale knew that instantly too.

'Keep sharp, lads,' he boomed out from Rooftop. 'They'll just be flanking away from the dam to have a go at us on the gates. You four Recce boys, get over to the south wall.'

Crump. Crump. Crump.

'Mortars incoming from Zinc! Three possible base plates!'

Everyone dashed for the sangars again and curled up into foetal positions.

Silence. There were no explosions. *Eh?*

'Where the fuck did them things land then, Des?'

'Two on the dam, one on Tigris Street. They were smoke rounds. I can't see a damn thing behind them now, just white smoke all over the shop.'

What the hell was the smoke for? It made no sense. If we couldn't see them to shoot at, they certainly couldn't see us. The small arms incoming suddenly stopped too.

Dale was the first to realize what was going on.

'Cease firing!'

'Why, sir, what if we see targets through the smoke?'

'You won't, lad. They're withdrawing. The smoke's to cover their retreat.'

Nobody could really believe it. All of us stayed stood-to in our battle positions until long after the last smoke cleared. The only enemy fighters to be seen were the dead and dying, scattered around the wasteland, the end of the pontoon bridge and Tigris Street. The only sound was the odd pathetic groan.

It was over. The enemy had had a damn good crack at us; they'd given everything they had, they'd got as far as our walls, and they weren't far from success. Yet just as they'd reached their closest point to overrunning us, they ran out of men. Dozens of their number were killed, many more again wounded.

I looked at my watch. 4 p.m. The battle had lasted four hours. It felt like twenty minutes. Just after five, more than an hour after the last round was fired, came the tired message over the PRR.

'Charlie Charlie One. Stand down.'

To a man, the whole company was exhausted. After such a long hit of adrenalin, we were all now totally drained of it; way too tired even to celebrate. Anyway, nobody said it was all over yet. If they had surprised us so badly by mustering that many fighters for an assault, who's to say they couldn't do the very same thing again with more? We'd beaten them, but for how long?

The roof was littered with debris. A carpet of empty brass casings, water bottles, sand and stone shards lay under our feet. The remnants of the Light Infantry's original half-sangar wooden frame had been blown totally upside down, and every sandbag in our sangars had rips and tears in them. It had been too dangerous to clear any of it up, or do *anything* but fight up there for days.

The rest of the compound was no better. Cimic resembled a disaster scene.

Barely a single square foot of surface inside it, vertical or horizontal, wasn't now pockmarked with bullet holes or shrapnel gashes. The house was so badly scarred it looked like something out of West Beirut in the 1980s.

All bar none of the Portakabins and prefab accommodation blocks were blown up, and every single room pepperpotted from floor to ceiling. In the washroom blocks, half the sinks had been shattered and the rest were hanging off the walls.

The OC's was the last to go, not that Charlie Curry ever moved into it. Since Major Featherstone found the blind in the floorboards, it had miraculously escaped any other attention from the OMS mortars. Then, around halfway through the all-out assault, it took a direct hit right through the middle of the roof.

Not just one but two kitchens had now been blown to pieces: the aluminium trailer from June and then the field kitchen under the green tent.

At least half of the perimeter fencing was either blown on the floor or simply not there any more. Ugly lumps of mortar shrapnel lined the paths and driveway. Every one of the garden's palm trees oozed sap from where they'd been slashed by flying metal.

I surveyed the damage from the roof with Dale at sunset.

'D'ya think the new governor will want his house back now, then?'

'No chance, Danny boy. It's just a scrapheap now, innit.'

I couldn't disagree.

'At least it's still our scrapheap I suppose,' he pondered. 'Anyway, ours not to reason why and all that. Give us a hand with doing the stock list will you, Dan? I'm not looking forward to this.'

Establishing what supplies we had left was grim work indeed. We weren't doing great on food. Most of the ration boxes had been broken open and plundered for all the best bits, with little more than pâté tins and stewed plums in custard left. There were many hundreds of those though, so we'd be shitting five times a day but at least we weren't going to starve for a bit.

Water was a different picture. We were very low. Dale and I calculated there were just four two-litre bottles left per man. In that heat we could probably get by on two bottles a day each, as an absolute minimum. We might still be thirsty, but we probably wouldn't dehydrate. We rationed them all out.

Most seriously of all, we were very low on ammo. The ceiling-tall wall Dale had built up inside the secure room was now almost entirely gone. It its place now were just a couple of tins and a red fire extinguisher.

'Jeez, is that all we got left?'

'Yeah. Still lots of stuff lying around in the sangars, but we ain't got nothing in reserve any more. All faarkin' gone.'

We worked out we had enough bullets to last around sixty hours at the siege's normal pace of fighting. A lot less, if the enemy mounted another all-out assault. We gave Captain Curry the bad news.

'Well that's it then,' he pronounced. 'The battle group is just going to have to come and get us. Neither we nor they have a choice in that any longer, do we?'

'No, sir. We don't.'

There was absolutely no doubt about it. Any convoy that tried to get through to Cimic was going to get the mother of all smackings. But there was simply no other option this time.

The message went back to Abu Naji. They'd been guessing as much, after having to sit through the all-out assault with nothing else to do but listen to events play out on the radio. During it, Captain Curry was told an emergency convoy would be dispatched the moment he genuinely thought we were going to be overrun. It had got close, but not close enough. Cool as ever, Curry kept his nerve.

The Ops Room gave Slipper City the news. Abu Naji had new orders for us within the hour. The resupply was set for around twenty-four hours' time, at some stage during the next night. They needed that long to pull together everything they had in mind for it. It was going to be close.

'There's something else,' Curry said, when he told us the news at a midnight O Group. 'We're being relieved. It was an order, I wasn't given a choice.'

The CO had decided that we'd more than done our bit, and it was time to pull us out. Exposing us to extreme combat with us in the state we were now in was simply not something he was prepared to take responsibility for any longer.

325

Crucially, it was a relief-in-place, not a withdrawal. The company of Royal Welch Fusiliers was going to take over our position. They'd come in with the resupply column, and we'd go out with it.

We were always going to leave Cimic at one stage or another, but when the notification of it actually came it was still funny to hear it. If given the choice at the time, to a man we would all have stayed on. The OMS weren't beaten yet, and the fear of life in Slipper City and the RSM's petty bollockings haunted us all.

The CO was probably right though. With the physical activity, the heat, the sleep deprivation and the dwindling supplies, we had become a force of skeletal zombies relying on little more than an intravenous drip of adrenalin to get us through.

Every man in the company had lost at least a stone during the siege, some double that. I was surrounded by odd creatures covered in grime, dried sweat and flecks of blood from head to toe, with two huge black circles around their eyes. Most worrying of all was the slightly crazed look we'd all begun to adopt – like we were all on the first rung on the ladder to insanity. No. It couldn't last.

Most importantly, a relief was something our pride could deal with. It meant the British Army in Al Amarah weren't losing an ounce of face.

The lads were resigned to their fate when I broke the news to them. There was a stunned silence for some time.

Pikey broke it, with the perfect comment.

'Oh, fuck it. All good things come to an end.'

Secretly, everyone also craved some decent nosh and a good night's kip. Almost as much as they craved killing OMS men.

At midnight, the mortaring began to pick up again. It kept

up throughout the night and into the next day.

The mood was tense. Several false alarms had the whole company repeatedly standing-to. Yet by 2 p.m. that afternoon, a repeat of the previous day's all-out assault hadn't materialized. Instead, there was just regular sniper fire from the usual locations – old town rooftops and the north bank. Curry ordered every soldier to conserve his ammo as much as possible.

All we needed was for the OMS to lick their wounds for another twelve hours longer, and they could come at Cimic as hard as they liked. Then, the battle group would be fully ready for them again.

So Abu Naji knew what to bring in, Dale had the unfortunate task of delivering to the battalion Quartermaster a battle damage assessment on all the military equipment in the camp. It was just one long list of misery.

I sat on the house's front doorstep beside Dale as he set up the portable satellite phone and dialled the Quartermaster's number.

Like most in his trade, our QM would never give anyone an easy run for what he saw as his own money if there was anything he could do about it. That day was no different. He insisted on Dale giving him a description of every single thing that had been signed off to Y Company. It was going to be a painful conversation.

It started with the Portakabins. Each one separately.

'Blown up, sir,' was Dale's response.

'OK. Portakabin number two?'

'Blown up too, sir.'

'Really? Portakabin number three . . .'

And so it went on. The QM decided to change tack.

'OK, well what about the vehicles then? Better news there I'd hope, or have they been mistreated too?'

'We've only got one out of the ten Snatches serviceable now, sir.'

'WHAT? What happened to the rest of them?'

'Blown up.'

'Every one of them?'

'Yes.'

'Are you sure? Even the civilian Land Rover Discovery that we paid to have air conditioning in?'

'Even that one, sir, yes.'

The more damage the QM heard about, the more irate he got. He could see money going down the pan left, right and centre. There goes his fucking OBE.

Dale then went on to tell him about the swimming pool, the chef's galleys, the TV trailer, the satellite and Internet dishes, the outdoor gym and weightlifting equipment, two giant JCB generators, all the compound's fencing and, the QM's most beloved articles of all, the two Mark 5 speed boats.

'No, Sarn't Major, not your brand new boats too?'

'Yes, sir, the boats too.'

'But we only bought them in June. And at some considerable cost, as you well know.'

'Yes, I do know that, sir.'

'Are you sure they are totally unusable?'

'You could put it like that. They're at the bottom of the Tigris.'

'Well, this is all very bad news, Sarn't Major. This is an appalling waste of perfectly good military equipment. Taxpayers' money all of it. It doesn't grow on trees, you know.'

The QM's rattiness had started to rub Dale up the wrong way. The bloke just couldn't have been living on the same planet as us. He clearly hadn't been reading any of our sit reps, and must have thought we'd only taken a couple of pot shots.

Finally, twenty-five minutes later, Dale got to the end of the list.

'I'm not happy about this at all, Sarn't Major. Not one little bit.'

'Yeah, well neither were we, sir.'

There was a silence.

'Look, can you go through everything again with me just to make sure?'

That was the final straw for Dale.

'Look, sir, it's real simple. Everything's fucked, all right? Everything I'm looking at has been fucking blown up. It's all faarkin' fucked, and there's not a bollocks I can do about it. Sorry, sir, I've got to go.'

He slammed the handset down into its bracket, breaking a small piece of plastic off the phone too.

28

Darkness fell with still no sign of another compound assault. The OMS and Abu Hatim clearly needed more than just one day to reorganize after the losses they'd suffered. Perhaps they'd been even bigger than we thought.

The message came through from Abu Naji that the resupply operation would begin at 9.45 p.m. By nine, we were all packed up and ready to go, and stood-to for the inevitable outbreak of mayhem as soon as the column put in its first appearance.

What a moment that was to be too.

The plan was really quite simple. The battle group had worked throughout the previous night to amass the greatest single column of British armour since the invasion of the country a year earlier. They were just going to pound their way through to us in the straightest and shortest line possible, with overwhelming brute force.

That meant a battalion-size war formation: an extraordinary total of seventy-two Warriors, led by the Queen's Royal Lancers' entire squadron of twelve Challenger II main battle tanks. Every spare armoured vehicle within 300 miles had been rustled up for the job. That meant not just the PWRR's A Company coming up from Basra again, but a full company of the Black Watch in Warriors too. Thickly armoured and tracked CRV recovery vehicles fitted with bulldozers were coming along too. Nothing must be allowed to get in the column's way.

All this, just to give Cimic House a fresh face and a few bombs, beans and bullets.

The route was just as simple as the plan. It was A to B. The column was simply going to come straight up the Red Route as fast as possible, and then stop at Yugoslav Bridge. The final leg round to us was always a surefire death trap. The north bank and OMS's stronghold estate Aj Dayya threw up a series of choke points perfect for ambush. So for once, they weren't going to give the bastards the chance to use them.

Instead, the Royal Welch Fusiliers would dismount, cover the kilometre of rough ground between us on foot, while crossing the Tigris on the dam and carrying in by hand the entirety of the resupply. Then, we'd come out the very same way. It was ballsy, and brilliantly simple.

The whole thing began with a deep rumble. We heard the 7th Cavalry coming long before we could see them. Almost 100 armed vehicles all moving in unison makes a hell of a noise.

As usual, the column got contacted on the city outskirts. This time, though, they were stopping for nobody. With bullets and RPGs pinging off their ultra-hard shells, the Challengers smashed through Mehdi Army defences with chain guns and main armaments blasting away, often at the same time. Anything that was deemed remotely hostile got the good news.

Again, we followed their progress from the roof, thanks to the light show of the white and yellow flashes of explosions, and the red tracer rounds pinging off in every direction from everything metallic – the column's armour, civilian cars and trucks, wrought iron gates and fences.

Their junction drills were spectacularly slick; two Challengers stopped off on each side and blazed away repeatedly to cover the rest of the column across it. They were making astonishing progress.

Finally, once the first tanks passed Red 11, they began to come into our view. It was mesmerizing, an awesome display of force that none of us had seen anything like before.

Gradually, the column's full might became apparent. Deploying a tactical spacing of 25 metres between each vehicle, the whole thing was almost two kilometres long from start to finish.

'Fuck me,' said Daz. 'It's bigger than Ben Hur.'

Chris just looked on stunned, his mouth wide open.

'It's like the wrath of God. Hey, maybe it *is* God.'

The closer it got to us, the more we could feel the armour's vibrations under our feet. It was rocking the whole of the city.

The enemy was in disarray. The column moved so quickly, it gave no time to plan a proper attack. In their determination to finish us at Cimic the day before, the rebel alliance had totally neglected their own town defences. The few fighters that did come were uncoordinated and got pulverized.

The lead Challenger reached Yugoslav Bridge and stopped. Behind it, the Red Route was now completely full up with our armour, as far down as the eye could see.

I was listening in to the battle group net on my VHF. Delta was the tanks' call sign.

'Cimic, Delta One Zero. We're in situ. Resupply beginning.'

Stage One was complete. Stage Two was more risky. Every round of ammunition, bottle of water and tin of food had to be carried by hand across a click of rough ground. That meant massive exposure to enemy gunmen and mortars, for some considerable time.

With eyes the size of oranges and ears the size of naan

bread, we were on maximum alert for the first sign of any OMS attack. It still never came.

One of the first faces into Cimic House was Major Featherstone. He'd come in to command the Royal Welch Fusiliers. It was vital they had an experienced and battle-proven leader who knew Al Amarah inside out. For all his faults, Featherstone was certainly that.

Reliefs-in-place mean nobody leaves their post until the bloke who's replacing you is in it first. Man by man, Cimic House's defenders were seamlessly swapped. Then I heard a familiar voice on the roof behind me.

'All right, granddad, you tosser. Some peacekeeping tour, eh?'

It was Ads. He'd come in on the column with De Villiers and H, the three snipers who'd been away on R&R. That warranted them an awful amount of abuse.

'Oh, nice of your fucking rear echelons to join us. Good break, then? You've missed all the fun.'

Ads knew all about that.

'No shit, Dan. I've been pulling me hair out in Abu Napa for a week. There was no way we could get back in, was there. Proper gutting it was, I can tell you.'

I knew where I'd rather have been.

'Anyway, what the fuck have you boys done to this place? Looks like we'll have to give it at least a new coat of paint.'

I was pleased they were there. It meant Sniper Platoon would still have a representation in Cimic House. But their arrival meant it was time for us to go.

My platoon was the very last to leave. With Bergens on, we huddled by the front gate awaiting our cue. Yet still there wasn't much sign of the much feared enemy attack. A little harassing fire on the sangars, but nothing on the waste ground and, even more rarely, no mortars either. It was mighty bizarre, and unnerved me.

'Right lads, normal drills. As soon as the rounds start coming in, dump everything straight away and then get into a decent covered fire position.'

Daz led off. Dale was coming out with us; he and I would be the last of Y Company to leave. He grinned at me as the rest of the boys filed by.

'You're gonna miss this place aren't you, Danny boy?'

'Yeah, like a hole in the head.'

Then it was just the two of us.

'Right, you jammy git, let's get the fuck out of here.'

Out on the wasteland, we could hear gunfire in the distance where the Challengers were still slapping the odd chancer back at Red 11. As I walked, I couldn't help tensing up to prepare myself for the first incoming mortar. That would be when it would all go horribly wrong, and right at the last bloody minute knowing our luck.

It never came. Sooner than I thought, we were on top of the brightly lit dam. If only Major Tait had shot out its fucking street lights too. Then we were over it, and on the home stretch.

Figures in combats and helmets waiting for us on the main road frantically beckoned us to hard-target the last 200 metres, then bundled us into the nearest Warriors with space.

The automatic door clunked closed. A minute later, the giant column juddered into motion. Every few minutes, our vehicle's chain gun rattled out a few rounds at some target, but there was less than half the opposition on the way out than the convoy had faced on the way in.

Then the chain gun stopped completely. We were out of

the town, and rumbling full speed through the last few kilometres of the dark arid desert before Camp Abu Naji.

One of the dismounts handed over a set of headphones. The Warrior commander wanted to talk to me. Turned out it was a sergeant who was an old mate of mine.

'Know why you had to hard-target the last 200 metres, Danny?'

'No. Why?'

'Surveillance report came in from the Lynx 2,000 feet above Aj Dayya. They spotted hundreds of enemy on rooftops and street corners. By the looks of it, that's where they were setting up for us. Stupid arseholes never once realized what was going on at Cimic before it was way too late.'

'Really? Gleaming.'

'Yeah, isn't it. Don't you love it when a plan comes together?'

Four things came together in beautiful synchronicity to make the night work like clockwork: enormous firepower, slick timing, smart tactics and a decent dose of luck. As we came to learn, luck was the most important of the four.

Only then did it dawn on me what a fantastic triumph the battle group had just pulled off.

The siege of Cimic House had been relieved. Fresh fighting troops were in there now, with enough supplies and ammunition for them to fight alone for a month. The physical blow this was to our enemy was bad enough, after all the losses they'd suffered trying to wear us down. But the psychological one was far more devastating. The battle group had proved it could go in and out of the town when it needed to. We were still the true masters of Al Amarah, and Cimic would never be taken. The OMS and Abu Hatim could all go fly.

29

We finally pulled into Abu Naji at 4.30 a.m., just as the sun was rising again. It was a nice feeling to step under a shower and get some fresh clothes on. I hadn't done that since I'd last left Abu Naji almost four weeks ago. Then we had breakfast, and got our heads down. Most of the platoon slept until after sunset. Chris didn't wake up until the next morning. That was OK though. We'd earned a lie-in.

For the next few days, the OMS alliance kept up a steady flow of mortar and sniper fire on Cimic. It meant the Royal Welch Fusiliers got the chance to get some scrapping under their belts. But after what we'd been through, it was hard to see it as anything more than keeping up appearances for Moqtada.

The enemy never attempted another proper assault on the compound. They either no longer had the men for it or no longer had the will; or both. Our all-out defence coupled with the resupply had broken the back of the insurgency in Al Amarah. They knew it, and we knew it. It gave everyone who'd been in Cimic House in August a tremendous sense of pride. We had stood up and been counted, we were tested to the extreme, and we had won.

When the ceasefire finally came a few days later, it must have been far more of a relief to them than it was to us.

Again, just as events in Najaf had started it, it took the final play of the game in the holy city to bring the August uprising to a final close.

Where the interim Iraqi government had failed after weeks

of fruitless negotiations, the most influential cleric in Iraq succeeded. As the Shia's equivalent of the Pope, Grand Ayatollah Ali al-Sistani was a very powerful man indeed in the south; probably the most powerful. Luckily for the Yanks, the 73-year-old preacher with a long white beard was still a moderate who generally gave the coalition his support. The Americans' masterstroke was to coax him into the fray on their side.

On 25 August, he was flown to Basra on an RAF C17 jet from London, where he had been undergoing heart surgery. A hospital bed abroad for three weeks had conveniently left Sistani without having to choose sides. From Basra, he set off to Najaf by road in a heralded 'peace convoy' to call a halt to the uprising.

Faced with having to defy the great man's word and take him on too, Moqtada blinked. Tactically, though, he was already in deep trouble. According to CNN, the Marines had finally come up with a way of taking the Imam Ali mosque without exploding Muslim sensitivities. Elite Iraqi Army troops had been trained to storm it with the help of US special forces disguised as Arabs. The operation to capture or kill Moqtada was just hours away from being launched.

After twenty-four hours of frenzied talks, Sistani brokered a new deal. If the Mehdi Army would disarm and leave Najaf, the US Marines promised to do the same. Again, there'd be no recriminations on either side. It was a compromise that suited everyone by that stage.

Moqtada sent out a proclamation asking all loyal fighters to put down their weapons. He even agreed to rejoin the political process and take part in the elections in five months' time. His loyal defenders in the mosque were escorted out of it by jubilant worshippers. The home of their belief system had been saved.

337

On 28 August, the Al Amarah OMS also declared a ceasefire, pending, of course, the outcome of their negotiations with the town's security forces, which really meant our CO. In other words, their murdering swine wanted immunity too. With orders from above, Colonel Maer reluctantly accepted the deal, which came into effect at midday.

With the quiet, the company finally got a chance to add up the statistics. They made terrific reading. During that 23-day period of concerted attack, we'd taken a total of 595 incoming mortar rounds on the compound during 230 different bombardments, 57 separate RPG attacks and 5 barrages from 107mm rockets. We'd fought 25 different firefights out in the town, and repelled 86 enemy ground assaults on Cimic itself.

In return, we fired back 33,000 rounds, countless Challenger, Warrior and mortar HE shells, and even managed to persuade the US Air Force to drop a 500lb bomb right into the middle of a built-up city.

We'd never had the time – or the opportunity – to properly count up all the enemy dead. During the siege alone, it must have been somewhere in the mid-hundreds. Thanks to a rough Ops Room estimation, Sniper Platoon alone accounted for 40 per cent of all of Y Company's kills.

The siege's fighting had certainly taken our platoon tally for the whole tour to over 200 confirmed kills; double that unconfirmed. We all knew how many of them we'd hit, but you don't often get the chance to take the pulse of some fucker you've just slotted when you're in the middle of the shit.

As for the company's casualties, we suffered one dead and six seriously wounded. How we didn't lose dozens rather than just Ray will remain the world's greatest mystery to all of us.

The locals in the houses surrounding Cimic had not been quite so lucky. A total of twenty-two had been killed by mortars intended for us dropping short or long.

The next day, I radioed Ads from Abu Naji to ask him to check up on the people in the corner house. They'd been playing on my mind. If any of them were still alive, I still wanted us to apologize for zeroing on their wall. Miraculously, they were all still there, albeit in little more than a pile of rubble now. They had all survived, and they had nothing but thanks for us for defeating the OMS. Amazing. Our presence next door had fucked their lives, and they still said thank you.

This time, the ceasefire held firm all over Iraq. Moqtada was well and truly a spent force now; for the rest of that year anyway.

The CO shared an anecdote with Captain Curry in the back of a Warrior on the way back to Abu Naji after the ceasefire signing ceremony in the Pink Palace.

'Well, Charlie, I take my hat off to you and Major Featherstone. The OMS told me they thought Cimic was being defended by an entire SAS squadron. Of course, it was a misapprehension I was comfortable to leave them with.'

The greatest irony of all had come a week into the peace. Chris heard the news first and couldn't wait to tell me.

'Guess what, Danny.'

'What, mate?'

He grinned. 'You'll love this. We're handing Cimic House back over to the Iraqis tomorrow. All UK forces are moving out for good.'

It had been all part of the long-term strategy to give the

place back to local government control as soon as it was feasible. It was about the Iraqi security forces taking on an ever greater lead. After all, we weren't going to stay in Maysan for ever. The handover had originally been planned for mid-summer. Then the uprising had begun again and everything was canned.

In peacetime, our priorities had changed again. We could hand it over now while looking all magnanimous – most importantly, at a time of our choosing, not theirs. A final fuck you to the OMS.

We knew the logic behind the decision full well. Yet Chris and I couldn't resist a wry smile about it all the same. It was hard for us, the grunts, to not feel a little bit of Hamburger Hill syndrome after everything we'd been through there. One of our men had even died for the right to call that place British. Two weeks later, the Grand Old Duke of York had decided the hill wasn't needed any more so we marched all the way back down it again.

In the end, nobody was really that massively bothered. We didn't actually give a fuck about the place. A poxy few lumps of concrete in the middle of Al Amarah; they can shove it up their arses for all we cared.

The only thing that mattered was we'd done our jobs when we were really needed. That would never be taken away from us.

With nowhere else to go now but Abu Naji, the platoon spent the rest of the tour chasing camel spiders up and down the corridors of its giant tents. There was the normal dull routine to keep us occupied: guard duties, Land Rover patrols, escort trips and admin days.

The only violence we ever witnessed was the odd mortar attack. In the Abu Naji cookhouse, you could spot the people who'd been at Cimic House in a flash. At the first sound of incoming, we were the only ones to stay at the tables calmly finishing our food. The rest of the battle group scrambled under the tables and lurched for their body armour.

At the end of September, I got posted. It had come sooner than I'd expected. I was being promoted to Colour Sergeant, and sent to the Infantry Battle School in Brecon as an instructor. My leaving date was in just one week's time, three weeks ahead of everyone else.

Truth be told, I was happy to get out of Iraq by then. The ceasefire bored us all to tears just like it had in July. Life also moves on. My priorities began to change; I was looking forward to my new job, seeing my kids again. By then, I'd done my bit for the place and the battalion. I'd also proved myself to everyone I'd needed to – most importantly, me.

Despite all that, leaving the platoon was always going to be hard. Having fought with them so hard for so long, we'd developed a bond the likes of which I'd never experienced before. Half of them had become men on the tour, and all of us had become soldiers. We'd also had the time of our lives.

On the afternoon before I left, I handed over command of the platoon to Daz.

'It's all yours now, mate. Take good care of it.'

'Roger that, Dan. We might, but somehow I don't think the QM will miss you.'

That night, Major Featherstone got special dispensation to throw a small party for a handful of us who were leaving the company the next day for good. It meant a barbecue, and a couple of beers each.

The OC gave a small speech, followed by an even smaller one from me. But I meant every word of it.

'I just want to say cheers, guys. The last six months have been the pinnacle of my career. It's been a privilege to serve in Y Company, and an ever greater one to command Sniper Platoon. Even on a boring peacekeeping tour like this. I never thought I'd have the chance to do even a tenth of what we've done. You're the best soldiers I've ever met, so here's to you.'

The OC was straight back on his feet.

'Before you sit down, Dan, the snipers have got something for you.'

A couple of the boys came forward and presented me with the Iraqi flag that had hung from Cimic and defied everything the OMS had thrown at it.

'This is for you, Danny. We thought it would make a fitting souvenir after all your close shaves.'

Every one of them had written a little good luck message on it. It was a very touching moment.

It's amazing how long you can make two beers last when that's all you've got, and we gassed the rest of the night away as a full platoon for the last time. Each of us retold the full stories of our own individual escapades. Then we relived all the fantastic stitch-ups. Smudge even admitted he was finally over Natalie.

Late on, Ads came up with an idea.

'Hey, why don't we all meet up on April the eighteenth next year? It could be our soldier's anniversary reunion? It would work if we all made the effort.'

April the eighteenth was the date of our first contact in Al Amarah when Daz got blown up. It was a nice thought, and everyone agreed to it. But we all knew it was very unlikely to happen. The battalion was moving from Tidworth to Germany, so half of us would be living in different countries by then.

A Hercules from Sparrowhawk took me down to Basra the next day. After an overnight in the air station's soulless camp, I flew out of Iraq on a Tristar back to Brize Norton on 7 October, exactly six months and a day after I'd first arrived.

It wasn't until I got to Kings Cross the following afternoon and changed into my civvies that I had a chance to sample my very first pint of the black stuff. To my parched lips, it tasted like darkened honey. I had an hour and a half to kill before my train left for Catterick, so I made it three.

I sat down alone to prop up the station's bar, and idly glanced up from time to time at its flatscreen TV. It was showing Sky News. Halfway through Guinness Number Two, a report came on from some grave-looking reporter who'd finally talked his way up to Al Amarah. Word of what had happened there must have begun to leak out. *You're a bit late for that, I'm afraid, laddie.*

Thanks to the wonders of modern technology, he wasn't though. All of a sudden, Sky started running clips from a couple of the battle group's contacts. One had even been filmed on Cimic's roof.

'Hah!' I blurted out loud.

It could only have been a matter of time before those home movies got on TV. They were simply too good to stay in PWRR hands.

Then to top it all, there was me. Crouching, helmet on, with the 51mm mortar tube clasped in my hand. That nailed it down to the day of the OMS's all-out assault.

'Yeeesss!' I leapt to my feet and toasted the screen with the remainder of my pint. It got me a whole load of funny looks. Just another drunkard in a train station with mental problems, the rest of the drinkers must have thought. I didn't give a stuff.

343

The camera shot panned down to my feet as I tugged on the lanyard to launch another round.

'Look at that silly fella on the telly,' said the barman to nobody in particular, as he polished a glass. 'He's fighting a war in his bleedin' flipflops.'

Epilogue

I was wrong about Ads's suggestion on my last night in Abu Naji. Most of us did end up meeting for a night out in London the next April the eighteenth. The few that couldn't make it sent texts instead, reading 'Happy April 18'. The year after that, we all went up to Leeds on Chris's invitation. A load of mates, just sitting in the pub, with a few beers and a lot of old stories. Old soldiers just talking about their war.

Most of all though, at our reunions, we talk about the fun.

Our QM had done something good for morale before we left. He'd managed to work out that the battle group had fired more rounds on the tour than the entire British invasion force had fired during the Iraq war.

The battalion handed over Maysan province to the Welsh Guards on 22 October. The first thing they did was to give the camp a thoroughly good tidy-up. Typical guardsmen, everything spick and span. I wouldn't deny it needed it though, after what we'd put the place through.

The regimental historians also got stuck into the record books. It turned out that the Siege of Cimic House proved to be not only the longest continuous action fought by the British Army anywhere since the Korean War, but also the lengthiest defensive stand since World War Two. In total, the battle group had also clocked up 963 different contacts, and suffered two dead and 48 seriously wounded.

Much of the bravery shown by everyone across the ranks was justly rewarded in the Operational Honours and Awards List published in March 2005.

Private Beharry was given the Victoria Cross; and became the first living recipient of the nation's highest award for bravery in thirty-six years. He's recovered enough now to leave hospital and wear a uniform, but he'll never see active service again. There were also two rare Conspicuous Gallantry Crosses (now the second highest medal after the VC), ten Military Crosses and seventeen Mentions in Dispatches.

Colonel Matt Maer got a Distinguished Service Order, the highest military honour for leadership in battle, along with the OC of C Company.

From Y Company, Dale got a battlefield MBE, Justin Featherstone got one of the MCs, and I got one of the MiDs.

With the usual smattering of 'well done' lower medals to boot, it made a grand total of thirty-seven different medals and awards. The list made us the most highly decorated serving battalion in the army. Even then, it could easily have been double that. All in all though, it's fair to say we put the regiment's proud name back on the military map.

The more time elapses, the more Cimic House and what happened there seems to grow in army folklore. It's funny, because none of it felt particularly legendary to us at the time.

Three years on now, I keep hearing the odd bloke in the mess coming out with the 'I was in Cimic House during the siege, you know' stories. I've never seen most of them before in my life. I don't bother embarrassing them, because it's just a compliment really.

After August 2004, the OMS of Al Amarah – or any other insurgents – never took the British Army on again in face to face combat. Since then, the city's streets have been by and large quiet and peaceful.

Moqtada al-Sadr may still be riding strong, but the local OMS's fortunes have flagged. They don't enjoy anywhere near the same level of popular support in Al Amarah as they did during the summer of 2004. A lot of Maysanis never forgave them for starting a fight they couldn't win. Not only had they smashed up large chunks of the city with us, but a lot of poor or stupid young men had gone to their deaths pointlessly.

However, that's not to say the violence against the coalition stopped in Maysan. Terrorism continued, but the killers just stopped showing their faces. Without the support of the general population, their activities were pushed underground. Arguably, that just made them ever more deadly.

At the time of writing, a further eight British soldiers have lost their lives in Al Amarah from enemy action – seven of them from a new type of roadside bomb supplied by Iran's Revolutionary Guards. The battalion's C Company ended up going back there for a second tour over the summer of 2006, picking up another Conspicuous Gallantry Cross and three more MCs for their efforts.

The British Army finally moved out of Camp Abu Naji in August 2006 as part of the gradual handing back of power to leave Maysanis largely to govern themselves. It's what they've always wanted.

Did our three and a half year occupation really make any difference? For Ray's sake, as well as for all those others, I'd like to think so. The place is a democracy now and there is the rule of law, of sorts. The economy has also got a little better – specifically, from really shit to just shit. But every

347

soldier who was there will also know that most of us spent the overwhelming majority of our time just trying to keep ourselves alive.

By any Western standards, Al Amarah is still the barbaric and remorseless shit hole that the Paras found when they first arrived. The bloke with the biggest stick is still king. It's how they bring their sons up. If you were to stop them fighting, you'd have to change an entire culture and identity. That's just how it works in Maysan. Always has been, always will be.

As far as the platoon goes, most of the boys are now out of the army.

Of the original eighteen, just Daz, Smudge, H, Rob, Ben and Sam are still in the battalion. All six were sent back to Iraq for its second tour of duty there in April 2006. Luckily for them, they all managed to avoid a return to Al Amarah.

Daz got made up to sergeant for the second time, having managed to keep his nose sufficiently clean for a bit.

Ads was promoted to lance corporal. Then he went AWOL after a scuffle with four German civvies outside a Paderborn bar. Instead of jailing him, the regiment offered him a fresh start with a transfer to the 2nd Battalion in Northern Ireland. He transferred to avoid the nick – and then got out. After a bit of security work, he decided to go back to broking in the City and start earning some proper money again. Wise lad.

Pikey is nominally still in, but only while he awaits court martial for allegedly smacking a Red Cap round the head with an ashtray in a German nightclub. The plonker then went AWOL, while the copper had to have twenty-five stitches in his neck. He's back now, but he's going to have to do some serious time in the glasshouse for that one.

The company hierarchy are all still in too.

Dale was promoted to Warrant Officer First Class and is now a Regimental Sergeant Major for another battalion. It's a shame he wasn't the battalion's RSM; he'd have been one of the best we ever had.

Major Featherstone was posted to the Royal Military Academy Sandhurst as a senior instructor. There, he taught, among others, Princes William and Harry leadership and adventure training. Tigris the mongrel lives with him in the Home Counties now. He smuggled her out of Iraq on a series of RAF helicopters and then on a BA flight back to London thanks to a campaign by the *Sun* when the army refused to fly her.

As for Redders, he learnt a lot in Iraq – so much so, he was appointed the battalion's Adjutant, one of the most responsible positions in it.

Three of the sniper lads chose women over the army.

Having repeatedly vowed to never settle down, Chris promptly got married in Las Vegas to a Royal Military Police-woman on his return home. Both of them left the army and moved to Leeds, where Chris now drives cranes. He says he likes it 50 metres up in the air on his tod because nobody can harass him with bullshit there.

Fitz also got out after ten years' service to settle down to a normal life with his wife and kids. He would have made a fantastic senior NCO, but he could never be bothered to put himself in for it. He loved shooting too much.

And Longy got out when his missus gave him a final ultimatum: the uniform or her. Self-pleasure was evidently no longer enough for him. Now he's a carpet fitter.

Des went back to Johannesburg to take over the family property business. He said he lost the desire to go for SAS selection because he got what he had wanted out of Iraq.

Oost is a security guard at a university, with a goatee, long hair and tattoos all up his arms now. A terrible waste of a really fine soldier. Hopefully he'll have second thoughts and get back in.

Gilly forgot about the 'RLCs' after Iraq for an easy life in Paderborn. But he signed himself straight out of the army as soon as he heard about the battalion's upcoming second tour.

Finally there is Louey, who's working as a bodyguard in London. He could be mine any day.

As for me, I'm now back with the battalion again. I leave the army soon as I'll have served out my full 22-year engagement. I've no idea what I'll do next.

Sgt. Dan Mills was decorated for his command of an eighteen-man sniper platoon during the siege of Al Amarah. During a long army career he has served in Bosnia, Kosovo, Northern Ireland, and the Falkland Islands. *Sniper One* is his first book.